THE KARMA OF WORDS

THE KARMA OF WORDS
Buddhism and the
Literary Arts
in Medieval Japan

William R. LaFleur

UNIVERSITY OF CALIFORNIA PRESS

Berkeley   Los Angeles   London

UNIVERSITY OF CALIFORNIA PRESS
Berkeley and Los Angeles, California

UNIVERSITY OF CALIFORNIA PRESS, LTD.
London, England

First paperback printing 1986

Library of Congress Cataloging in Publication Data

LaFleur, William R.
  The karma of words.

  Bibliography: p. 187
  Includes index.
  1. Japanese literature—900–1700—History and
criticism.   2. Buddhism in literature.   3. Japan—
Civilization—Buddhist influences.   I. Title.
PL726.33.B8L34   1983   895.6′2′09382   82-45909
ISBN 0-520-05622-1 (paper)

PRINTED IN THE UNITED STATES OF AMERICA

    3   4   5   6   7   8   9

To My Parents

CONTENTS

PREFACE   ix

MAJOR ERAS OF JAPANESE HISTORY   xvi

1. "FLOATING PHRASES AND FICTIVE UTTERANCES":
   THE RISE AND FALL OF SYMBOLS   1

2. IN AND OUT THE ROKUDŌ: KYŌKAI AND THE FORMATION
   OF MEDIEVAL JAPAN   26

3. INNS AND HERMITAGES: THE STRUCTURE OF
   IMPERMANENCE   60

4. SYMBOL AND YŪGEN: SHUNZEI'S USE OF TENDAI
   BUDDHISM   80

5. CHŌMEI AS HERMIT: VIMALAKĪRTI IN THE "HŌJŌ-KI"   107

6. ZEAMI'S BUDDHISM: COSMOLOGY AND DIALECTIC IN
   NŌ DRAMA   116

7. SOCIETY UPSIDE-DOWN: KYŌGEN AS SATIRE AND AS
   RITUAL   133

8. THE POET AS SEER: BASHŌ LOOKS BACK   149

NOTES   165

JAPANESE NAMES AND TERMS   183

BIBLIOGRAPHY   187

INDEX   197

He has gradually vanquished the demon of wine
And does not get wildly drunk;
But the karma of words remains;
He has not abandoned verse.
                    —Po Chü-i (Hakurakuten)*

PREFACE

T HE ORIGIN OF THIS STUDY lies in the simultaneous frustration and fascination I felt nearly two decades ago when for the first time I saw a performance of nō drama in Japan. I was greatly moved by what I saw, but I was also greatly perplexed by the presence in this form of drama of energies, assumptions, and aesthetic values that seemed very different from those present in the classical theaters of ancient Greece and Renaissance Europe. Here was a form of drama that had evidently been shaped by a set of religious and philosophical assumptions—but these were neither those of Aristotle nor those of European Christianity. My curiosity about this led me to search for relevant books and to question people who I thought might provide information.

I soon discovered a certain consensus; it was that, although the components in nō are many and complex, it is probably Japanese Buddhism which did most to shape the world of nō. Beyond this, however, my frustration continued, since the available materials in Western languages provided information about Buddhist *elements* in this form of drama but stopped short of a real reconstruction of the way the Japanese in the medieval period of their history saw their world and envisioned their destinies in and through Buddhist terms and concepts. Footnotes gave definitions of things like arhats, ashuras, and Amida, but these things collectively never added up to a satisfying account of the intellectual and religious assumptions of the Buddhist poets, dramatists, and writers of prose in medieval Japan.

This book is first an attempt to provide what I could not find then and was subsequently forced to pursue in the original texts and in modern scholarly studies in Japanese. It considers a number of concepts, symbols, figures, and strategies but, above all, tries to see them as *interrelated parts* of problems and arguments that dominated the intellectual and religious life of medieval Japan. This is not, however, to claim that the Buddhist component in medieval Japanese civilization was always structured, coherent, or unitary. In fact, one of the things that became increasingly clear to me in the course of my research was the existence in medieval Japan of at least two very different, often conflicting, ways of viewing the world. Moreover, both of these were Buddhist and had their pedigree of origin on the Asian continent. The story of this disparity and of the attempts to reconcile these two ways of being Buddhist is one of the most interesting aspects of the intellectual and religious life of this period of Japanese history. In the chapters that follow I refer to these with a bit of conceptual shorthand, calling one Buddhism as cosmology and the other Buddhism as dialectic. Yet it is the tension and exchange between these two that is important. Not confined to learned discussions behind monastery walls, it reached out from there to leave a very deep impression on the practice of poetry, the purposes of narrative, the emergence of particular aesthetic values, and the shape of what unfolds in the theater. In brief, it was a tension and exchange from which Japan's literary arts profited greatly. As will become clear in the following chapters, Mahayana Buddhism in Japan also became a rich resource for those concerned to articulate aesthetic theories—especially for those who wished to define what they saw as an intrinsic connection between Buddhism and the literary arts. This relationship represented an especially fertile development in the Japanese medieval period, more fertile than, for instance, the relationship between Christianity and literary theory in medieval Europe. Though I have not tried in this book to make such comparisons between the Japanese and European medieval experience explicit, I hope they will be of interest to students of the literatures and religions of the West.

Between the inception and the completion of a book, however, many things are likely to happen, and these have a way of augmenting the original plan. Three such things on the way to this book are worthy of mention here. The first arose from my growing conviction that, since I was making a close scrutiny of old literary and religious texts, I would do well to take advantage of some rather fascinating approaches to texts developed within the past few decades. These new ways of looking at texts have, to my knowledge, been virtually untested and untried by scholars dealing with Japanese literary and religious materials. Here I have done nothing more than experiment with these approaches to see to what degree they can help illumine old texts. In some cases it is the approach of structuralism which I have adopted, but in others I have followed the admonition—primarily of Michel Foucault—that all texts and the ideas they embody must be seen as embedded in the social history of a given era. For the purposes of this book, I think the synchronic scope of structuralism and the diachronic scan advised by Foucault and others complement one another. I have also found a special usefulness in Victor Turner's studies of structure and antistructure; these studies have a rich potential for assisting our understanding of the complex relationships among Buddhist thought, literary texts, the various genres of theater, and historical developments within medieval Japanese society. Throughout this book I have tried to use these new approaches rather than be used by them; I have attempted to keep the texts themselves in view at all times. This cautiousness will be well rewarded if the following chapters are viewed simply as experiments with new techniques for the purpose of learning new things about medieval Japan. There is no attempt to be definitive or final in terms of a theory of textual analysis.

The second development on the way to this book was my growing aspiration to look at Buddhism in medieval Japan from outside the perspective of the various schools and sects that were spawned in this period. During the past few decades, the West's scholarship on Japanese Buddhism has made impressive progress and I am indebted to the many superb studies by scholars whose vocation is that of the Buddhologist. There is, however, an often natural and, I think, forgivable tendency among Buddhologists to identify with one person or school and see that person or school as having reached an unparalleled point in a long development. My own approach is somewhat different. I try to see medieval Japan as a period in which Buddhism and its variegated schools presented not only great solutions but also great problems for the Japanese living then. By the time it reached Japan, the Buddhism of continental Asia was already an entity of monumental proportions—in its spectrum of philosophical options, bureaucratic structures, architectural developments, commentorial treatises, and so forth. It also had within it certain conceptual problems and points of great debate. Its thinkers certainly did not always agree with one another. Thus, when the Japanese imbibed deeply from this continental source they inherited not only the treasures of the Mahayana but also many of its problems. My general approach in the following chapters is to leave these problems and tensions in place. I am more interested in defining the arena and the bases for the debates of the time than in focusing on a particular thinker or school seen as having resolved the large questions with a higher harmony or synthesis. As a result of this approach, I hope this book will complement the work of the various Buddhologists and at the same time be of interest to students of the general history of man's religions.

The third item not on my original agenda was increasingly forced on me by the nature of the materials. It consists of the need to give greater specificity and precision to what we mean when we refer to an era of Japan's history as the *medieval* one. I must confess to having been over the years somewhat uneasy with the protracted concern of Western scholars over the question of Japan's sudden and surprising "modernization." To me this has always seemed to border on what might be called Western narcissism—a too great fascination with the question of how Japan became to such a remarkable degree like the modern West. To me it has always seemed inherently more interesting to explore the reasons Japanese civilization is so different from European and American. In order to deal with the idea of modernization, it would seem essential to study premodern Japan. But this too is a division of history into only two parts, the modern and all else; it again reflects our willingness to use *modern* as the ruling rubric.

It is, at least in part, in an effort to wriggle free from the implicit constraints of the modernization problematic that I deliberately call the era under study medieval. In the first chapter I delineate the content I give to that term and try to state the criteria I have used to define its borders in time. My usage is, to be sure, unorthodox and irregular; it follows neither the usual meaning of medieval as that term is used by Western students of Japan's institutional history nor the use of the term *chūsei* by Japanese scholars. The hypothesis offered in the following pages is one that arose from my engagement with the texts I was reading. I felt compelled to the position by the texts, especially those of the eighth and ninth centuries, which seemed to be loudly insisting that the Japanese were entering not just a new era but an entirely new epoch. There is in these texts a sense of amazement that a whole new mode of understanding reality had been set forth and a whole new mode of discourse begun. These new concepts served as the principal substance of discussions and debates for many centuries afterward. They still structured the world of nō's greatest creativity in the fifteenth century. It seems to me that, at least in intellectual terms, the entity outlined in this book constitutes what some now would call an *episteme*, an era during which certain assumptions are commonly held and certain epistemic possibilities widely entertained.

By referring to this era as medieval I do not wish to claim that it was in some special sense an "age of faith." It was, of course, an age in which religious institutions had great power over the minds and lives of most people. But this does not imply that faith as some kind of quantifiable element in human existence was more present in that era and, by contrast, less present in an earlier or later epoch. In saying this I am trying to pursue the implications of some of the more recent developments in the history and philosophy of science, especially the rejection of the older positivist predication of human progress as a movement away from an age of faith toward one of science and knowledge. In this I follow Quine, Kuhn, and others in order to view the medieval epoch in Japan as one in which people tried on the basis of evidence and guesswork to represent the world and its workings to themselves with as much accuracy as possible. Their view of the world may have been very different from ours, but like ours, it was a composite of things known and unknown—that is, a "scientific" view that filled in the conceptual holes and uncoordinated places with elements of guesswork and stands taken on faith. I share the perspective of postpositivism and recognize an ingredient of belief in every moment and movement of scientific knowledge.

It will be clear in the following pages that I am much more interested in defining the inception of Japan's medieval period than in depicting its close with precision. Perhaps that is the work of a different book or to be dealt with by historians of the rise of "modern" Japan. I suppose this refusal to depict the end of the medieval arises out of my original intention to delineate the world view that gave shape to nō. When I have gotten to that apogee (I call it the high medieval), I become less concerned to follow the descent. It is interesting, however, to reflect on the implications of the poet Bashō's perception that he was living either at the close of one era or at the beginning of a new one. My refusal to be precise about the "end" of medieval Japan constitutes, I suspect, a certain connivance with Bashō. The last chapter of this book shares his mood of retrospection and nostalgia. What I like most about his longing for an era he called good are the power and possibilities implicit in the very act of recollection. Recollecting the past and bringing it again before the mirror of memory is, according to Mircea Eliade, one of the most powerful ways of keeping it alive or, if necessary, bringing it back to life.

Conversations with Professor Joseph M. Kitagawa at the University of Chicago a decade ago did much to shape this book; he encouraged my desire to explore the nexus between Buddhism and Japanese literature, guided me to key resources, and forced me to deal with certain important, though difficult, concepts. Among my teachers I am most grateful to him. Among my teachers in Japan, I especially appreciate the help of Professor Masamichi Kitayama, who read poetry and the essays of Zeami with me and gave freely of his time and knowledge. Mr. Rikuzō Kamikawa served as an unparalleled tutor, applying the rigor for which he has a great reputation among those fortunate enough to have had him as a teacher. Professor Masao Abe guided me through the more intricate moves made within Buddhist philosophy. Professor Kōsai Fukushima and Mr. Senshō Kimura of Otani University read the *Mo-ho Chih-kuan* with me in Kyoto in 1976. Masatoshi Nagatomi sharpened my thinking about Tendai and the importance of Fujiwara Shunzei. Earlier, Professor Kensuke Tamai led me to good sources as did Professor Jin'ichi Konishi. Among the many others who offered comments, criticism, and encouragement I am especially grateful to Robert N. Bellah, Marius B. Jansen, Martin Collcutt, Anthony Yu, Nathan

Sivin, James Sanford, Karen Brazell, Henry D. Smith, Jeffrey Stout, S. F. Teiser, Kazumitsu Katō, and my colleagues at the University of California, Los Angeles. My wife, Mariko, wrote the characters in the glossary.

Generous grants from the Japan Foundation and the Social Science Research Council enabled me to spend the 1975–76 academic year in Kyoto doing research. Assistance from Princeton University enabled me to return during the summer of 1977. Many of the chapters have had an earlier debut in one form or another. The second and fourth chapters were presented and discussed at the first and third conferences, respectively, of the Project for the Study of Buddhism in Japanese Civilization sponsored by Harvard University's John King Fairbank Center for East Asian Research and with a grant from the National Endowment for the Humanities. Chapter three was presented to the Topical Seminar on Time and Space in Japanese Culture, sponsored by the American Council of Learned Societies and the Social Science Research Council, and later to the Regional Seminar of the Center for Japanese and Korean Studies of the University of California, Berkeley. Chapter five was given before the American Oriental Society at Washington University in 1979, and six was part of the annual meeting of the American Academy of Religion in New Orleans in 1978. The seventh chapter in an earlier version was presented at the Conference on High Culture and Popular Culture in East Asia at Harvard in 1978. Through the auspices of Professor Tōru Haga of Tokyo University the third chapter has already appeared in Japanese; it was published in *Hikaku Bungaku no Kenkyū* in 1981. The final chapter, in a slightly different version, appeared in 1980 in *Transitions and Transformations: Essays in Honor of Joseph M. Kitagawa* and is used here with permission of E. J. Brill of Leiden.

Finally, I wish to express my gratitude to the University of California Press for the care taken in making this book. My editor, John R. Miles, gave the manuscript a very intelligent initial reading and suggested numerous improvements. Then, with her own very careful reading Cheri Derby made not only the sentences but also the overall substance more readable.

NOTE ON JAPANESE NAMES

For the sake of readers unfamiliar with Japanology it would be nice to be able to say that everything here is simply the reverse of our Western practice and that people are referred to by their surname first, followed by their given name. This is generally the case, and it can usually be assumed here that the first name given (also in the case of Chinese names) is the surname or family name, which initially identifies the person. There are, however, important exceptions. Many of the writers discussed were Buddhist monks who in taking the tonsure also received a completely new name with religious significance; usually they are properly referred to by this name rather than that of their family—as, for example, in the case of Saigyō, Jien, and Dōgen. In some other instances, however, when a poet or writer has had great fame among the Japanese over some centuries, or at least some decades, he is known merely by his given name—thus, simply "Teika" rather than Fujiwara Teika and "Bashō" instead of Matsuo Bashō. To further complicate matters there are now an increasing number of modern Japanese scholars who publish both in their original language and in one or another of the languages of the West. It seems right to me to refer to them differently and in accord with the two systems of attribution; thus, the same writer is "Hisamatsu Shin'ichi" when I refer to his "Yūgen-ron" in Japanese but "Shin'ichi Hisamatsu" when I cite his English book *Zen and the Fine Arts*. Japanologists will understand the problems involved and nonspecialists are asked to use this guide and tolerate our peculiar practices. Some respite lies in the bibliography, where East and West agree on listing people by their surname.

MAJOR ERAS OF JAPANESE HISTORY

Jōmon	5th millennium to ca. 250 B.C.E.
Yayoi	ca. 250 B.C.E. to ca. 250 C.E.
Tumulus	ca. 250 to ca. 500 C.E.
Asuka	ca. 500 to 710
Nara	710 to 784
Heian	794 to 1191
Kamakura	1192 to 1333
Muromachi	1334 to 1573
Azuchi-Momoyama	1574 to 1600
Tokugawa	1600 to 1867
Meiji	1867 to 1912
Taishō	1912 to 1926
Shōwa	1926 to present

1

''FLOATING PHRASES AND FICTIVE UTTERANCES'': THE RISE AND FALL OF SYMBOLS

> They say that poetry at its height
> extols the All which escapes us,
> and they deny that the tortoise
> is more rapid than lightning.
> You alone knew that movement
> is not different from stasis
> that emptiness is fullness and clarity
> the most diffused of clouds.
> —Eugenio Montale, *Xenia*[1]

THE INTERPRETATION OF SAIGYŌ'S DREAM

SOME OF THE world's poetry and prose seems to have such directness and simplicity that, even when translated from one language to another or from one epoch to another, it seems clear and compelling. It has what we sometimes call an obvious universality. Other fine examples of literature, however, lie hidden in the opaque recesses of a particular culture or era in history and need a good deal more than mere translation to be understood in later time and in another place.

Much of the literature of medieval Japan is, for us in the modern West, decidedly of this second type. It does not charm us with the terse but clear action of a haiku, a comparatively late development in Japanese literature. Nor does it engage us as does a novel by Yukio Mishima with its neatly structured plot line and its twentieth-century interest in explorations of the psyche. Instead it hides away from us. It has literary modes, techniques, and values quite different from those of our own time. But perhaps even more important, it originated in a culture that had intellectual assumptions at variance not only with those of the modern West but also somewhat at variance with those of modern Japan.

Such poetry and prose might sometimes be so dense and full of cultural presuppositions that we are tempted to turn it aside, or dismiss it as unimportant and unworthy of our time. To do so, however, would be to overlook that it is often the past's most recondite and forbidding texts which enable us to reconstruct and understand the particular shape and scope of an era. Moreover, it is often from such texts that we can expand our perception of the literary experience and the history of human thought. The following poem with prose introduction by Saigyō, a Buddhist monk of twelfth-century Japan, is an apt illustration:

> At the time that the priest Jakunen invited others to contribute to a hundred-poem collection, I declined to take part. But then on the road where I was making a pilgrimage to Kumano, I had a dream. In it appeared Tankai, the administrator of Kumano, and [the poet] Shunzei. Tankai said to Shunzei: "Although all things in this world undergo change, the Way of Poetry extends unaltered even to the last age." I opened my eyes and understood. Then I quickly wrote a verse and sent it off to Jakunen. This is what I composed there in the heart of the mountains:

sue no yo no	'Even in an age
kono nasake nomi	gone bad the lyric's Way
kawarazu to	stays straight'—
mishi yume nakuba	Not seeing this in a dream,
yoso ni kakamashi	I'd have been deaf to truth.[2]

Although it has not gained much attention even in Japan in recent centuries, this is a fascinating poem in many ways. The autobiographical element is fairly clear. Saigyō tells us that an invitation to contribute a poem to another monk's poetry collection arrived at what seemed to be an inconvenient time, namely, as he was about to begin a pilgrimage to an important Shinto shrine. Therefore, he at first declined. Along the way, however, he had a dream in which there occurred a conversation between Tankai, the head of the shrine to which he was going, and Fujiwara Shunzei (1114–1204), the doyen of poets in that era. The former told the latter that the practice of poetry was an abiding human discipline, and this resolved Saigyō's dilemma. The experience became the material for the poem he wrote and sent off to the collection.

But this is scarcely all that is needed for us to understand the poem today. At least, it neglects to point out ways the situation and the poem it brought into being were deeply implicated in the world view and characteristic problems of medieval Japan. That is, the cognitive dimension of this poem cannot be overlooked, since the mind of the poet who composed it was shaped by the questions and answers—primarily Buddhist questions and answers—of his epoch. In order to illustrate this, three elements can be singled out.

First, it is important to realize that people in the twelfth and thirteenth centuries of Japan's history were deeply absorbed in a debate as to whether the entire world had just entered a necessarily evil era called *mappō*, the final epoch of the current Buddhist cycle. Many of those who embraced this idea had calculated that as of the year 1052 (or approximately 130 years before this poem was written) there had commenced a lengthy period during which the correct understanding and practice of Buddhism had been virtually nonexistent.[3] In Saigyō's own day there was enough change and chaos in society to give what looked like empirical support to those who fixed on this idea.

Although this was a question of paramount importance for the era, there was anything but unanimity about it. Some took the calculations to be correct and the current laxity of monastic discipline as proof that the theory was true. Others, especially the Zen master Dōgen (1200–1253), argued against the mappō theory; they held that the possibility of understanding and practicing Buddhism was as good as it had ever been and that theories such as that of mappō were merely mental contrivances by which shallow understanding and loose practice were rationalized.[4] One scholar, the Tendai abbot and important poet Jien (1155–1225), was able to use the notion of mappō very creatively in his great work of historiography, the *Gukan-shō*.[5]

Saigyō was a man of his era in that he too was vexed by these questions. To him, a monk, they were not esoteric or arcane but had immediate implications. These implications had to do with the nature, possibility, and value of his austerities as a monk. In the following poem, for example, he seems quite clearly to be referring with disapproval to adherents of the mappō idea. ("Vulture Peak" refers to the place in India where the *Lotus Sutra* was said to have first been promulgated.)

On that chapter of the *Lotus Sutra* called "Duration of the Life of the Tathagata":

Washi-no-yama　　　　　　　　Those who view the moon
tsuki o irinu to　　　　　　　　over Vulture Peak as one

miru hito wa   now sunk below
kuraki ni mayou   the horizon . . . are men whose minds
kokoro nari keri   confused, hold the real darkness.[6]

In the poem quoted earlier, however, Saigyō seems to give the mappō concept at least the benefit of the doubt. He claims to have finally understood through his dream that the way of poetry remains as strong and vital as it has always been; this is so even in an era some call the final era ("sue no yo")—by which they mean that it is an evil epoch because there has begun a serious deterioration of mankind's knowledge of the truth of Buddhism. To see poems such as these two in the context of discussions going on in that era, and as reflecting Saigyō's own struggle over such questions, is to identify an important node where the world of poetry and the world of medieval Japanese intellectual life intersect.

The second thing that locates Saigyō's dream poem in a medieval Japanese context—and so hides it behind a veil for us—is Saigyō's assumption that conversations that take place in dreams cannot be dismissed but have some very special significance and message that must be accepted by the dreamer. It is one of the hallmarks of this era that *muchū mondō*, "conversations taking place in dreams," are highly valued and are considered so directly relevant to the problems faced by the dreamer that they require no act of interpretation. They are not cryptic messages that need to be decoded by someone with expertise in such things but direct exchanges between dead persons and living ones. The conversation in Saigyō's dream was between Tankai, an old friend of Saigyō's who had died about six years earlier, and the poet and critic Fujiwara Shunzei, who was still living.

Although the origins of this belief may lie in the most archaic levels of Japanese society and in religious practices that antedate the introduction of Buddhism, it would be wrong to view the attitude to dream conversations as merely a naive and primitive folk-belief that survived, although very oddly, in the practice of Buddhists such as Saigyō and his contemporaries. On the contrary, this belief fit rather nicely into some fairly sophisticated philosophical discussions carried on by Buddhist thinkers throughout most of Asia at this time.[7] For, in the opinion of large numbers of Buddhists, man's capacity for dreaming posed serious questions about the nature of reality—questions that were more philosophical than psychological. Dreams raised questions about the stability and reliability of what we ordinarily regard as the "reality" of the world we experience when awake.

Perhaps it would be most accurate to say that the Buddhists of this period were interested in flattening or relativizing our habitual and easy distinction between what we identify as the *reality* of the world we experience when awake and the *illusion* of all the events that take place in our dreams. As Buddhists, their claim and conviction was that the difference between ordinary waking consciousness and ordinary dream consciousness pales to insignificance when both of these are set in contrast to something else, namely, the consciousness of the mind that has achieved enlightenment. In other words, the Buddhists made it their business to point out that it is not a matter of a black-or-white difference between waking consciousness and dream consciousness but rather of both of them being *on a continuum* of consciousnesses. To them our ordinary juxtaposition of only two types of consciousness divided sharply into the categories of reality and dream was inadequate, itself an illusion.

This was a philosophical move that had a direct effect on the status of both waking and dreaming consciousness. Especially in the traditional considerations of the Hossō school, one of the continental schools of Buddhist philosophy, which established itself during the Nara period of Japanese history (710−784) and set the problematic for subsequent centuries, the phenomenon of dreams was a subject of close scrutiny. The reality status of ordinary waking consciousness was radically lowered by placing it on a continuum with dreaming consciousness. This was emphasized through language describing the fact that, contrary to our hopes and projections, all the phenomena and relationships we experience in our daily lives are bound to disappear with time. Nothing is permanent; all things succumb willy-nilly to the law of impermanence (*mujō*) —often almost as quickly as the things we see at night in our dreams.

Any acquaintance with the prose and poetry of the Heian period reveals that it is replete with references to all things of this world as in reality as "fleeting as a dream." The literature of the period abounds with such statements, so much so that they sometimes seem almost hackneyed and mechanical. But what we usually tend to overlook is that this was the extension deep into belles lettres of serious philosophical discussions going on concurrently within the confines of Buddhist monasteries, and quite probably also in the salons of the educated courtiers. The repeated statements about impermanence must be viewed against the background of the era's discussions about the nature of reality, the propensity of the human mind to delude itself, and the variety of complex relationships that can exist between the world and the mind. The rich literature of the Heian period—that of both men and women, clergy and laity—abundantly shows that people carried their fascination with these questions concerning reality, illusion, and knowledge into the concretely imagined poetry and prose they were composing.

The corollary of the Buddhist philosophical preoccupation with dreams was equally interesting and important. People in medieval Japan assumed that, if it were demonstrated that things experienced in waking consciousness were little different from those experienced in dreams, it must also be true that things experienced in dreams are at least as real as those encountered in waking consciousness. Saigyō reflects lyrically on this in the following poem:

utsutsu o mo	Since the "real world" seems
utsutsu to sara ni	to be less than really real,
oboeneba	why need I suppose
yume o mo yume to	the world of dreams is nothing
nanika omowan	other than a world of dreams?[8]

Saigyō seems to be saying that the hard edge of distinction that we raise between the world of perceived phenomena ("utsusu") and that of dreams ("yume") can be honed down and, as a consequence, dreams can be seen to have more of "reality" in them than was expected.

For the Buddhists, this seemed especially true of certain dreams, dreams that appear to press in on the dreamer with even more reality and more significance than things experienced in ordinary diurnal consciousness. Such a dream even lay at the beginning of Buddhism—at least according to legend. As retold in Japanese literature in the opening episode of the *Konjaku-monogatari* of the early twelfth century, Śākyamuni Buddha's birth in India many centuries earlier had taken place because he, while still a bodhisattva or Buddha-to-be in the Tusita heaven, had decided to be born on earth and then deliberately entered the womb of Queen Māyā. The rather fabulous account in the Japanese retelling of this foundation tale continues:

> As the Queen lay sleeping in the night, she dreamed that the Bodhisattva descended from the skies riding upon a white elephant with six tusks, and that he entered her body through her right side. Her body was transparent, and he was visible through it, like an object inside a beryl jar. The Queen awoke with a start. She went to the King and told him her dream. "I too," said the King, "have had such a dream."[9]

They then sought an interpreter who explained to them that this was a wondrous sign that indicated the child in the Queen's womb would become a Buddha.

Thus, even in the continental tradition of Buddhism, there was a good precedent for the seriousness with which dreams were taken in medieval Japan. Especially significant to the Japanese, however, was the kind of dream incident that seems to indicate to the dreamer that a problem in his life could be readily solved or that he must take some definite action. For example, the author of the *Nihon ryōi-ki*, who wrote at the end of the eighth century, tells us that his purpose for becoming a Buddhist monk was made clear to him through a concatenation of strange events and a preternatural dream.[10]

Saigyō, then, in stating that the solution to his dilemma came through a dream in which two important figures had a conversation about that very problem, was being neither pretentious nor simpleminded. He was merely participating in the mental structure of his era, in what everyone at the time would have regarded as common sense, the expectations about the world that are implicitly held as true by the vast majority of people in a society. Saigyō's trusting the contents of his dream as genuine reality was a way of drawing practical benefit from a long tradition in Asian Buddhism and from fairly sophisticated discussions in contemporary Buddhist circles concerning the relationship of illusion to reality.

The third and perhaps most important element lying in the intellectual background of Saigyō's dream poem is one that engaged many of the best minds of that era. It has to do with attempts to comprehend the exact nature of the relationship between Buddhism and the composition of poetry. It is obviously the basic problem of this episode, and it was a problem Saigyō struggled with during most of his life.[11] But he was not alone. Throughout this period many of the practicing poets were Buddhist monks and nuns, and so it became for them a matter of considerable importance to define the relationship between the writing of poetry and their religious vocations.

Part of the problem arose because a good poet or poetess was expected to be capable of writing poems on a whole range of topics. This included poems on love between the sexes, which Buddhist monks and nuns were supposed, at least, to be beginning to transcend. Ever since the publication of the *Man'yōshū* in the middle of the eighth century, the Japanese world of poetry had included a tradition of poems of passion and of gently handled eroticism. For Buddhist clerics who wished to be both traditional and spiritually serious, this obviously created a dilemma.

This was only part of an even larger problem, however, a problem that arose because the writing of poetry and involvement in the world of lyrical exchange and competition constantly threatened to deflect the energies of those who had chosen a religious vocation. The conflict of interests was potentially very serious. Once having left life as a householder (*shukke*) and taken the tonsure, monks and nuns in medieval Japan often feared that the whole purpose of that decision would be compromised—perhaps even totally lost—if they were to become deeply involved in writing lyrics and start hankering after the praise, prizes, and prestige lavished on good poets in this era. Yoshishige Yasutane (?−1002), who had once been a famous court poet, took the name of Jakushin when he became a monk and eventually gave up writing poetry completely.[12] Especially during the late twelfth and early thirteenth centuries, there came into

Japanese Buddhism a strong emphasis on single-mindedness and concentration on one and only one kind of religious practice. Different schools placed the emphasis on different kinds of practice and different foci of concentration, but almost all alike stressed the importance of focused rather than diffused and scattered energies. Even the great Zen master Dōgen (1200−1253) is quoted as having said that the writing of poetry was a dangerous diversion for those who really ought to be single-mindedly sitting in meditation. In such a climate the monk or nun who went on writing verse had reason to be anxious about his or her attainment of Buddhahood. Saigyō seems to have experienced a special agony in his attempts to resolve this problem.

This is not to say that the clergy stopped writing poetry, however. It is merely to note that for those who went on writing while in clerical robes there was a serious intellectual and religious problem. The result was a discussion that went on for centuries. It was one of the most interesting sources of disagreement and debate in medieval Japan, as this was a period when both poetry and Buddhism were taken with great seriousness and were important in the lives of all literate Japanese.

The presupposition of many in this period was that at bottom the practice of poetry and the practice of Buddhism were fully compatible; but this had to be proved and demonstrated, not merely asserted. Those who shared the problem shared also the task of locating good precedents in the past and constructing new arguments in the present. For precedents none served better than Po Chü-i (772−846), the Chinese poet who was known affectionately to the Japanese as Hakurakuten and whose poetry and personality were much revered throughout this period. Part of the reason for Po's popularity lay in the comparative simplicity and directness of his verse. However he was also seen as something of a paragon for having worked out a rapprochement between that part of him which was a Buddhist and that part which was a poet.[13] Late in his life, during the year 839, Po Chü-i gave a copy of his poetry to a Buddhist library. His written explanation referred to his poems as nothing more than "floating phrases and fictive utterances" ("k'uang-yen i-yu") but expressed the hope that even as such they might in the future somehow bring honor to the Buddhist dharma. For many Japanese this phrase, which they rendered as "kyōgen kigo" or "kyōgen kigyo," and the hope that even such ephemeral utterances might serve the Buddhist dharma, were important, and the phrase became much celebrated.[14] Since Po had found a way to reconcile the writing of verse with the practice of Buddhist disciplines, the Japanese poets of the medieval period were much encouraged. The phrase and its implicit suggestion that the problem had been or could be resolved reverberated down the centuries for those

Japanese who wished to retain the best of both poetry and Buddhism.[15] It was their way of reconciling the "Way of poetry" (*kadō*) with the "Way of Buddhism" (*butsudō*).

This problem will be examined in greater detail in the chapters that follow. Here my purpose has been simply to throw some light on the context of an otherwise puzzling selection from Saigyō in order to suggest the dynamics of the many-faceted relationship between Buddhism and the literary arts in medieval Japan.

THE ARC OF JAPAN'S MEDIEVAL EXPERIENCE

To continue on in this same fashion, however, would be to cast this entire study in the format of lengthy footnotes appended to dense texts. These might illuminate aspects of those texts to some degree, but the study as a whole would fail to provide what is most needed in our knowledge of medieval Japan—namely, a reconstruction of the basic intellectual and religious *shape* of that epoch. This is to say that all the bits of seemingly esoteric information and the lines of seemingly arcane discussions were not esoteric or arcane to the medieval Japanese, and we will really understand that era and its texts only if we see these disparate things as parts of a framework. This framework was one of interrelated problems and concepts shared jointly by all literate Japanese and possibly a portion of the illiterate population as well.

In other words, when medieval Japan is described in terms of its intellectual shape and suppositions, it can be seen to form what today is often called an *episteme*. It was a period during which there was a general consensus concerning what kinds of problems needed discussion, what kinds of texts and traditional practices constituted authority worthy of citation and appeal, and what kinds of things constituted the symbols central to the culture and to the transmission of information within it. This means that we are able to come to an approximate definition of medieval Japan in intellectual terms.[16] I would suggest that we can best account for the vast array of materials in this period by defining *medieval* Japan as that epoch during which the basic intellectual problems, the most authoritative texts and resources, and the central symbols were all Buddhist. This is not to say that Buddhist problems, texts, and symbols were the sole ones of the era; it is merely to claim that they held intellectual hegemony during that period of time. I would further suggest that through a careful analysis of materials at our disposal we can not only observe and describe the inception of this epoch but can also see that, at a point in time many centuries later, Buddhist problems, texts, and symbols ceased to hold the central place they once occupied. Although they continue to exist and even have a certain vitality in the twentieth century, they now live alongside serious competitors in the intellectual and cultural arena.

A serious concern to depict the intellectual and religious history of Japan forces us to redefine the edges of the medieval experience of the Japanese in such a way that it does not remain entrapped in the rubrics found useful by institutional historians. During at least the past decade, a number of Japanese scholars have demonstrated the need to take a new look at the problem of periodizing Japanese history.[17] When it comes to describing what makes medieval Japan really medieval in intellectual terms, we need to see that events such as the growth of feudalism or boundary marks such as "the end of Nara" or the "beginning of Kamakura" can blind us through their very familiarity and handiness. There is no reason to assume simply that a sudden radical change in the political order had an immediate and pervasive effect on all the literary and intellectual endeavors of the time.

The so-called idealist alternative may be just as problematic, however. There is no reason to assume that ideas float freely through history, completely impervious to the changes in society, the pull of power politics, and the intellectual's lurking need in every era to demonstrate to himself and others that ideas in general, and his own ideas especially, have real relevance. The influence of contemporaneous events on a writer's program of writing is fairly obvious, for example, in the case of the priest Jien and his writing of the *Gukan-shō*. It often seems much less important when it is a piece of poetry or a random essay that is being considered, but even then we should never assume that literary and intellectual life exist in a world apart. With only a few exceptions, the poets of the Heian period wrote as if power politics and social struggle did not exist; but this was a very conscious ignoring of part of their world and constituted a constriction of the perceptual field that was almost a litany inviting anything outside that field—social and political change especially—to leave the world of their experience.[18] Through their very genteel tastes and constricted vision they asserted what they took to be their right to social preeminence.

The view that a literary world is a world unto itself unaffected by other things makes it possible to do literary history in a tidy, hermetic environment; but it belies the fact that writers are also people with concerns other than writing and that those concerns will inevitably find a place in what they write. Yet to attempt to view literary or intellectual history as something that merely takes its shape in the powerful wake of politics and social change is to forget that writers are also readers. As literati they are influenced not only by contemporaneous

events but also by the books they read and the past, which through that reading
is made contemporaneous. Literati are, by definition, men and women who are
bound to be influenced to an unusual degree by the past—that is, by the
manuscripts with which they are in almost daily interaction. These books are
not only a source but also a standard; they comprise a canon that cannot be
lightly dismissed. It might be best, then, to take the complex view: a literatus is
neither the pawn of social pressures nor the purveyor of pure ideas. His role
might be best described as that of a mediator between books from the past
regarded as classics and the particular problems and opportunities of his own
time.

Recognition of the essential engagement on the part of a literatus with a
collection of books widely regarded as canonical provides a useful tool for
defining the arc of the medieval experience in Japan. It gives none of the usual
comfort and convenience of a date fixed on a time line—as when a seat of power
changes location or a great ruler dies; but it does provide greater specificity to
the attempt to define medieval Japan as an epoch dominated by the problems,
texts, and symbols of Buddhism. By thinking of this epoch in terms of its
canon, we can describe Japan's medieval period as that span of time during
which the literate people of the country held the classics of Buddhism to be the
ultimate norm—that is, the canon for integrating, interpreting, and judging a
much wider range of books and experiences they also accepted as valuable and,
to a lesser degree, authoritative.

The Japanese inherited from the continent not only the sutras of Buddhism,
in a flow that lasted for centuries, but also, and at the same time, the non-
Buddhist classics of China. They also came to possess in written form a record
of indigenous experiences, narratives, and mythologies all of which were
authoritative in some sense even though they were not overtly Buddhist. Still,
in what is here defined as the medieval epoch, scholarship and learning were
largely carried on in Buddhist monasteries. It was, then, an era in which the
Buddhist works had an edge in importance. They were usually referred to as
naikyō, "inner scriptures," and distinguished from *gesho*, "outer books," the
non-Buddhist works that, while great and valuable, were given a position
subordinate to the sutras of Buddhism.

The temper of the times was to be as synthetic and syncretic as possible.
Great effort was expended in harmonizing Shinto, Confucian, Taoist, and
Buddhist perspectives. The ancient practices of indigenous Shinto and the
imported doctrines of Buddhism especially were seen as fully compatible
within the scheme of *honji-suijaku*, according to which the various deities of
ancient Japan were understood to have been local manifestations of an under-

lying Buddhist reality. The assumption was that no conflict between the two need arise since each was an expression of the other.[19]

A synthesis is an accomplishment, however, not a given. And it is, moreover, an accomplishment attained through the assertion of priorities. Even within the most tolerant of intellectual and religious frameworks, there is often the assumption that one form, maybe because it is seen as the basis for the others, has a higher place as an articulation of truth. Such was the case in medieval Japan, where the Buddhists held sway over the era because they were in a position to define the issues and the answers to those issues. We can detect evidence of opposition to this, and we can see how the Buddhists fashioned the intellectual tools that would guarantee their hegemony. Both the possibility of conflict and the formula for harmony are present in the opening sentences of the *Nihon ryōi-ki*, an early Heian work:

> The Inner [Buddhist] scriptures and the outer [non-Buddhist] classics originally came to Japan through the [Korean kingdom of] Paekche in two waves. The latter came during the reign of emperor Ōjin who lived at the palace of Toyoakira in Kurushima, whereas the former arrived during the reign of emperor Kinmei who lived at the palace of Kanazashi in Shikishima. It seems fashionable these days for those scholars who study the outer classics to slander the teachings of Buddhism, and for those who read the inner scriptures to neglect the outer classics. They are all foolish and delude themselves. The wise, however, are well-versed in both the inner and outer traditions; they have a sense of awe and believe in the law of karmic causation.[20]

Although this is a call for social and intellectual harmonization, it is offered with Buddhist terms and concepts as the guidelines. The very use of the inner/outer distinction implies the priority in importance of the former; it is understood to be the more profound and penetrating of the two types of books. In addition, the implication is that the Buddhists are less culpable than their opponents; theirs is merely the fault of neglect, whereas the non-Buddhists are actively slandering Buddhist teachings. Finally and most tellingly, the consequences of failing to achieve harmony are depicted in classically Buddhist terms; those who upset the needed harmony deceive themselves and will suffer the consequences of bad karma. The price to be paid by those who refuse to synthesize Buddhism and other teachings is to be paid in distinctively Buddhist currency.

A roughly contemporaneous work, the *Sangō shiiki* by the Shingon master Kūkai (774–835), is more polished and literate than the *Nihon ryōi-ki*, but it too articulates the need for synthesis within a framework in which Buddhism clearly has preeminence. It is cast in the form of a conversation in which representatives of Confucianism, Taoism, and Buddhism debate one another and enter a competition to win the adherence of a young profligate. In the end, all the participants, even the Confucianist and Taoist, are convinced by the arguments of the Buddhist mendicant and recognize the comprehensive superiority of the teaching he espouses. They tell him:

How superficial the teachings of Confucius and Lao Tzu are: From now on we will observe faithfully your teaching with our whole beings—by writing it on the paper of our skins, with pens of bone, ink of blood, and the inkstone of the skull. Thus your teaching will be the boat and wagon by which we may cross over the ocean of transmigration.[21]

It is a plea for harmony but also for the hegemony of Buddhism within that harmony.

Works such as the *Nihon ryōi-ki* and the *Sangō shiiki* appear at the beginning of the epoch here called medieval; they are argumentative and insistent because they came into being at a time when it was still less than obvious that Buddhism would be the dominant intellectual and religious framework of Japan. This situation had changed greatly by the twelfth and thirteenth centuries, when there were arguments within the Buddhist establishment as to which school was preferable but there was no longer any need to defend Buddhism as a whole against serious alternatives. According to the perspective offered in this book, in the late Heian to the Muromachi periods the arc of Japan's medieval experience reached its apogee: although there were often fierce debates within the camp of Buddhism, there was no question that Buddhism in one form or another was the final authority in all matters of the mind and social behavior.

In the Tokugawa period things changed rapidly. As Tetsuo Najita notes, "Whereas the governing intellectual force during the past 1,000 years may be characterized as being primarily Buddhist, Japan during the Tokugawa era concentrated with sudden and conspicuous intensity on Confucian studies."[22] Adherents of Neo-Confucianism and National Learning began to feel restive with the old synthesis; they began to assert that something other than Buddhism deserved to be aired and possibly recognized as more valuable than what had for centuries held intellectual hegemony. Certainly, Buddhism did not seem to offer what many now were searching for, namely, what Najita calls the "intellectual foundations of modern Japanese politics." But this is not to say that the Buddhist hegemony disappeared overnight. To see this period as one in which the taken-for-granted truth of the Buddhist episteme began to collapse is only to note that Buddhists were forced once again to recognize competitors and to defend themselves where possible. It was a time during which alternative models and modes of understanding were presented to the Japanese, and

Buddhism was no longer the sole canon for thought and experience. In addition to Neo-Confucianism and the Neo-Shinto texts of the Tokugawa period, there was also the science of so-called Dutch Learning and an ever-growing acquaintance with the classics, methods, and criteria derived from Western sources. In this expanding intellectual bazaar Buddhists discovered that their ancient framework, problems, and symbols were only some among many. When Buddhism's implicit hegemony could no longer be taken for granted, Japan had come to the end of its medieval experience.

The focus of this book will be on the beginning rather than the end of the medieval epoch. There is an important sense in which Buddhism even today remains as a source, power, and influence in Japanese intellectual and social life. After passing through paroxysms of opposition during the *haibutsu-kishaku* movement of the 1860s, Japanese Buddhism has experienced something of a renaissance in the twentieth century among intellectuals interested in the continuation of the past into the present. Though Buddhist problems, texts, and symbols no longer dominate the intellectual life of Japan, they retain a very important presence. And, because ritual is often the most resilient aspect of culture, the perpetuation of the medieval into the modern is still very much a part of the ceremonial and ritual experience of today's Japanese.

THE BUDDHIST SYSTEM OF SYMBOLS

The medieval Japanese were like one of the various peoples of medieval Europe in having a distinct language and identity, while also being part of something larger. That is, they were part of the intellectual life of continental Asia and were involved in a lively exchange of ideas brokered primarily through the great Buddhist monasteries and temples of China. In the early portion of the Japanese medieval period, Buddhism was at the height of its influence in China. Many of the literati of T'ang China were still seriously involved with forms of Buddhist thought and practice that continued to arrive there from India. In terms of the exchange of both material and intellectual culture, it was an open and creative period; Japan lay at the far eastern end of an ecumene that stretched through Korea and China and along the Silk Road to India and Afghanistan. The treasures that were housed in Nara's Shōsō-in during the eighth century are an unmistakable, concrete index to the period's ready and wide exchange of goods and ideas.

It was under the aegis of Buddhism that most of this exchange was carried on. This was the first, and perhaps also the last, time in Asia's history that virtually all literate people from Afghanistan to Japan shared a basic set of books they regarded as the ultimate authority and fund of knowledge. They had these books in different renditions and languages and certainly would not have agreed as to which was the preeminent text, or, the canon of the canon; but they would not have disputed the supreme value of the library that housed the words attributed to Śakyamuni Buddha. The institutional organization of Buddhism was never as sophisticated or as centralized as that of the Roman church in medieval Europe; nor was its concern for doctrinal orthodoxy quite as exacting. Nevertheless, the books, rites, and meditational practices of Buddhism gave to much of Asia during these centuries a single, common "universe of discourse."

The literate part of the Japanese population participated fully in this common episteme. Some did so as monks by traveling to China or by studying in Japan with an immigrant master such as Chien-chen (686?–763), known in Japan as Ganjin and by the posthumous title the Great Master Who Crossed the Sea. Others, both clergy and the wider community of lay practitioners, participated in this same intellectual milieu by reading and copying the multitude of Buddhist texts in Chinese and by attendance at rituals and debates held in the great temples constructed during that era.

Not only the clergy but also the literate laity were involved in the digestion and dissemination of Buddhist learning. The proliferation of manuscripts was possible because of the extensive copying carried on as an exercise in piety for anyone who could read and write.[23] Whether the practice of copying manuscripts indicates that Buddhism was deeply internalized is a question that has vexed scholars of this period of Japanese history. Many have pointed out that the copying of the Chinese characters of a text may have been a rote, mechanical exercise and that it in no way proves the text was understood or that there was any serious engagement with the content of the manuscript. The suspicion that the Buddhism of the courtiers may have been quite superficial is reinforced, for instance, by Sei Shōnagon's suggestion in her *Makura no sōshi* (*Pillow Book*) that it is really the prettiness of priests that she most likes in Buddhism.[24] We have no way of knowing how typical her tenth-century statement was; nor do we have any means of access to the minds of people copying texts in a long-ago age. We are probably correct in assuming that it was sometimes a mechanical exercise and sometimes one in which the copier internalized what he or she wrote down.

Perhaps the entire question is wrongly put; the real engagement with Buddhism on the part of the literate laity was through sustained exposure to the various symbols with which the texts and rituals of the period were replete. Even if the laity did not participate in the dialectic and debate carried on in the monasteries, they were very much involved in the pursuit of poetry, and the sutras of Buddhism were a natural, available, and rich repository of concrete symbols and subtle metaphors. A scripture such as the *Hokke-kyō (Lotus Sutra)* was for these courtly writers a treasury that seemed to overflow with an abundance of images;[25] for most of the medieval epoch it was important not only for its teaching but also for its vivid manner of presentation. Likewise, the *Yuima-kitsu-gyō* was important to these Buddhist laymen because its main figure, the Indian Vimalakīrti, was an urbane and witty layman whose profound understanding of Buddhism was praised by Śākyamuni himself.[26] The poetry and prose written by the laity adopted, used, and reinforced Buddhist symbols and tropes received in the scriptures from the continent. For that reason, much of the literature of this period in Japan forms a part of one continuous and ever-evolving tradition.

Recognizing this partially resolves the long disputed question whether the Buddhism of the courtiers was or was not superficial. Although, from our distance, we cannot read "hearts" to judge the degree of understanding, we can read texts, the texts the courtiers themselves have left us. And from these texts—poems, random essays, tales, drama scenarios, and treatises—we can see that that the symbol-system of classical Buddhism was imbibed deeply by the medieval Japanese.[27] Since the adoption and reiteration of the symbols pertaining to a religion or philosophy are tantamount to participation in its most fundamental aspects, we have every reason to conclude that Buddhism was part and parcel of Japanese intellectual and literary life at a fairly early point. It therefore seems a mistake to assume that it was for many centuries a veneer and only really came to be understood by the Japanese in the thirteenth century and the Kamakura era.[28] Although the impressive thinkers and charismatic leaders of that time brought Japanese Buddhism to a new stage of development, communicated Buddhism to the masses, and wrote important treatises still read today, we cannot (without ourselves becoming parties to their debates) judge the Buddhism of the earlier Asuka, Nara, and Heian periods to have been superficial or less than "real" Buddhism.

In connection with this it is also important to note that the extensive rituals of Tendai and Shingon Buddhism in the Heian period were actually modes through which the people of that time participated fully in the received Buddhist tradition and its teachings. These rituals should not be dismissed as some kind of excrescence or superfluity, not properly part of what we imagine the true intellectual or spiritual form of Buddhism ought to have been. They should not be seen by us as merely bodily, rote, or superficial—thereby implying that the Japanese had to wait many more centuries to gain a real understanding of Buddhism. As many modern anthropologists have shown, ritual is a mode of cognition.[29] It is a way of learning, reiterating, and retaining something new and important. That ritual is done with the body rather than with the mind alone is not only fully harmonious with Buddhism's traditional discomfort with mind/body dichotomies but is also harmonious with what is increasingly recognized to be a salient feature of the Japanese *intellectual* tradition,[30] going at least as far back as the insistence by Kūkai (774—835) that enlightenment for a Buddhist occurs "with this very body" ("sokushin jōbutsu").[31] Even the Kamakura figures, although they are sometimes compared to the Protestant reformers, did not denigrate ritual or propose a dualism between body and mind.

We have, then, ample grounds for assuming that the literati of medieval Japan were involved both bodily and mentally with the primary symbols of Buddhism. These became and remained a central and natural part of their writing, as much so as did the symbols and narratives of Christianity for people writing poetry, prose, and drama in medieval Europe. To try to understand what the medieval Japanese wrote without some grasp of the symbol-system to which they appealed is like trying to understand the *Divine Comedy* without a knowledge of Christianity.

The use of symbols suggests that language is two-tiered. When transformed into a symbol a thing remains what it was and becomes something else as well. So it was with the symbols of Buddhism. Chapter three of this book will show how, once it had been nourished and made more complex by being given Buddhist implications, as simple a thing as a travelers' inn was no longer simply that; likewise, the simple hut of a hermit became in Japanese Buddhist literature a symbol of much more. Though the focus will be on how these particular symbols or literary topoi developed their specific resonances, it should be pointed out that these were only two items in a vast system of Buddhist significations. Throughout the medieval period, an entire array of everyday items was drawn into a web of secondary and even tertiary meanings. Lotuses signified the purely lived life, and the quickly falling cherry blossom told the tale of the transience of all things. The era's penchant for seeing Buddhist meanings was very strong. The moon, the web of a spider, the stillness of a boulder, the direction west, the chirp of a mountain bird, the distant shore of a body of water—all these and many more became part of the Buddhist system of symbols that pervaded medieval Japan. If it was a central tenet of Buddhism that things are not what they seem to be, it was as if the mind of the epoch was determined to illustrate that truth in thousands of ways. And it was appreciated most by poets and writers, as symbols were, after all, the stuff of their lives and art.

This way of viewing Buddhism—as primarily a system of symbols shared almost universally throughout Japan's medieval period—perhaps also helps to solve another problem that has plagued students of East Asian literatures; that is, the problem of knowing how to handle the didacticism of the poetry, prose, and dramatic scenarios we study. Often the dilemma arises because, as modern researchers working on East Asian materials, we are caught between indigenous literary traditions, which take the didactic elements in Chinese and Japanese works very seriously, and the assumption in the modern West that fine literature ought not to be didactic and true literary analysis should not be concerned with the didactic intention of an author. On the one side, we have ancient or medieval writings by East Asian literati for whom it would have seemed a shameful waste of a good narrative or poem to fail to include a lesson to be learned. On the other side, we have the tradition still strong in our century—to which New Criticism contributed its own version of the art-for-art's-sake theory—holding that the presence of didactic elements in a piece of literature soils it as a work of art. Caught between these two opposing traditions of literary studies, we have sometimes been forced to argue for the value of a poem or a piece of prose by stating that it is good in spite of its didactic elements. In this way we have found ourselves forced to engage in the winnowing of literature—that is, in the attempt to separate the aesthetic wheat of pure belles lettres from the chaff of elements that seem to sully the purely literary goals of literature.

This erects a false wall between ideas and art. It makes of literature a separate domain, when in fact the literati we study—whether it be Po Chü-i, Han Yü, Kamo no Chōmei, or even Motoori Norinaga—were people to whom ideas mattered greatly. We cannot try to ferret out the "purely literary" without also sacrificing the intention of the author or poet. We cannot lift the work up for a purely literary inspection without removing it from its place in the history of ideas and from the competition among different versions of the world.

I would like to suggest that, instead of seeing didactic elements as faults in a writer's work, they may be worthy of aesthetic evaluation; and this evaluation is most easily done if we are aware of the work's place in the history of ideas. In this regard we can learn something from recent developments in the history and philosophy of science.[32] Many of the writers we most admire in East Asian literature lived and wrote during what historians of science call an era of "epistemological crisis"; that is, they wrote at a time when a Buddhist system of symbols was replacing a Confucian or Shinto one or was itself being replaced by something else. Certainly China in the ninth century was such a place, and this accounts for the passion with which Han Yü (768–824) wrote against Buddhism and in behalf of the Confucian way of representing the world. Likewise, in the Japan of Kūkai and the author of the *Nihon ryōi-ki*, both writers felt compelled to set forth very didactically the Buddhist episteme as they saw it. And in a similar way Motoori Norinaga (1730–1801) much later took up the cudgels against both Buddhism and Confucianism as pernicious, foreign ideas that sullied the Japanese soul and the archaic literature it had once produced. All these writers were important in literature but also very didactic.

Because they are deeply involved in defending or repudiating a given symbol-system in the intellectual milieu, such writers will make their didactic purposes very overt and sometimes even strident. But this is due at least in part to the writer's intense involvement in issues that seem about to make or break his world, not to a mere lack of literary finesse. Because he lives at a time when one set of epistemic assumptions is in a life-and-death struggle with another, the writer cannot do other than defend the one he prefers. He cannot tell a story or sing a song just "for its own sake."

It is for these reasons that in the following chapter I treat the *Nihon ryōi-ki* with what some might consider undue charity and that I consider the work's blatant moralizing interesting not only from the point of view of the history of Japanese thought but also from that of the literary historian. Its didacticism is due to its author's conviction that he is the possessor of a whole new set of cognitive possibilities, which he must share with his countrymen by using every rhetorical device at his disposal. His sometimes strident language is intimately connected to his intention as a writer, and that intention is related to his place in history.

Kyōgen, the dramatic form described in chapter seven, is equally didactic, though in contrast to the *Nihon ryōi-ki*, it seems to have been conceived by people among whom there was a growing skepticism about the validity of the medieval Buddhist episteme. The authors of kyōgen state what they have in mind through satire rather than by moralizing, but it is fairly obvious that they do have something they wish to say—and teach—about the fragility and vulnerability of the Buddhist symbolic system.

It is in fact difficult to find a piece of literature that has no didactic program whatsoever. Sometimes the purpose stands out quite conspicuously on the surface of a work, creating what we might call "hard didacticism." At other times the purpose has been worked more deeply into the grain of the work and seems less obvious—a didacticism we might place at the "soft" end of the continuum.[33]

The softer form of didacticism in literature, in addition to being attributable to the skill of the writer, may also come into being because the age is not one of intellectual crisis. Consequently, the author can assume his readers share in his system of symbols. Much of the literature examined in this book is of this more softly didactic type. It was written during a portion of Japan's medieval epoch when a writer, fully confident that his readers understood and found intellectual pleasure in the symbols of Buddhism, could play with those symbols. This is what happens in much of the best poetry of the era. Still, inasmuch as it reinforced and extended the Buddhist system of symbols, even poetic play was not completely without didactic import and effect. Such literature appeals to us as more relaxed and perhaps more sophisticated; but this is because of the manner in which ideas are presented, not because it is somehow "purely literature" or "purely art."

THE BUDDHIST CRITIQUE OF SYMBOLS

The preceding may seem to imply that medieval Japan can be adequately comprehended simply as an Asian counterpart to the religious and intellectual structure of medieval Europe, with Buddhism playing the role played by Christianity in the West. This would not be entirely accurate, however, primarily because of a basic philosophical difference between European Christianity and the Mahayana form of Buddhism that shaped medieval Japan. The implications of this difference are examined closely in chapters four and six, which deal with Fujiwara Shunzei's use of Tendai thought and Zeami's theory of drama; but because the Buddhist critique of symbols and its basis in Mahayana thought are crucial to this entire study, they merit some initial attention here.

One of the most fascinating features of Japanese Buddhist culture in the medieval period is that it pursued, on the one hand, the elaboration of an extensive system of Buddhist symbols and, on the other, the subjection of the entire symbolization process to a radical critique that was itself grounded in Mahayana Buddhist thought. The seeming paradox is that the Buddhist symbolic system was forced to undergo analysis on bases that were themselves Buddhist.

This paradox must be viewed in the context of what was probably the central philosophical problem for medieval Japan, namely, the correct understanding of *hongaku*, or "original enlightenment." For the Japanese, the most important source of the term was the *Daijō-kishin-ron*;[34] it entered from there into the thought of Kūkai, the major Tendai scholars, and the scholars of the Zen and Pure Land schools. In fact, if there was one philosophical point on which these various schools generally agreed, it was probably that of hongaku. Though there were a variety of formulations, they can perhaps be summarized in this way: Hongaku expressed the insight that the nature of *kaku* or *satori* (usually translated "enlightenment" or "realization") is of something already in existence rather than envisioned as a future possibility.

The *Daijō-kishin-ron*, along with many other texts, begins with the assumption that it is of fundamental importance to move from the state of ignorance about reality to that of enlightened knowledge of it. But, since one of the principal characteristics of the enlightened mind is that it sees reality without "two-ness"—that is, free of the lens of our usual differentiating consciousness—the very distinction between "ignorant mind" and "enlightened mind" is itself problematic and needs to be overcome. Since it postulates an enlightened mind somewhere in a place or time completely removed from where I am at present, this distinction must be a total projection.

Actually, the thought of wanting to be enlightened—often called the "seed of enlightenment"—appears or sprouts in the midst of ordinary mind, otherwise thought to be deluded mind. With a literary finesse and logical consistency all its own, the *Daijō-kishin-ron* demonstrated this by a deliberate inversion of Buddhism's traditional "four characteristic states" (*shōjūimetsu*).[35] Based on analogy with the life cycle of an ordinary human or other animate form, the classical depiction of the progression to full enlightenment was as follows: (a) the coming into being of the thought of enlightenment, comparable to the birth of a child into the world; (b) abiding and discipline, comparable to the continuity of growth and development from childhood to manhood; (c) the transformation, comparable to the change from prime of life to old age; and (d) the cessation of all delusion, comparable to old age and expiration. This sequence is deliberately *reversed* in the *Daijō-kishin-ron* in order to demonstrate that thinking of enlightenment in terms of process, sequence, and the projection of a future possibility is itself an illusion. In the beginning or base (*hon*) of this apparent process, enlightenment (*kaku*) can already be found. Without enlightenment at the origin, there can be none at the end.

This was not an affirmation of ignorance but a way of collapsing the distance or gap between ordinary mind and enlightened mind and, thus, abolishing the dualism that is itself the stuff of delusion. As developed in the Japanese context by Kūkai, the founder of Japanese Shingon Buddhism, it would seem to be the basis of his emphasis on "sokushin jōbutsu," "enlightenment with this very body." If we recognize the hongaku principle to be one of radical nondualism, it becomes clear why Kūkai rejected a number of dualisms.[36] He insisted that it was folly to project enlightenment somewhere off in the future after a lengthy process of transmigration, maintaining instead that enlightenment is of "this very lifetime." In a similar vein he collapsed the division between body and mind and conceived of man as an undivided unity—what Yoshito S. Hakeda calls Kūkai's conception of man as "body-mind."[37] It was natural, then, for him to articulate Buddhism as a teaching that exfoliates in body-expressive rituals, almost dancelike mudras made by the hands, mandalas that are complex patterns of figure and color, and mantras that literally vibrate the Buddhist teaching in the ear and vocal chords of a human being. This ensconcing of truth in physical form was for Kūkai never a move downward or an incarnation from some loftier, more spiritual, plane but a natural and in no way condescending articulation of truth in the physical world. It was also a way of maintaining the radical nondualism of the Mahayana tradition; body and mind were not permitted to become separate or opposable realities.

The principle of hongaku was also very important in the tradition of Japanese Tendai. There it was translated into an entire panoply of philosophical moves, each of which stressed in one way or another that the world of birth and dying is also the world of true enlightenment. The emphasis throughout was on *being* enlightened rather than on *becoming* enlightened, and in Tendai there was even a refusal to make a sharp distinction in this matter between mankind and other sentient beings. It was therefore a logical consequence for Tendai thinkers such as Ryōgen (912–985) and Chūjin (1065–1138) to use the principle of hongaku as the basis for their extended arguments in favor of recognizing that even plants and trees are in possession of Buddha-nature ("sōmoku-jōbutsu").[38]

Likewise, the Zen master Dōgen (1200–1253) pursued the consequences of hongaku in his own way to arrive at possibly his most characteristic teaching, namely, the indissoluble "oneness of practice and attainment" ("shushō ittō"). Dōgen felt that there was something wrong in the usual distinction between ends and means in talking about the relationship between enlightenment and the discipline or practice needed to reach enlightenment.[39] He disliked the way this implicitly subordinated practice to attainment and made the former into no more than a means to a goal conceived of as apart from that means. He concluded that the practice a Buddhist engages in—for him this was seated meditation—is itself the reality of enlightenment. A person doing *zazen* is not doing it as a means or strategy to get something or somewhere else, that is, to a condition in which the need for practice has been eliminated. Dōgen wanted to collapse the means-versus-ends distinction and thus fortify the value and meaning of practice.

This is only a sample of how hongaku shaped the intellectual concerns of medieval Japan. Perhaps its most conspicuous feature is the persistent removal of any basis for dualized thinking. That is, it radically challenges our customary relegation of some phenomena to the category of "merely means," subordinate to another category considered ends in themselves. In hongaku ways of thinking, the hierarchy implicit in dualism is wiped away, and imbalanced value judgments are erased. There is no such thing as mere instrumentalism; philosophically speaking, all phenomena are on an equal footing. This idea dominates the *Lotus Sutra*, one of the major texts of the era.

The implications of hongaku for a Buddhist theory of symbols are quite clear. We noted earlier that symbols by definition suggest that language is two-tiered: that when something is transformed into a symbol it is both what it always was and something else as well. For the medieval Japanese Buddhist, the inn where a traveler stopped for the night became a symbol pointing to the entire process of transmigration between lives and worlds. But even Buddhist symbols themselves had to be subjected to the hongaku insistence that no thing is ever merely a pointer or means for recognition of another thing. Because the principle of hongaku required absolute egalitarianism among phenomena, the values implicit in the very process of symbolization—in which a phenomenon serves as a pointer toward something else—came under the critique of Buddhist philosophy.

The exact format of this critique was considerably more subtle and positive than what we usually mean by the term. It was not made just for the sake of formal philosophical consistency but because it was a basic component in what the Buddhists perceived to be the realization of truth. For example, it was clearly implied in the following well-known statement by the Sung dynasty Zen master Ch'ing-yüan (1067–1120):

> Before I had studied Zen for thirty years, I saw mountains as mountains and waters as waters. When I arrived at a more intimate knowledge, I came to the point where I saw that mountains are not mountains and waters are not waters. But now that I have got the very substance I am at rest. For it is just that I see mountains once again as mountains, and waters once again as waters.

The relationship between this type of formulation and the collapsed dualism of hongaku thinking is apparent.

It might be said that in Buddhism the problem posed by the symbolizing process of the mind is not unlike that posed by the habitual daydreams, fantasies, and projections that disturb our capacity for "right seeing." In a sense, the symbolizing process is itself a digression, a move away from the clear recognition of mountains as merely mountains, waters as merely waters. In the end, inns are also merely inns and hermitages merely hermitages.

This critique of symbols brought into being a very specific aesthetic mode—one we customarily associate with Zen; but it appeared in Japan even prior to the great growth of Zen in the thirteenth century and is in many ways the consequence of the logic of *hongaku*. It requires the return of a poet's perceptions and mind to the simple recognition of phenomena. This recognition is powerful because it represents a *renewed* simplicity rather than a naive simplicity. This aesthetic mode lives off the way it *redirects* our focused attention to phenomena for their own sake. It does so with stunning effect by reversing the symbolizing habit of the mind.

The poetry that results from and expresses this aesthetic mode invites us to see things in and for themselves; it deliberately rejects the attempt to discover "meanings," implications hidden or coded into a poem. Thus, Saigyō, who had earlier been a master of symbolization, late in life began to write poems that read much more like records of an act of bare, clear, unadorned perception.

furu hata no	Old field run to ruin
soba no tatsu ki ni	and in the sole tree starkly
iru hato no	rising on a bluff
tomo yobu koe no	sits a dove, mourning its mate:
sugoki yūgure	the awesome nightfall.[40]

In this poem it is as if nothing is "attached" or added to what is seen and heard. Another example, which is discussed in more detail in a later chapter, is the following celebrated verse by Fujiwara Teika:

miwataseba	Gaze out far enough,
hana mo momiji mo	beyond all cherry blossoms
nakarikeri	and scarlet maples,
ura no tomaya no	to those huts by the harbor
aki no yūgure	fading in the autumn dusk.[41]

These poems serve to illustrate the aesthetic quest to return to what the early Buddhists had called "right seeing."

Iriya Yoshitaka has wisely pointed out that in the case of the Chinese Zen poet Han-shan, it can be said that: "His best work, those examples successful as genuine poetry, are not those which attempt religious statement, but those in which the poet disports himself in a free, effortless revelling in the Way—the joyful outpouring of a 'sportive samadhi.' "[42] The same can be said of some of the best Buddhist poets of Japan. It is as if—for reasons clearly connected with their understanding of Buddhism—they decide to turn away from a poetry or prose freighted with symbols drawn from the Buddhist symbolic tradition.

The result is a tension and ambivalence that existed even in the middle of Japan's medieval period. Many poets, essayists, and people articulating a theory of literature appear to have been simultaneously involved in constructing and demolishing the system of Buddhist symbols; and this was the case *because* they pursued the implications of their understanding of Buddhism and tried to express it in literary form. Chapter six of this book discusses this phenomenon as it is reflected in Zeami's thinking about nō drama; his profound understanding of the principle of hongaku carries him to some surprising and fascinating places.

Perhaps the deep ambivalence within Japanese Buddhism about the adequacy of Buddhism's own symbolic system also helps to explain the difficulty of locating the point at which the medieval episteme in Japan yielded to a distinctly modern one. Because the critique of the Buddhist symbol-system came in part from within Buddhism itself, the clash of rival systems as Japan moved into the modern era was much less overt than that which characterized Europe's torturous move from the Catholic medieval epoch to the "secularized" modern one. This is to say that a move toward the secularization of Buddhist symbols may have taken place fairly early in Japan, coming out of the heart of Buddhist philosophy itself. Paradoxically, the result may be that more of the medieval is retained by modern Japan than modern Europe retains of her own medieval past.

The question is a tantalizing one. It is implicit throughout the chapters that follow and surfaces explicitly in the final exploration of Bashō, who is seen as an extraordinarily self-conscious poet whose work suggests that, in intellectual and artistic terms, much that was medieval was still available in his day and much that would prove to be modern could be found in the heart of the medieval period.

2

IN AND OUT THE ROKUDŌ: KYŌKAI AND THE FORMATION OF MEDIEVAL JAPAN

Natura nihil agit frustra, is the onely
indisputable axiome in Philosophy; there are
no *Grotesques* in nature; nor anything
framed to fill up empty cantons; and
unnecessary spaces.
　　　　—Sir Thomas Browne (1605–1682),
　　　　　　　　　　　　　　Religio Medici

B UDDHISM GAINED ASCENDENCY IN medieval Japan largely because it
successfully put forward a coherent explanation of the world and of
human experience; it was the single most satisfying and comprehensive
explanation available to the Japanese people at the time. This is to deny neither
that Buddhism was espoused by persons who had great social and political
power nor that it provided justifications for their power and prestige. Moreover,
this is not to disembody it or overlook the impressive technological and artistic
side of the Buddhism that came to Japan from China and Korea—its magnificent architecture, paintings, icons, vestments, illuminated scrolls, and choreo-
graphed ritual. It is merely to call attention to the cognitive dimension and to
observe that Buddhism provided not only salvation but also explanation. That
is, as a religion in a medieval context, it was considerably more comprehen-

sive, than religion in modern settings. In many ways, Buddhism performed in medieval Japan much of the role now customarily assigned to science.[1] It did so by giving to the epoch a basic map of reality, one that provided cognitive satisfaction not only to learned monks in monasteries but also to unlettered peasants in the countryside. This chapter attempts to reconstruct that map of reality as it seems to have been universally accepted throughout Japan's medieval era.

I shall argue that Buddhism's cognitive framework was characterized by both simplicity and comprehensiveness. It functioned quite effectively as what Max Weber called a *theodicy*; that is, it made the world and the vast variety of individual destinies rational and acceptable—something needed perhaps equally by princes and peasants.[2] In addition, it provided a relatively simple framework within which a vast amount of varied and complex data could be located and described. The basic portrait of the universe in terms of a taxonomy called the *rokudō*, or "six courses," was universally accepted by all the schools of Buddhism and included the belief that karmic reward or retribution for anterior acts pushed every kind of being up and down the ladder of the universe.

Ironically, however, though Buddhism's portrait of the universe was cognitively satisfying, it was not necessarily personally reassuring. Medieval Japan was a context in which virtually everyone believed in multiple lives and the system of karmic causality; but most people, while believing in it, found it distressing at best and terrifying at worst. So they sought personal salvation in one way or another from the causal sequence. In many ways Buddhism gave an explanation but also presented a problem. The reconstruction essayed in this chapter will therefore move in two stages: first, an overview of the formation of the medieval paradigm as shown by close analysis of a basic Buddhist text; and second, a survey of a number of specifically Buddhist remedies for the personal anxieties aroused by the paradigm. The relationship of these things to the literary arts of the era will also be a continuous concern here.

What I shall describe as the taxonomy of medieval Japan is what the Chinese called the *liu-tao* and the Japanese the rokudō.[3] It was a pervasive idea in East Asia although its origins were in India. Thus, it is present in the sutras of Indian origin, the most important commentaries in Chinese, and the basic Buddhist texts by the Japanese themselves. It is found in the *Saddharma-puṇḍarīka sūtra*, which the Japanese called the *Hokke-kyō* (usually rendered as *Lotus Sutra* in English),[4] the *Ta-ch'eng ch'i-hsin-lun (Daijō-kishin-ron)*,[5] the *Mo-ho chih-kuan (Makashikan)*,[6] the *Wu-men kuan (Mumon-kan)*,[7] the *Ōjō-yō-shū*,[8] the *Shōbō-genzō*,[9] and the *Tanni-shō*,[10] to name only a few of the important texts of this era. Its use and acceptance cut across the various differences of doctrine and practice among the schools, and it is, therefore, appropriate to view it as having been universally accepted. In all these works the depiction of the universe as constituted by six basic modes of being and by a karmic causality that pushes all beings through the taxonomy is simply assumed to be true and immediately evident. The idea was reinforced with every mention, a cognitive scheme so basic and pervasive that it found its way into virtually every major literary work. The notion of karma and transmigration appears not only in overtly Buddhist works, such as the *Shaseki-shū* or those groups of lyrics specifically devoted to Buddhism, but also in all the major collections of verse, in all the *monogatari*, and in all the major dramas of the period. For nō, it is an essential part of its histrionic mechanics and meaning. It pervades the literature and art of medieval Japan.[11] According to Watsuji Tetsurō:

> Belief in transmigration through the six courses was made into a view of things that made complete common sense, so that it lay at the basis of ordinary observations of life. Through it the whole of people's lives was explained as demonstrations of the principle of karmic rewards and punishments. And it is not too much to say that the literary arts of medieval Japan were completely and uncritically under its sway.[12]

An interesting and perhaps coy reference to the rokudō is already in a *Man'yō-shū* poem by Ōtomo Tabito (665-731); this poem is included in a section of thirteen of his poems celebrating the pleasures of drinking:

ima no yo ni shi	Getting my pleasures
tanoshiku araba	This way in my present life
komu yo ni wa	May make me turn
mushi ni tori ni mo	Into an insect or a bird
ware wa narinan	In the life to come.[13]

That the poet does not seem to experience any great anxiety over his karmic fate possibly reflects the early date of the poem.

The rokudō taxonomy was not, of course, indigenous to Japan. It has been integral to the Buddhism the Japanese absorbed from the Chinese and Koreans. Through it, the process of transmigration was concretely imagined. It consisted of a classification of all beings into six types: gods, mankind, asuras, animals, hungry ghosts, and the creatures of hell. Slight variations in the order were possible, but that it was a hierarchy of value was always implicit.[14] Perhaps only two of the rubrics need definition: asura *(ashura)* are titans whose killings in the past have given them a warlike and ever-warring nature; and hungry ghosts *(gaki)* are beings with literally insatiable cravings and desires (they are often represented as having enormous stomachs and needle-thin throats). The six were usually ranked as follows:

gods	(*kami*)
humans	(*ningen*)
asuras	(*ashura*)
animals	(*chikushō*)
hungry ghosts	(*gaki*)
creatures of hell	(*jigoku*)

As a system for classifying the beings of the universe, this includes and combines types seen every day with types seen scarcely, if ever. Thus it gives to the unseen an aura of greater presence and positivity. In some ways it bears a similarity to the taxonomy widely accepted in medieval Europe. There is, however, at least one decisive difference, and it is due to the Indian notion of transmigration. Each of the six is not only a rubric but also a route. Each being in the universe is involved in an ongoing journey and, against the backdrop of nearly infinite cosmic time, is only temporarily located in its present slot. Death will result in rebirth, and rebirth always poses the possibility of either progress or slippage to another location in the taxonomy. In strict interpretations, everything depends on the life lived now and the karma engendered in the present. The system thus makes each person individually responsible for his or her own future. Injustice is an impossibility.

Erik Zürcher has pointed out that the Indian teaching of karma and transmigration had captured the imagination of the Chinese quite early, when Buddhism was first making its entry there. Ironically, the Indian Buddhist idea of *anatman*, that is, the rejection of any perduring self (including the notion of a soul), an idea many modern scholars interpret as the key notion in Buddhism, appealed to the Chinese Buddhists only later in their engagement with the Indian Buddhist tradition. For the early Chinese Buddhists, transmigration was a process that involved successive incarnations of a *soul*.[15] If it were to be judged with the Indian Buddhist concept of anatman as the standard of orthodoxy, Chinese Buddhism, at least during its earlier centuries, would probably fare badly. Here, however, it is the historical process that is at issue and it seems clear that a simple notion of karma and transmigration fascinated first the Chinese and then the Japanese as Buddhism entered East Asia. These were new ideas, but they provided a fairly simple explanation of the workings of the universe and the destinies of human beings and could be quite easily adopted.

The best way to observe the Japanese fascination with this new way of

viewing the world in terms of karma and transmigration is through an early
Heian work, the *Nihonkoku genpō zen'aku ryōi-ki*, usually abbreviated *Nihon
ryōi-ki*.[16] It is prized by historians as a rich vein of information about the late
Nara and early Heian periods and by students of literature as the first of the
setsuwa, a very large and remarkable genre of legendary literature in Japan.
The analysis of this work undertaken here, however, will be in order to
demonstrate that the *Nihon ryōi-ki* can serve in a remarkable way as an aperture
through which to view the formation of the medieval episteme in Japan. It is a
uniquely valuable text because through it we can witness the transition from the
archaic to the medieval paradigm. This is because it presents, according to
Taketori Masao, "the basic world view of Buddhism."[17]

This view of the *Nihon ryōi-ki* stands in need of some defense, however.
Because it is an assemblage of narratives characterized both by a surface
rusticity and by an often blatant moralizing, it has sometimes been taken to be
an interesting but unsophisticated work, the product of a pious monk who had
excellent intentions but little learning.[18] Such an approach sees it as an
important source of historical information but scarcely systematic and certainly
not a critically important document in the intellectual history of Japan. My
argument, by contrast, is that rusticity does not preclude sophistication and that
both subtlety and system lie within and below the surface of the *Nihon ryōi-ki*. I
hope to show how it may be regarded as a very significant work, in spite of its
graphic details and carrot-and-stick moralizing. Although it is abundantly clear
that its author, a monk of Nara named Kyōkai (perhaps Keikai), was not among
the most erudite of the age in his knowledge of the Buddhist sutras, he
composed a literary and intellectual work that is in its own way a tour de force.
Although it had precedents in China, Kyōkai's work stands as a unique
creation, a work that related Buddhist teachings to earlier Japanese experience
while at the same time arguing for the wholesale adoption of the Buddhist
paradigm of reality.

The *Nihon ryōi-ki* is a watershed work. In arguing as it does for the Buddhist
ideas of karma and transmigration, it reflects a time when these ideas were still
novel, unacceptable, or unintelligible to large portions of the populace in
Japan. In this way it contrasts sharply with all the great literature of medieval
Japan—the *Tale of Genji*, the great military romances, subsequent legendary
literature such as the *Konjaku-monogatari*, the poetic anthologies beginning
with the *Kokin-shū*, as well as the private collections of both clergy and laymen,
histories such as the *Gukan-shō*, and the classical drama of nō. The critical
difference is that in all of these works the taxonomy of rokudō and the
operations of karma are simply presumed to be true, universally applicable, and

intelligible. The *Nihon ryōi-ki* makes no such presumption. It assumes that they
are not well known and therefore require demonstration and argument. This is
why, I think, it represents the introit to a new era of epistemic possibilities in
Japan and is probably the key work for understanding the arc of the Japanese
medieval experience.

A portion of the introduction to the *Nihon ryōi-ki* will illustrate how
Kyōkai's excitement at the inception of a new epoch comes out directly in the
text.

Here at the temple called Yakushi-ji in Nara, I, Kyōkai, am a monk. I see
human society very clearly and notice able people who are doing evil things.
Some have a greed and eagerness for profit that is mightier than the magnet
that pulls iron out of the mountain. They covet what others have and yet hang
on to everything that is their own with a tight-fistedness more than that of the
miller who squeezed even a chestnut shell trying to get something out of it.
Some cheat Buddhist temples; they will certainly be reborn as calves and pay
off by work what they have now taken. Some slander Buddhist monks; they
will meet with disaster while still in their present lives. Others, however,
follow the Buddhist path and discipline themselves; they are rewarded
already in this life. Others have deep faith, practice what is good, and enjoy
happiness here and now. Good or evil deeds make their own reward or
retribution the way a shape in the sunlight makes its own shadow. Pain and
pleasure are produced by such actions in the same way that a sound in the
valley produces its own echo. Those who see and hear such things immediately think of them as marvels but forget that they are real events in our own
world. The person with reason to be ashamed finds that his heart is pounding
wildly and looks for some way to make a hasty exit. If we did not have such
illustrations of what is good and what is evil, what could we use to straighten
out those whose lives are crooked and how could we differentiate the evil
from the good? And, without these examples of the workings of the law of
karma, with what could we rectify the evil-minded and pursue the path of the
good?

Long ago in China the *Ming-pao chi (The Record of Invisible Karma)* was
written and in the great T'ang dynasty the *Po-jo yen-chi (The Record of
Wonders Connected with the Vajra-Prajñāpāramitā-sūtra)* was composed.
Why is it that we stand in awe before records compiled in other countries but
do not believe in and marvel at the strange things that happen on our own
soil? Having with my own eyes seen such things happen right here, I cannot
be indolent and indifferent. I have spent a good deal of time sitting and
thinking about this, but now it is time for me to break my silence. Therefore,
I have here compiled the rather limited number of such stories that has
reached my ears; I have entitled my work the *Nihonkoku genpō zen'aku
ryōi-ki [An Account of Wondrous Cases of Manifest Rewards and Retribution for Good and Evil in Japan].* [19]

Later works of Buddhist literature in Japan perhaps had more finesse; their authors worked their didactic purposes more deeply and subtly into the grain of their writing so that they stood out less sharply and stridently. The *Nihon ryōi-ki*, by comparison, seems primitive and naive. Kyōkai reviews his purpose directly: ''By editing these stories of wondrous events, I want to pull the ears of people over many generations, offer them a hand of encouragement, and show them how to cleanse the evil from their feet.''[20] Nevertheless, it would be a mistake to conclude on the basis of such ingenuousness or from the rusticity of specific narratives that the work is unimportant in Japan's literary and intellectual history.

It is one of the peculiar ironies of the Heian period that the work of many of its most erudite intellectuals went largely unread. Kyōkai's contemporary Kūkai (774-835) wrote sophisticated, highly literary prose and even verse in Chinese. Yet, his impact on history was not directly through his writings but through the force of his personality and the mystique that came to adhere to his name. His writings were ''not widely known outside of a restricted circle of Buddhist scholars and Shingon clergymen.''[21] Examples like that of Kūkai make it increasingly clear that intellectual or literary history cannot proceed solely by the presentation and analysis of the works of thinkers and writers who strike us now as sophisticated intellectuals or literati worthy of the name. Certainly, a figure such as Kūkai looms large in Japanese history in what Joseph M. Kitagawa has called the roles of ''master and savior.''[22] As regards Kūkai's role as a writer, however, it is probably one of the ironies of history that his treatises may have had much less historical impact than the 116 tales collected and edited by an obscure monk named Kyōkai. That is because, although they too were written in Chinese, the tales of the *Nihon ryōi-ki* were easily adopted as temple homilies by Japanese priests; they appealed to the popular imagination; and they spawned a whole genre of legendary literature that retained importance throughout the medieval period.

There is, however, an even more significant reason to stress the importance of the *Nihon ryōi-ki*. More than any other work of the period the *Nihon ryōi-ki* demonstrates both the excitement and the problems of a revolution in thought. Though it is based on the central conviction that the Buddhist notions of karma and transmigration can explain the world, Kyōkai makes his point through a reinterpretation of old stories. And, whereas at times this interpretative scheme works well, on other occasions the heterogeneous nature of his sources makes it difficult for Kyōkai to reinforce his argument through such narratives. Rather than exclude them, however, he leaves them in as if on some deeper level of understanding they too help establish his case. The result is a certain degree of intellectual untidiness in the work but not a vitiation of its intended structure.

The work is therefore critically important for observing the historical adoption of a new paradigm for understanding the world, a process not unlike those described in different contexts by Thomas S. Kuhn in *The Structure of Scientific Revolutions*.[23] Kyōkai's paradigm has its problems, but the *Nihon ryōi-ki* becomes a fascinating document if we think of its author as a man excited by the prospect of offering his contemporaries on every stratum of society a new way of explaining their world and experiences. He was not, of course, the only one to account for reality in such terms; the wide sharing of this interpretation of reality is what makes it possible to speak of the medieval episteme in Japan. Karma and the rokudō taxonomy eventually did become what Watsuji has called the "common sense" of people on every level of society.

Kyōkai's basic strategy as a writer was to begin with accounts of strange, bizarre, believe-it-or-not events. He tried to be precise in telling their geographical and temporal locations; and his accounts have an unusual amount of detail that enhances the sense of verisimilitude. Such exactness and positivity was likely intended to offset incredulity about the events themselves. He probably retold what he had heard with a certain amount of embellishment. His focus was on what he called "ryōi," bizarre happenings and freakish phenomena in the city and the countryside. Kyoko Motomochi Nakamura has translated *ryōi* as "miracle," but I prefer the translation "anomaly." The difference is more than verbal; it derives from a difference in our interpretations of Kyōkai's book.

It is true that both *ryōi* and *miracles* refer to highly unusual and atypical events. There is an important difference between them, however. In the religious and intellectual history of the West, miracles have usually been understood as suspensions of the laws of nature or the irruption of divine will into the normal patterns of the cosmos. Traditional understanding has been that such interruptions revealed the existence of a concerned deity, who as creator of the cosmos had the capacity to suspend its laws at will. The complete cosmology of medieval Europe thus included not only the world and its laws but also the creator, who having made the world, now providentially sustained it through law, and occasionally intervened in the world and its laws through miracle.

By contrast, the cosmos in Kyōkai's view has neither a functional role for a creator deity nor any real suspensions of basic law (that is, the law of karma and transmigration).[24] This does not mean that suspensions of karma were not present within Buddhist thinking[25] but merely that they were not conceptually important for Kyōkai.

In fact, Kyōkai collects and presents a wide variety of ryōi, events reputed to be bizarre and wondrously strange, because he holds that they are fundamentally capable of being completely understood and explained in terms of the Buddhist concept of law. That is, he takes events people had widely regarded as totally inexplicable and attempts to render them fully intelligible. He sees them as "freaks" that are, when understood, really law-abiding phenomena. He holds that he has an explanatory system that can potentially make perfect sense of even the most anomalous events. Karma and transmigration through the six courses becomes the fundamental paradigm for understanding, and because it possesses and transmits this superior paradigm for understanding, the Buddhist monastic institution receives Kyōkai's lavish praise. Kyōkai never fails to suggest to his readers that he has knowledge of the basics of an explanatory system that makes sense of even the most bizarre and wondrous occurrences. These, he argues, are not things that happened by chance or because of some flaw in the fabric of the "natural"; rather, when properly interpreted, they are the most telling examples of the underlying law of the universe, manifestations of the karma that is really operative in events the uninformed think of as miracles. Kyōkai claimed that for those who see the system there is no anomaly, nothing really irregular or outside the law of karma.

Though, as we will see, Kyōkai employed rhetoric to make things fit his explanatory system, the fact is that his tales and the system they exemplified did not reach the masses directly but by way of temple homilies and imitative works of literature. In this way, though the *Nihon ryōi-ki* may not have single-handedly changed the mind of the Japanese, it did much to shape the epistemic possibilities of medieval Japan. It contributed to the presentation of a new paradigm that seemed much more comprehensive than older ones. It explained things that had been mysterious. In this sense it became part of a scientific revolution, a new way of depicting the world. Kyōkai's work asked for the credence of its era and seems to have had considerable success in receiving it.

In the following excerpt Kyōkai can be observed engaging in his favorite activity of explaining how the world works:

In Kawachi province there was once a melon merchant whose name was Isowake. He would load huge burdens on his horse, far in excess of what it could carry. Then, if it would not move, he would get furious and drive it on by whipping it. The horse would then move along with its burden, but tears would be falling from its two eyes. When the man had sold all his melons, he would kill the horse. He, in fact, killed a good number of horses this way. Later, however, this fellow Isowake happened to be just looking down into a kettle of boiling water one day when his own two eyes fell out of his head and were boiled in the kettle. Manifest retribution comes quickly. We ought to believe in karmic causality. Even though we look upon animals as mere beasts, they were our parents in some past life. In fact, it is passage through the six courses and according to the four modes of birth that constitutes our real family. Therefore, it will not do to be merciless.[26]

This account is quite obviously based on a local legend that had probably gained credence through many retellings and become widely accepted as fact. Kyōkai never misses an opportunity to display the poetic justice of his cases[27]—as here the tears falling from the eyes of the overburdened horse result in the eyes of its master falling into the water of his kettle. The coincidence is more than thematic and poetic, however; it reinforces the exactitude and perfect balance Kyōkai holds to be the chief characteristics of the cosmic system of karmic reward and retribution.

With this story Kyōkai explains a double anomaly. He not only provides an explanation to people who may have wondered what lay behind the extant tale of a man whose eyes fell out (however embellished and farfetched the original event may have become) but he also explains a much more common but still anomalous phenomenon, namely, that of animals whose eyes ooze with water. Kyōkai's contemporaries would have known well that one of the perceptible differences between man and animal is that beings in the latter category do not weep; pain or emotional distress brings no tears to their eyes. Nevertheless, there are exceptions, animals with eyes that water for reasons we would today describe as medical. Kyōkai's explanation for such phenomena was, of course, not medical but in terms of karma and transmigration. For him, the weeping horse is a clear instance of residual activity from a former incarnation, that is, of the earlier human who is in some sense still "in" the horse making his presence known. Kyōkai makes his point: "Beasts in the present life might have been our parents in a past life. We pass through the six modes of existence and four manners of being born. Reflection shows us that we cannot be without mercy." The intellectual work done by this simple illustration is striking. Thus, the anomalies examined are seen to be epiphanies of the underlying system, and the system itself is thereby both illustrated and reinforced. There may be something circular in such a process of interpretation, but in its own way and for its own time it did the work of paradigm replacement and construction.

Another case in which Kyōkai's interpretative technique is remarkably in evidence is the following:

Tanaka no Mahito Hiromushime was the wife of the governor of Miki district in the province of Sanuki, a man whose rank was lower junior sixth and whose name was Oya no Agatanushi Miyate. She had given birth to eight children and was extremely wealthy. Horses, cattle, slaves, rice, money, and fields—all these and more were hers. However, she had never showed any devotion to the way of Buddhism and was very greedy, refusing to give anything to another. She would add water to the rice wine she sold and make a huge profit on such diluted saké. On the day she loaned something to someone she would use a small measuring cup, but on the day of collection she used a large one. When lending out rice her scale registered small portions, but when she received payment it was in large amounts. The interest that she forcibly collected was tremendous—often as much as ten or one hundred times the amount of the original loan. She was rigid about collecting debts, showing no mercy whatsoever. Because of this, many people were thrown into a state of anxiety; they abandoned their households to get away from her and took to wandering in other provinces. No one ever went beyond her in sheer greediness.

But then she, Hiromushime, fell ill on the first day of the sixth month of the seventh year of the Hōki era (776) and was confined to a sickbed for many days. On the twentieth day of the seventh month she called her husband and their eight sons to her and related to them the details of a dream she had had. She said: "I was summoned to the palace of Yama, the king of death. There I had my three types of sins pointed out to me. The first was the sin of borrowing a good deal from the Three Treasures [the Buddha, the dharma, and the sangha] and failing to return it. The second was the sin of making enormous profits by selling diluted saké. The third was the sin of using unequal measures and scales and that of giving out seven-tenths when making a loan but of taking twelve-tenths when collecting a debt. Then King Yama said to me: 'I have summoned you here because of these sins and because I want to show you that you will be punished by manifest retribution.' "

Having related the details of her dream, the woman passed away that same day. They left her uncremated for a period of seven days and made arrangements for a group of thirty-two monks and laymen who were to spend nine days praying for her repose and well-being. But then on the evening of the seventh day she revived and herself opened the lid of her own coffin. Those who came to look at her encountered an indescribable stench. From the waist up she had already become an ox with four-inch horns protruding from her forehead. Her two hands had become the hooves of an ox, her nails were now cracked so that they resembled an ox hoof's instep. From the waist down, however, her body was that of a human. She disliked rice and preferred to eat grass. Her manner of eating was rumination. Naked, she would put on no clothes and lay in her own excrement. From both the east and the west many people hurried to get a look at her; there was no let-up in the steady stream of people who came to view this strange phenomenon. Her husband, the governor, and his children were deeply humiliated and distressed; they prostrated themselves and made innumerable religious vows. To expiate her sin they presented all kinds of precious things out of their own household to the temple called Miki-dera, and to Tōdai-ji they gave seventy oxen, thirty horses, fifty acres of rice land and four thousand bundles of rice.

For those who owed them anything, all debts were cancelled as if already paid. The provincial and district officials saw her, and at that point, just as they were about to dispatch a report to the central government, she died, having been like that for five days. All the people of that district and province who had seen this event were in a state of grief and worry. This woman had never kept the law of karma in mind. And, for her violations of what is both reasonable and right, she had to receive immediate and manifest retribution. How much more, then, will be the karmic effects in future lives! It is as one sutra says: When we do not repay the things we have borrowed, our payment becomes that of being reborn as a horse or an ox. The debtor is like a slave; the creditor is like a master. Or again: A debtor is a pheasant and his creditor a hawk. If you are in a situation of having granted a loan, do not put unreasonable pressure on your debtor for repayment. If you do, you will be reborn as a horse or an ox and be put to work for him who was in debt to you, and then you will pay many times over. [28]

Once again the feature of poetic justice is present: the woman who gains profit by diluting rice wine or saké with water is herself eventually "diluted" when she takes on a mixed form, half human and half ox.

This tale is worth close scrutiny. It is, of course, impossible to know exactly what event in Sanuki province (modern Shikoku) was the germ of the story. It is not difficult to recognize what today we would call a case of severe psychosis, a woman whose behavior suddenly began to resemble that of a beast more than a human being. This may have been accompanied by secondary, physiological changes, perhaps sufficiently severe to cause people to see in her body signs of incipient bestialization. Kyōkai's own explanation is once again not medical but moral. For him this is a clear case of "immediate penalty [*genpō*] for unreasonable deeds and unrighteous acts." The woman's exact crime was excessive greed, which led her, in spite of great wealth, to all kinds of unjust practices. Not unrelated or unimportant was the severe social unrest she precipitated: because of her acts, "many people worried a great deal, abandoned their homes to escape from her, and wandered in other provinces." Her greed harmed not only individuals but the very fabric of society, causing unrest and movement.

The nature of the woman's transformation is interesting and important. She has a dream in which she is told by Yama, the king and judge of hell, that she will receive a penalty of the *genpō* type. This term, *hsien-pao* in the Chinese texts, had often meant karmic retribution or reward during one's present life—as opposed to *sheng-pao* (*shōhō*), reward or retribution in one's next lifetime, and also distinguished from *hou-pao* (*gohō*), karma that comes to fruition during an even later lifetime. [29] In this story, the problem with the usual interpretation of genpō is that immediately after hearing her fate in a dream and telling it to her family the greedy woman is thought to have died. Moreover, her real punishment seems not to be death but the things that happen to her during the five days when, having recovered from her death, coma, or whatever, she visibly and publicly undergoes transformation into a freak, a being half human and half ox.

In this story and in other crucial episodes in the *Nihon ryōi-ki*, the primary force of the term *genpō* is of a kind of karmic retribution or reward that is empirically and publically observed, or at least described as such by Kyōkai. This is why the case of the greedy woman from Sanuki province is critical for understanding his mode of argument. For Kyōkai relies on what was probably wide public knowledge of a case of highly erratic behavior and perceptible physical change; he refers to the fact that "streams of people from the east and west hurried to gather and look at her in wonder." And, for this widely observed and talked about anomaly, Kyōkai has an explanation that takes the mystery out of the event. He declares it to be a case where transmigration took place not at the invisible node between death and rebirth but before the very eyes of the family, neighbors, and curious crowd gathered in Sanuki.

His point is that what people had seen in Sanuki was not a freak but an empirical case of the workings of karma and the six-course transmigration system. The physical and behavioral changes they had observed were the result of transpecification (in this case from the human to the bestial) taking place before their eyes. Usually such a change of species occurred between death and rebirth, that is, at a time and place beyond human observation. But cases of genpō did not wait for this; they occurred where they could be empirically observed. The workings of the entire cosmic system were made patent in such cases. In this way Kyōkai was able to explain away an anomaly and, through that anomaly and its explanation, gain greater credence for the basic paradigm he set forth. He concluded with the logic of an a fortiori: "For her violations of what is both reasonable and right, she had to receive immediate and manifest retribution. How much more, then, will be the karmic effects in future lives!"

Although all cases of physical malformation or disfigurement in the *Nihon ryōi-ki* are interpreted to be the karmic result of past actions, an unusual body is not necessarily an indication of retribution and of slippage *down* the scale. Interesting examples of freaks which suggest upward or positive change also occur, as in the following example:

Niu no atai Otokami was a man who lived in Iwata district in the province of Tōtōmi. He had once made a vow to build a Buddhist pagoda, but the years went by and the pagoda remained unbuilt. He did not, however, forget that he had made such a vow and, therefore, he continually regretted being unable to fulfill it. During the reign of Emperor Shōmu, this man Otokami, even though seventy years of age, conceived a child with his wife of sixty-two, and she gave birth to a baby girl. When the infant was born, however, her left hand was clenched shut. Perplexed by this, the parents tried to pry open the clenched fist, but it seemed then to get even tighter. No matter what they did, it would not open. Lamenting what had happened, they said, "The wife was too old to have a child, and therefore it was born with a defective limb. It is very humiliating for us. But you, child, have become our child because of some karma in the past." They did not, then, dislike or neglect their child; on the contrary, they gave her their warmest love and the best of care.

Gradually she grew up to be a very good-looking girl. And when she was seven years old, she one day opened her clenched hand and showed it to her mother, saying: "Look at these!" It could be seen that what she had inside were two particles, sacred ashes of the Buddha. The parents saw reason for both joy and amazement in this event and let many people know what had happened. Everyone shared their rapturous joy. The provincial and district magistrates were also delighted and headed a commission to build a seven-story pagoda. In it they enshrined the sacred ashes in a service of dedication. This pagoda stands today in Iwata district and is the pagoda of the temple known as Iwata-dera. Once the pagoda was built, the child suddenly died. This is something that can be definitely known: A vow once made does not come to nothing. This shows what is meant when it is said that a vow, once made, will certainly be fulfilled.[30]

This story illustrates a number of virtues. Buddhist piety is demonstrated in both the idea of building a pagoda and in the idea of unswerving maintenance of a vow. There is also the more typically Confucian virtue of domestic harmony and parental responsibility even for a child born deformed. The mechanism that makes the story work, however, is the denouement that occurs when the anomalous or crippled child at seven years of age turns out to be not at all what the parents had thought. That is, she is not a child born impaired because of some sin of her parents in the present or in earlier lives. On the contrary, she turns out to be a child whose unusual palm enclosed the ashes of the cremated Buddha, the material that was traditionally the most revered relic and the best reason for constructing a shrine. For seven years, unknown to her loyal parents, this child housed, or enshrined, a physical residue of Śākyamuni in her own body. She had been a human pagoda. Once this is recognized and the ashes are installed in an architectural shrine, her reason for being in that form is fulfilled and she dies.

Once again we have no precise information from a modern and medical point of view about what occurred in Tōtōmi province; we can only guess what it was that served as the germ for this fascinating narrative and interpretation. The story simply tells us that a child was born with a clenched fist that opened when she was seven; the skin on the inside was, as could be expected, flaked and granular. Modern medicine might see this as a partial recovery from some kind of paralysis of the hand.

Such was not Kyōkai's frame of reference. His own paradigm for understanding such an anomaly was transmigration through the six courses. In order to follow his mind in the interpretation of this event, it is important to recognize that, for Kyōkai, the "human" rubric was not the highest; it was surpassed by that of the gods, or *kami*. Moreover, in his interpretation, Buddhas and gods generally occupied the same position on the scale, that superior to mankind and all other beings. Modern studies of early Buddhism in India and of the texts in Pali have placed emphasis on a normative homocentricity in those sources, one that regarded Buddhahood as a high form of humanity, not as a distinct and separate species. Such, however, is not the view implicit in the *Nihon ryōi-ki*. This text clearly holds that gods and Buddhas exist on a level superior to humans in the received taxonomy.

This being the case, the narrative concerning the girl with the hand of ashes becomes even more fascinating. Her deformed hand indicates her peculiar, but empirical, movement between two species, man and the gods or Buddhas. Regarded in terms of the rokudō system, she is important not only for what she carried but for what she was. For, during the seven-year period before she opened her hand, she had been a bodily fusion of Buddha and man. Kyōkai thus presents her as another case of a rare mixture that was widely known and witnessed, another empirical example of the workings of transmigration. She was moving in a direction precisely the opposite of that of the usurious woman turned into an ox. Nevertheless, they are alike in being genpō, immediate and supposedly witnessed cases of transpecification. Also interesting, then, is the girl's death immediately after the building of the pagoda. Though it is now obvious to everyone in the Iwata district that she had been a mixture of the human and the divine, her death is noticeably unlamented; even her aged parents seem not to mourn. This may be partially because they see the possession of the actual ashes of the Buddha as sufficient compensation; but it is also probably because, given the upward movement of karmic rewards in this story, continued existence as a mere human would, for this girl, be less than just. The proper reward for her is to move unambiguously and unmixedly into the category of a divinity or a Buddha. Knowing that their karma had been good rather than bad, her aged parents rejoice and see no reason for lamentation at the passing of their child. She is, in a most literal sense, passing upward into a higher category of being.

The girl's presence for seven years in the home of Otokami and his wife could also be interpreted in other, equally Buddhist, terms. Without changing the frame of reference, it would also be possible to view the girl as an incarnation, that is, as a voluntary movement down the taxonomy on the part of a superior being who, in order to bring beneficence in general and the reliquary ashes in particular, had metamorphosed into human form. In the precedents and texts of Buddhism, this downward movement of self-sacrifice or kenosis was characteristic of the bodhisattva; but in the general looseness of Kyōkai's system, it could be the act of a bodhisattva, a Buddha, or even a kami.

The looseness of Kyōkai's system was fortunate in many ways; through it he was able to make an important contribution to the intellectual and social harmonization of Buddhism with earlier forms of Japanese belief, especially Shinto. Because of the text's insistence on the preferability and viability of the Buddhist paradigm, it had to carve out a place for older forms of understanding and practice within the new episteme. It formed part of a vast investment of intellectual and artistic energy by medieval Japan into the negotiation of a relationship between Buddhism and Shinto. Studies in Japanese and in Western languages have shown that this was a complex process, since the Japanese set up neither simplistic equations nor facile oppositions between Buddhism and Shinto. Rather, through conceptual models such as *honji-suijaku* and *ryōbu-shintō*—all embraced within the exoteric-esoteric (*kenmitsu*) Buddhist umbrella of the epoch—there was a sustained and sophisticated attempt to reduce the possibility of conflict and work out an accommodation between the two forms of understanding.[31] My purpose here is to see how the *Nihon ryōi-ki*, with its characteristic vividness and rhetorical agility, serves as an interesting and important aperture into this medieval process. Particularly revealing is a story in many ways like that of the girl born with Buddha's ashes in her hand; this tale has other surprising features as well.

> In the village of Toyobuku in the Yatsushiro district of Higo province, the wife of Toyobuku no Hirogimi became pregnant. In the year 771, around four in the morning of the fifteenth day of the eleventh lunar month, during the winter, she gave birth to a ball of flesh. Its shape was that of an egg. The man and his wife took this as a bad omen and put the flesh ball in a box and stored it in a mountain cave. Seven days later they went back to the cave and saw that the cover of the flesh ball had split apart and that a baby girl had emerged from it. The parents took her and the mother nursed her. Many people came to witness this phenomenon and there was no one who was not impressed. After eight months, her body suddenly became very large. Her head was continuous with her neck because, unlike all other people, she had no chin. She was three-and-a-half feet tall. She was also born intelligent and

had a natural brilliance. Even before she was seven years old, she had memorized and could recite the whole of the *Lotus Sutra* and the eighty fascicles of the *Kegon Sutra*. Nevertheless, she was not one to boast, and she didn't even mention these abilities to other people. Eventually, she sought to leave secular life, had herself tonsured, wore the surplice of a nun, and converted others to the practice of good deeds. There was no one who refused to believe what she taught. The quality of her voice was excellent— so that all those who heard her were deeply moved. Her body differed from others' in that she had no vagina, and therefore she could not marry; her body did, however, have an opening for urine.

Some stupid lay people mocked her and called her "saru hijiri," that is, someone who, like an ape, mimics sagehood. One time, two monks, one from the provincial temple in Takuma district and the other from Daijin-ji in Yahata in the Usa district of Buzen province, became extremely jealous of this nun and said to her: "What you are teaching is not Buddhism at all!" Looking down on her, they ridiculed her and made her the object of their sport. Just then, a supernatural being came down out of the sky and made as though he was going to impale them with his halberd. The two monks were terrified, let out shrieks, and eventually died.

Sometime in 776 or 777 it happened that His Eminence, the monk Kaimyō of Daian-ji, was given the honored position of being a National Teacher in Tsukushi province. Then the governor of the Saga district of Hizen province, a man who had upper senior seventh rank and the name of Sagano kimi Kogimi, sponsored a Buddhist retreat. He invited His Eminence, Kaimyō to give lectures on the eighty fascicles of the *Kegon Sutra*. During all of these lectures the above-mentioned nun sat in the audience, never missing one of them. The lecturer noticed this and censured her with these words: "Where did that nun come from? And why is she sitting there among the monks in open violation of Buddhist rules?" The nun responded with these words: "It was because of his great and undiscriminating compassion for all sentient beings that the Buddha spread the teachings which are true. Why do you wish to exclude me alone from this company?" Then she posed a question in the form of a poem composed on the basis of the sutra, but the master was unable to respond with a religious verse of his own. Amazed at her, a large group of famous and wise monks put her through intense questioning and testing. And this nun never failed to give the right answer. In this way, they came to realize that she was an incarnation of a Buddha; wanting to rename her, they called her "Sari Bodhisattva."[32] Both clergy and lay-people embraced her teaching with great reverence and considered her to be their master.

Long ago, it happened that during the lifetime of the Buddha, Sumanā, a daughter of a rich man of Śrāvastī named Sudatta, gave birth to ten eggs. These hatched and produced five males, all of whom renounced the house-holder's life, became arhats, and were enlightened. Likewise, the wife of a wealthy man of Kapilavastu became pregnant and gave birth to a single ball of flesh, which at the end of seven days hatched to reveal 100 children inside it. These all together renounced the householder's life, became arhats, and were enlightened. Our country of Japan is small and narrow, but even here we have received something as wonderful as the girl described in this account. This, too, is a wondrous phenomenon.[33]

The narrative begins with an anomalous birth, a flesh ball that resembles an egg. This ball of flesh is first put in a box and then in a cave for further incubation. After seven days, it "hatches" but retains unusual physical characteristics, a chinless face and a largeness that suggests exceptional rotundity. The child also has no vagina.

The representation of the girl as having been born in the shape of an egg and as requiring a period of incubation before being fully born is a detail of crucial importance for the narrative. A theory current in Kyōkai's time, and one he mentions directly in another episode, was that of the four modes of birth (*shishō*). These were live birth from a womb (the mode of animals and humans); birth in the form of an egg (the mode of birds); birth from moisture (the mode of insects); and birth by metamorphosis (the mode of kami and demons). Derived originally from India and sources in Sanskrit, this was another classificatory system that entered Japan as part of Buddhist science. Its argument is easy to follow. It begins with an empirical observation, namely, the difference between live and oviparous births. It then moves to something at that time considered equally obvious but which seems to us somewhat mistaken— the assumption that, since insects seem to come from swamps and pools, they are born from moisture itself. The fourth kind of birth, that of gods and demons through metamorphosis, is the jump from the seen to the unseen, from the physical to the metaphysical. Its inclusion with the other three gives it an aura of being equally verifiable; extrapolation from the seen to the unseen becomes a form of "proof."

Both archaic Shinto and the kind of Buddhism espoused in the *Nihon ryōi-ki* maintained that superior beings do not always stay in place; at times they incarnate themselves in the forms of lower species, or at least take on behavioral characteristics of other species. In Shinto it was believed that this capacity for rapid change was the salient characteristic of kami: foxes sometimes become men, trees sometimes talk, and great beings such as En no Gyōja can walk on water and fly in the sky like birds (as narrated also in the *Nihon ryōi-ki*).[34] Likewise, in Kyōkai's understanding of Buddhism, a superior being such as a bodhisattva or Buddha undertakes to be born as a mere human and hides himself or herself by living incognito in human society. The classical understanding of this was in terms of the bodhisattva who, having practiced the path and fulfilled everything required for entry into nirvana, decides instead to become incarnate—perhaps disguised and lowly—in order to work for the salvation of all sentient beings.

All this is illustrated in the story of the girl born of a ball of flesh, a story that is quite carefully structured and narrated. In it there is a protracted struggle between the obvious intelligence and deep wisdom of the young girl and the bigotry and sheer nastiness of the male monks. At the end of the tale, it is revealed even to them that all along she had been a *hijiri*, a type of being that in the *Nihon ryōi-ki* is a rare but important incarnation of a Buddha or a bodhi-sattva. The wise ones recognize this fact and call her "Bodhisattva Sari." All along she had been a rare incarnation of another species.

There is a problem with such metamorphoses, however, in all religious traditions. Although they are thought to represent the rare entry by a divine being into another, lower, species—usually human or animal—there is nothing about incarnation or metamorphosis that itself gives any hint of the extra-ordinary transpecification going on. The movement from a celestial realm and the rubric of the gods into a lower form is not detectable. In contrast to live birth, egg birth, or, presumably, birth from moisture, metamorphosis takes place beyond the sight of man; therefore, it must be attended by circumstances and effects that testify to the extraordinary nature of the event. It is necessary to signal the presence of a divine being appearing incognito among men. Most often this problem is handled by a birth narrative that places the *mode* of birth outside the sphere of the usual: virgin birth, emergence from someplace other than the birth canal, or, as in this case, birth from a flesh egg that requires incubation. All these are presented in birth narratives as widely known signals that something extraordinary has taken place—that is, an incarnation, a rare movement within the received taxonomy. The frequency of such occurrences varies greatly from tradition to tradition—in that of Christianity it happened only once, whereas in Hinduism it has happened many times—but, as cases of transpecification downward, such incarnations have a remarkably similar structure.

This, then, is the role of the references to flesh-ball births at both the beginning and the end of the Bodhisattva Sari episode. They stand as sup-posedly witnessed and well-known anomalies signaling that a behind-the-scenes metamorphosis has occurred in which a Buddha or a bodhisattva is born human. In the taxonomy implicit in Kyōkai's system, such a *keshō* is the transfer of a distinctly superior type of being into ordinary human flesh, or possibly into a form of life even lower on the hierarchy.

This formulation placed the traditional appearances of the Shinto kami within a penumbra of interpretation that allowed them to be viewed as partaking of exactly the same *structure* of behavior as the classical bodhisattvas of the Buddhist tradition: that is, as the movement downward of superior beings, temporarily, for one purpose or another. The implicit assumption was that, whatever might be the epiphenomenal differences between the kami and the bodhisattva, an underlying structural similarity was deep and strong. In this way an ancient mystery was given a new explanation, one that reinforced its importance and its role. In such cases as this, explanation does not imply the evaporation or dismissal of what had been thought inexplicable; on the contrary, it validates its antique charm and power.

In a similar fashion the *Nihon ryōi-ki* revalorized the archaic Japanese tradition of the shamanistic seer, perhaps the most important religious functionary in pre-Buddhist times. An example of this is the following episode:

> In the old capital in the village surrounding Gangō-ji, there was once a ritual gathering of Buddhists who had invited His Eminence Gyōgi to expound the dharma to them for seven days. Both clergy and laymen gathered to listen to his preaching. In the audience listening to the sermon there was one woman who had on her hair the body-oil of a wild boar. Gyōgi saw this and reproached the woman with the following words: "To me that smells awful. The woman has blood spread on her hair. Take her far away from here." With that, the woman was greatly ashamed and went away. Our ordinary eyes would see nothing more than oil on such a woman's head. The farseeing eye of such a sage, however, sees clearly the blood of the slain animal. Right here in Japan, such a one is an incarnation of the Buddha, a divine one in disguise.[35]

Kyoko Motomochi Nakamura has rightly called attention both to the role of Gyōgi in the *Nihon ryōi-ki* and to the "heavenly eye" he is said to have possessed. She writes that, in the Buddhist tradition, such an extraordinary, penetrating eye is "the faculty that distinguishes the Buddha and bodhisattva from ordinary men. With such an eye a person can see into the past and the future, as well as the present; they can also see into another person's mind."[36]

Much about Gyōgi remains obscure. Although elevated to the position of archbishop (*sōzu*) late in life, he spent most of his years as a peregrinating holy man who had such immense popularity among commoners that he was at times held in suspicion by the central powers. The account of him in the *Nihon ryōi-ki* bears out the judgment that he was very much a shaman; the austerity of his demeanor and his powers as a seer are both features of the shamanic role in archaic Japan.

What the *Nihon ryōi-ki* does with Gyōgi is quite remarkable. First, it refers to him as a *keshin*, or "incarnation," thereby reinforcing the popular notion that Gyōgi had actually been a special incarnation—as was also indicated by the early tradition of referring to him as "Gyōgi Bosatsu," that is, Bodhisattva Gyōgi. At the same time, as Nakamura points out, here and elsewhere in the *Nihon ryōi-ki* it is suggested that Gyōgi possessed an optical organ different from that of ordinary men. Often referred to as *tengen*, "heavenly eye," this organ was traditionally the possession of those extraordinary beings who could see the rokudō system behind the epiphenomena of life. In a tradition that began in Indian Buddhism and continued in China and Japan, it was believed that a person with such an eye could see another being's past and future lives in the cycle of transmigration.[37] In the tale considered here, Gyōgi's sight is an extension of that capacity since he saw not just the oil but beyond it to the blood of the animal killed to produce it.

The author of the *Nihon ryōi-ki* has provided a concrete example of what Joseph M. Kitagawa has called "the Buddhist fusion with primitive shamanism and divination, the creative impulse which was elicited in the Heian period as well as in the subsequent history of Japanese religion."[38] By presenting Gyōgi as it does, this work reinterprets the unusual capacities of a shaman, such as Gyōgi, as having all along been in possession of the heavenly eye. The shamans and seers of archaic religion are thus revalorized as exceptional beings able to see the whole rokudō system and the procession of individuals through it. Even archaic shamans are interpreted as having been seers not only of individual fates and fortunes but of an entire *system* understood to be basically Buddhist.

In this way, the *Nihon ryōi-ki* legitimizes the archaic role of seers, shamans, and holy men such as Gyōgi and En no Gyōja. It also utilizes their high reputations among the general populace to validate the rokudō system and the Buddhist notion of karma. The work does what it can to reduce conceptual and institutional friction between the two forms of thought and religious practice. Such syncretism is sophisticated in its own way, rather than facile.

This does not represent simply a fusion and intermeshing of two *equal* systems of thought, however. Kyōkai presents Buddhism as able to enfold archaic Shinto and shamanism *within* the new paradigm it offers. The new way of viewing things is understood to be more comprehensive and satisfying than the old, but at the same time, the *Nihon ryōi-ki* fulfills a criterion set by Alasdair MacIntyre for such a shift of paradigm. MacIntyre notes that in order to be successful such a transition involves "not only a new way of understanding nature, but also and inseparably a new way of understanding the old science's way of understanding nature."[39] This applies well to Japan's entry into a medieval episteme; a work such as the *Nihon ryōi-ki* provided not only a newer, more satisfying paradigm but also a new way of understanding why the older forms had been satisfying and useful to so many for so long. A kind of intellectual hegemony is claimed for Buddhism (a hegemony that was to be undercut by the Kokugaku and other movements in the Tokugawa era), [40] but Kyōkai and other Buddhists gave a rationale for retention of the older systems even while urging the adoption of the new one. This not only made for conceptual accommodation but also reduced the potential for social disruption between institutions that had large stakes in these systems.

Of utmost importance to Kyōkai throughout the *Nihon ryōi-ki* was defense of the sangha, which at the end of the Nara period had been under severe attack for its corruption and laxity. In 798 emperor Kammu had tried, in fact, to extend complete state control over it. This is undoubtedly the background against which Kyōkai defends the clergy, using his customary argument that appearances can be deceiving:

> One must even tolerate monks who have ordained themselves. And the reason for this is simply that a holy one sometimes lives incognito among, and mixes in with, ordinary people. Do not strain to find defects in people who have no obvious faults; that is like blowing hair aside to look for scars. [41]

Kyōkai also defends the contemporaneous emperor Saga (Kamino) (786-842) who, from the evidence in the text, was also under attack. Kyōkai's defense of Saga is that he is a reincarnation of a famous and holy Buddhist master by the name of Jakusen who had died twenty-eight years before. [42] For Kyōkai, this is a particular instance of a more general rule. Those in positions of authority or those born into wealthy households are rightly there—as long as they do not disturb the sangha. They are where they are as the karmic reward for good done in earlier lives. This being so, they are permitted offenses that pose real dangers for others. The transmigration theory had clear and obvious social implications and social uses for Kyōkai.

A further note on the author's rhetorical technique is essential before concluding this discussion of the *Nihon ryōi-ki*. The work argues its case in the following way. Kyōkai claims that he sees the world closely and has an explanation for events and phenomena that mystify most of his contemporaries. The citation of names, exact locations, and people's social status at the beginning of each episode lends an aura of verisimilitude to the whole work. This is intended not only to convince his contemporaries that such things happen in Japan but also to present Kyōkai's argument as built on cases that could, if someone so wished, be empirically verified. A potential challenger would have to reckon with the wide public credence given the stories Kyōkai employs—though in another sense his evidence is no more than hearsay.

Among the tales, Kyōkai presents some that are for him clear cases of trans-migration occurring before the eyes of witnesses. He insists his explanation shows that even "freaks" are really examples of accelerated, here-and-now, karmic reward or retribution. He tries to dissolve what had previously been thought to be abnormal and mysterious, claiming that a rational explanation exists for all such things. From this explanation, he argues that, a fortiori, transmigration along the rokudō taxonomy is the most important feature of the universe, indeed its most basic law.

Extrapolating from the seen to the unseen, the author of the *Nihon ryōi-ki* then suggests that an infinite number of changes and transactions occur hidden away from our perceptions. This enables him to present the vast majority of stories with explanations that are tantalizingly vague. Many of them he leaves in an explanatory limbo, doing little more than note that these are also cases of "wondrous events." The implication is that they too are potentially explicable by the principle of karma and transmigration, and by such events as the incarnation of kami, bodhisattvas, and Buddhas. The fact of the matter may have been that, given the heterogeneity of his materials, Kyōkai could not easily integrate a number of his narratives into his transmigration argument; so he approached them in a roundabout fashion by simply claiming that they reinforce his central theme. In this way he makes his paradigm "work." As Kuhn has noted, "to be admirably successful is never, for a scientific theory, to be completely successful."[43] Kyōkai apparently convinced his contempo-raries, though a close analysis reveals that he stitched and pieced a few things together to make them fit. For centuries this interpretative system was accepted in Japan as coherent and compelling.

This notion of karma in the *Nihon ryōi-ki* was closely related to the various modes of salvation that proliferated throughout the medieval period in Japan. The concept of karma and that of the rokudō system provided an answer to one kind of question but also posed, or, at least, exacerbated, an old problem. Like most explanatory systems, the Buddhist one satisfied on one level and disturbed on another. My discussion of the *Nihon ryōi-ki* up to this point has focused on the way its basic paradigm provided a cognitive explanation of the world's workings and a way of classifying various kinds of beings both seen and unseen. But it is necessary to recognize that there was also something deeply disquieting about the notion of karma.

As presented in the *Nihon ryōi-ki*, there is an inexorability in the way karma works: rewards and punishments are exactly equivalent to their corresponding good or bad deeds. Scholars have noted that the work is not necessarily pessimistic, however; Kyōkai is fairly sanguine both about the possibility of evading dire effects and about achieving upward mobility along the six courses. For him it is simply a matter of recognizing the way the system works. Such knowledge, he holds, will change behavior and produce good results. It is, he claims, a matter of "pulling the ears of people over many generations, offering them a hand of encouragement, and showing them how to cleanse the evil from their feet." Although there are references to Buddhas and bodhisattvas in the work, these do not cancel the karmic results of earlier actions; they are not savior figures in that sense.[44] The author of the *Nihon ryōi-ki* holds that knowledge of the system will so change behavior that people will move voluntarily and effectively up the ladder of transmigration.

Some of his contemporaries and people of later times were, however, much less sanguine. A satisfying answer to questions concerning the basic functioning of the cosmos did not remove the fears of individuals about their personal destinies. Natural fears vis-à-vis death's uncertainties were now exacerbated by deep anxiety about the danger of transmigration downward in the taxonomy and a fall into hell. There is abundant evidence that people in all strata of society, fully convinced of the workings of karma, were anxious—perhaps, especially during periods of warfare, when many found themselves killing their fellows in battle.

Unless they were to be in a state of continuing despair, the people of Japan needed to have some relief from the conception of karma and transmigration as exact, inexorable, and unmitigated. They required what has been called *rokudō-bakku*, or "escape from suffering in the six courses." In the medieval period, theories of salvation proliferated. Though it would be impossible to survey them all here, each in its own way contributed to the possibility of optimism and hope. I shall attempt to sketch briefly what I see as four basic types of rokudō-bakku, trying not to be exhaustive but to demonstrate the intellectual creativity that was invested in an embellishment of the basic rokudō system to make of it a schema that would explain the world without throwing individuals into a state of complete terror and panic. Though each of the four is a different way of alleviating suffering in the rokudō, they all recognize the existence of the six courses as an established given. I refer to these four basic types of response as infiltration, transcendence, copenetration, and ludization. Their importance for the literary arts of the entire medieval period cannot be overemphasized.

The alleviation of suffering in the rokudō by infiltration is typified by the devotion directed toward Kannon (Avalokiteśvara), the Bodhisattva of Compassion, and Jizō (Kṣitigarbha), the Earth-Store Bodhisattva. One important index to the conception of these bodhisattvas as infiltrating the six courses is the iconographic evidence. Early in the medieval period both figures appear in assemblies of six, the *roku Kannon* and the *roku Jizō*.[45] The implication, as articulated in texts as well, is that there is one each of both Kannon and Jizō on each of the rungs of the rokudō taxonomy. They populate it thoroughly so that the devotee who thinks of himself as still very much a suffering traveler moving along the six courses can take comfort in the assistance and direction given by these bodhisattvas *within* the world of transmigration. Although very often Kannon and Jizō were iconographically presented as attendants to a Buddha such as Amida,[46] there is an important nuance of difference between a Buddha and a bodhisattva. Amidist piety retains the idea that Amida, as a Buddha, is the most exalted being of all, with power to transfer the believer directly from the samsaric to the nirvanic realm. By contrast, the cults of figures such as Kannon and Jizō articulate the concept of the bodhisattva, who voluntarily remains within samsara, the realm of transmigration, in order to negotiate passage up the taxonomy for devotees. The two forms of piety were compatible, and it is easy to see that the Buddhist wanting comfort and security on every level and for every eventuality would practice both types.

Piety directed to an assembly of six representations of Kannon (Kwan-yin) had its origin in China; such figures are found on the walls of Tun-huang and are referred to in what is probably the most important T'ien-t'ai text, the *Mo-ho chih-kuan* of Chih-i (538-597).[47] In the case of Ti-ts'ang, the Chinese precedent for Jizō, however, there seems to have been no development of a set of six figures corresponding to the six courses.[48] In Japan, Jizō already appears as able to negotiate escape from suffering along the six courses in the latter half of the ninth century. There is abundant evidence that the figure of Jizō struck especially deep roots in the popular imagination of the Japanese people. For example, the *Konjaku-monogatari*, an important Heian literary work with great popular appeal, depicts Jizō as the one and only bodhisattva engaged in relieving the sufferings of beings in hell.[49] The *Shaseki-shū*, the most important work of legendary literature of the thirteenth century, expressly portrays Jizō as different from Śākyamuni and Amida in that he chooses not to dwell in the Pure Land but prefers the six courses, where he can associate with those who have sinned greatly and can alleviate their sufferings.[50] Japanese iconography gradually preferred to represent Jizō as a young (or child) monk, and by the Muromachi period (1334-1573), a special connection between this figure and children, especially dead children making the passage from one life to another, was firmly established; certain *otogi-zōshi* (moralizing tales for children) show this clearly. Subsequently, an especially felicitous popular development was the placing of icons of Jizō—often extremely rough, or scarcely hewn at all—at crossroads or roads that forked. The homology with the nexi of the six courses was apt; throughout the countryside of Japan there were visible reminders of the invisible bodhisattva who was able to give direction to beings, especially children standing at the most critical juncture of all, between death and the next rebirth. Thus, both the entire medieval taxonomy and an especially potent means of acquiring a favorable rebirth were symbolized by the roadside icons of Jizō—even more forcibly when a cluster of six figures of Jizō was placed at a crucial junction. Some have speculated that the somewhat ithyphallic form of Jizō may have simultaneously made for easy mental association with fertility,[51] thus making Jizō a doubly effective figure for recently bereaved parents wishing good for their dead child and also wishing to enhance their prospects for new progeny.

The second way of escaping the suffering of the six courses (rokudō-bakku) was through the notion of a place that transcended all of them. The most popular was the Western Paradise of Amida. According to Watsuji Tetsurō, the Western Paradise (Jōdo) was really a seventh metaphysical level located above and beyond the original six.[52] It was conceived of as the locus of nirvana; *all* the original six were, by contrast, the world of samsara. Those reborn into the Pure Land need never again be reborn in any of the rokudō, having been pulled out of them through the divine power of Amida Buddha. The most efficacious way of realizing an indissoluble link between Amida and the devotee was through chanting of the *nembutsu*. According to Amidist thought, rebirth is not determined simply by an exact calculation of good and evil deeds as judged by Yama, the king of the land of the dead (the notion that appears in the *Nihon ryōi-ki*). Rather, in Amidist belief, the final hours of a person's life, and the final moments, are exceptionally important. It is a time of passage, of danger, and of opportunity. To the devotees of the Pure Land in medieval Japan it was an unparalleled opportunity; they made the most of it by chanting the nembutsu and by holding five-colored threads that led from the hands of the dying person to an iconographic representation of Amida.

The most important early Japanese text of Amidist piety was the *Ōjō-yō-shū*, written by the Tendai abbot Genshin (942-1017) in 985. This text had an enormous impact on the mind and literature of medieval Japan. In it, the relationship between the rokudō and Amida's paradise is mainly a contrastive one. The text begins with depictions of the various hells—the lowest rung of the rokudō—and then continues up the other five rungs with descriptions that make none of them especially desirable. Even the realm of heavenly beings is somehow painful and objectionable. Of Hisō-ten, the highest of the heavens, Genshin writes at the end of his survey of the rokudō: "Finally even in Hisō heaven one does not escape from karma. From this we must conclude that even

heavenly pleasures are not to be desired."[53] Then, with a descriptive power
equal to and perhaps even surpassing his depiction of the hells, Genshin
describes the Western Paradise in vivid detail. It is not difficult to understand
why this work became a favorite of literate people for many centuries, a model
for emulation in both the graphic and literary arts. Subsequent graphic representations derived from Genshin's work were the *Jigoku-zōshi* and the *Gaki-
zōshi*, pictures that disseminated such ideas widely among the common people.

In an important study that contrasts Genshin's work and the *Nihon ryōi-ki*,
Bandō Shōjun notes that, whereas Kyōkai's narratives demonstrated karmic
rewards and punishments very concretely, the *Ōjō-yō-shū* is primarily concerned to "make it clear that the nembutsu is the core of the way to transcend
the law of karma."[54] The difference between the two works is thus much more
than stylistic; it is the difference between karma conceived of as inexorable and
karma thought to be cancelable. Certainly, the possibility of personal optimism
was much enhanced when devotees of Amida could conceive of themselves as
being drawn by a compassion and power that negated all the effects of bad
deeds. The connection between Genshin's conception and those of Hōnen
(1133-1212) and Shinran (1173-1262) is clear; the transcendence of karma and
the conviction of rebirth in the Pure Land gave people in medieval Japan a
potent way of alleviating anxiety about transmigration in the rokudō.

Although Watsuji was probably correct in observing that most people
conceived of the Pure Land as a seventh level transcending the whole rokudō,
the optimism that adhered to belief in Amida's power to cancel karma had a real
impact on the way people viewed their present lives as well.[55] At the end of the
twelfth century, Retired Emperor Goshirakawa composed the poems that
became the *Ryōjin-hi-shō*; many of these equate the most beautiful things of this
world with those in the Pure Land. In these poems there seems to be an
awareness that a polarization of nirvana and samsara is in conflict with the
deeper principles of Mahayana philosophy. Fujiwara Shunzei (1114-1204)
sought to transcend the very notion that the Pure Land is transcendent and
forged a new literary aesthetic, *yūgen*, out of this realization. Those who
pursued the logic of the Mahayana realized there could be no nirvana apart from
samsara; as Amidists, they applied this to the Pure Land as well.

A third way of handling personal anxiety vis-à-vis death and transmigration
combines infiltration and transcendence and is thus somewhat more complex
than either. A development that took place largely within the Tendai school, it
is the mode I call copenetration. It has two phases that together constitute its
uniqueness. The first phase is a move to transcend the rokudō using a somewhat
similar method to the Amidist: that is, by building something above and beyond
the six courses. In this case it is an additional four courses, all taken from the

Buddhist tradition in general and the *Lotus Sutra* in particular. Although all four are conceived of as constituting a nirvanic level that transcends the samaric one (i.e., the underlying six courses), even within the superimposed four there is a hierarchy of value and position. In ascending order, the sequence of the four new rungs is, first, *śrāvaka (shōmon)*, those who were literally contemporaneous hearers of the preaching of Śākyamuni; second, *pratyekabuddha (engaku)*, self-enlightened Buddhas; third, *bodhisattva (bosatsu)*, Buddhas-to-be; and finally, actual Buddhas. In Tendai there occurred a change in terminology causing the ten courses to be referred to as ten stratified "worlds"; they were called the *jikkai* and the term included both the underlying six courses and the additional four.

Tendai thought did not stop there, however. In an intellectual move made previously in Chinese T'ien-t'ai there occurred references to *shih-chiai hu-chü (jikkai goku)*, or the "copenetration of the ten worlds." Chih-i was probably the first to use this phrase and others nearly identical to it. In his greatest work, the *Mo-ho chih-kuan*, he wrote that, although we ordinarily speak of the ten worlds as ten unmixed places where each act has its own karmic effect, in reality "each world is equipped with its own ten worlds."[56] The implication is of total interpenetration; each of the ten worlds includes the others within it. This means not only that there are Buddhas in hell but also that there is something of hell in the Buddha.

Many modern students of East Asian Buddhism see this as an intellectual move of critical importance in the Mahayana since it negated and removed the dualism implicit in the ordinary mental sketch of the six courses or the ten worlds; it rejected the notion that the universe may be conceived of merely as a hierarchy of value strung between two polar opposites. Tamura Yoshirō, for example, sees this as a crucial move expressive of the nondualism that is the fundamental point in Mahayana dialectics. Because of it, good and evil are not seen as absolutely opposite but, on the contrary, mutually dependent.[57] In addition to its adoption by Tendai, many Amidists also took this as an important development and incorporated it into their thinking about the Pure Land; certainly Hōnen and Shinran utilized this logical move made in the Tendai tradition that was originally their own. Nichiren, too, wrote of the copenetration of the ten worlds in his *Kanjin-honzon-shō*.[58]

The importance of this development in Tendai was not limited to its influence on Buddhist leaders usually associated with new movements of the Kamakura period. Next to the *Lotus*, *Kegon* and *Vimalakīrti* sutras, the treatises authored by Chih-i—especially the *Mo-ho chih-kuan (Makashikan)*—were possibly the works in Chinese most widely read by literate people in the Heian period. We will later see the importance of Chih-i's thought for the Heian poets;

his influence on poetry extended throughout the medieval period. I will also try to show that it lies at the root of Zeami's thinking and pervades nō drama. Nondualism was not only a basic problem with which Buddhist thinkers struggled in the medieval period; it became a conceptual context and stimulus for impressive artistic achievements as well.[59]

In this brief typology of means of escaping the sufferings of transmigration, the fourth and final means may also be the most subtle. It has points in common with the other three but also has an important nuance of difference. For want of a better term, I call it the *ludization* of transmigration along the taxonomy of value, to indicate that the entire *rokudō* system is conceived of as an arena of play.[60] It is extremely important for many aspects of the relationship between Buddhism and the various arts of medieval Japan. It is also of great value for understanding how, on orthodox Buddhist grounds, the mind of medieval Japan evaded the pessimism implicit in notions such as mappō[61] and instead displayed a remarkable capacity for enjoyment—one that over the centuries produced much humor, festival, spoof, the pleasures of a "floating world," the lyrics of an Ikkyū or a Ryōkan, and the comedy of kyōgen. In short, the medieval Japanese displayed a capacity for *ludus* in its many forms.

The evidence, both conceptual and textual, for this point exists in a variety of sources. A later chapter of this book considers, for example, how the *Vimalakīrti-sūtra (Yuima-gyō)* functions as the basis for some brilliant verbal play among literati. The following discussion by Kajiyama Yūichi concerns the element of play (*asobi*) in the Prajñāpāramitā (Hannya) literature and the *Avataṃsaka-sūtra (Kegon-kyō)*. He makes an important point about the conception of the bodhisattva as working within the realm of suffering so that he might help all sentient beings (*shujō*) to find release.

> A bodhisattva is not one who pursues the perfection of wisdom while all the time thinking of his activity as painful austerities. He will never be able to do anything good for sentient beings while having the idea that he is an ascetic; on the contrary, it is only when he begins to enjoy what he is doing that he will be successful. The reason for this is that, because there is to be no self whatsoever, even that of the bodhisattva is emptiness.[62]

Kajiyama then refers to what is often called the "Jūji-kyō," a chapter of the *Kegon Sutra* in which ten of the most important *bhumi*, or "stages in the development of a bodhisattva," are described. He summarizes what the sutra says concerning the highest stages:

> Then all the bodhisattva's activities are performed freely, not with the notion that some kind of effort must be expended [*muku yūgyō*]. This means that his

actions are not things he intends in order to realize his own definite goals; they are, therefore, not conditioned by such intention. This implies that salvation is by easy practice, something equivalent to "play" [*asobi*, or *yuge jintsū*]. Even compassion is not thought of as compassion but becomes, so to speak, unconcerned compassion, because in it there is no attachment to goals. This is why the actions of the bodhisattva are empty and pure.[63]

Although this emphasis on the bodhisattva's freedom and detachment from self-actualizing goals is characteristic of much of the Mahayana tradition, the most concrete examples of his actions being seen as a kind of play are in the literature of Zen. According to Yanagida Seizan, this concept had a direct effect on the entire notion of karma and transmigration through the rokudō. Yanagida suggests that, beginning with Ma-tsu Tao-i (709-788), the tradition put a positive construction on transmigration: "[Zen] placed emphasis upon explanation of transmigration in terms of going right into other species [*irui-chūgyō*], which is to say, shouldering the karma of earlier lives and going to play in and through the six courses and four modes of being born [*rokudō shishō*]."[64] The idea of *irui-chūgyō* is extremely valuable because it collates and connotes at least three things simultaneously: first, the free movement of transpecification through the rokudō; second, the movement on the part of a Buddha whereby he leaves his own world of enlightenment to enter the world of delusion in order to save others; and third, the Zen master's use of a number of different techniques and methods to facilitate the realization of his disciples. The emphasis is on freedom rather than necessity; and each of these meanings implies the others as well.

The hierarchy of value that places Buddhas at the top and hell sufferers at the bottom is thus radically relativized—at least for those who have come to stress *irui-chūgyō* and attained the freedom of a bodhisattva, that is, freedom from attachment to self-projected goals. Even Buddhahood is, then, nowhere other than where one is. In the words of the *Lin-chi lu*, the Master said: "Bring to rest the thought of the ceaselessly seeking mind, and you'll not differ from the Patriarch Buddha. Do you want to know the Patriarch Buddha? He is none other than you who stand before me listening to my discourse."[65] The *Lin-chi lu (Rinzai-roku)* portrays the man who has not realized that "Ordinary mind is Tao" as terrorized by the notion of transmigration. In the following passage of this classic text, however, Yanagida finds an attitude that positively valorizes the karma of earlier lives by making use of it to the point of actual enjoyment: "The True Man of the Way . . . makes use of his past karma; accepting things as they come he puts on his clothes; when he wants to walk he walks, when he wants to sit he sits; he never has a single thought of seeking Buddhahood."[66]

Perhaps the ludization of the rokudō is best described in a classic koan in the *Wu-men kuan* entitled ''Pai-chang and a Fox'':

Whenever Master Pai-chang gave a *teisho* on Zen, an old man sat with the monks to listen and always withdrew when they did. One day, however, he remained behind, and the Master asked, ''Who are you standing here before me?'' The old man replied, ''I am not a human being. In the past, in the time of Kāśyapa Buddha, I was the head of this monastery. Once a monk asked me, 'Does an enlightened man also fall into causation or not?' I replied, 'He does not.' Because of this answer, I was made to live as a fox for five hundred lives. Now I beg you, please say the turning words on my behalf and release me from the fox body.'' The old man then asked Pai-chang, ''Does an enlightened man also fall into causation or not?'' The Master said, ''He does not ignore causation.'' Hearing this the old man was at once enlightened. Making a bow to Pai-chang he said, ''I have now been released from the fox body, which will be found behind the mountain. I dare to make a request of the Master. Please bury it as you would a deceased monk.''

The Master had the officiant strike the gavel and announce to the monks that there would be a funeral for a deceased monk after the midday meal. The monks wondered, saying ''We are all in good health. There is no sick monk in the Nirvana Hall. What is it all about?''

After the meal the Master led the monks to a rock behind the mountain, poked out a dead fox with his staff, and cremated it.

In the evening the Master ascended the rostrum in the hall and told the monks the whole story. Huang-po thereupon asked, ''The old man failed to give the correct turning words and was made to live as a fox for five hundred lives, you say; if, however, his answer had not been incorrect each time, what would he have become?'' The Master said, ''Come closer to me, I'll tell you.'' Huang-po then stepped forward to Pai-chang and slapped him. The Master laughed aloud, clapping his hands, and said, ''I thought a foreigner's beard is red, but I see that it is a foreigner with a red beard.''

Wu-men commented:

''Not falling into causation.'' Why was he turned into a fox? ''Not ignoring causation.'' Why was he released from the fox body? If you have an eye to see through this, then you will know that the former head of the monastery did enjoy his five hundred happy blessed lives as a fox.

Wu-men's poem:

> Not falling, not ignoring:
> Odd and even are on one die.
> Not ignoring, not falling:
> Hundreds and thousands of regrets![67]

In keeping with the mode of Ch'an or Zen, this koan negates the customary understanding of transmigration; the old monk's ''fall'' into the body of a fox for 500 lives is interpreted by Wu-men as the living of 500 happy, blessed lives and therefore no fall at all. This is not a simple negation, however, but a much more complex move. The ludization of the rokudō does not mean that it is rendered ludicrous. Nor does turning it into an arena of play and enjoyment for the true man of the Tao mean it is reduced to being merely symbolic. The Zen texts acknowledge that transmigration throws the unenlightened into a state of panic and fear even though, ironically, it is their self-preoccupied fear itself that keeps them from learning how to play along the six courses.

Nevertheless, a considerable change in attitude can be readily recognized by comparing the episodes of the *Nihon ryōi-ki* with ones such as this in the *Wu-men kuan*. Though both are narratives about transmigration, there is an important difference between them which is not just a matter of rusticity versus sophistication; there is, as we have seen, a good deal of rhetorical skill demonstrated in the *Nihon ryō-iki*, and as others have noted, the *Wu-men kuan* has its rustic elements. The difference lies in the degree to which the *Wu-men kuan* sees the hierarchical values in the rokudō taxonomy as themselves conditioned and relative. The man of the Way has the freedom to turn them upside down or even to "kill the Buddha" because, in the words of the *Lin-chi lu*, he is "a true man without rank,"[68] one who "gaining true insight, is not affected by birth-and-death, but freely goes or stays."[69] His freedom is part of the play of bodhisattvic detachment.

Although the ludic mode of overcoming the pain of transmigration receives special emphasis and expression in Zen, it is by no means limited to that tradition. Because it is based on a conception of the bodhisattva that is common to most of the Mahayana, the idea of salvation experienced as a form of play appears in one way or another in a number of the schools. We have already noted that in the poems of Emperor Goshirakawa, the *Ryōjin-hi-shō*, the believer in Amida is portrayed as at play in the present world as though it were the Pure Land. More than likely, the vast panoply of rituals that were central to Shingon Buddhism ought, even though they are stately, to be viewed as deeply ludic. Certainly the practice of *odori nembutsu* ("dancing nembutsu") was a mode of salvation through play. With roots that go back as far as the dancing and chanting of the holy man Kōya (903-72), dancing was made into a regular part of Amidist worship by Ippen (1239-89) and the Ji school he founded. Whole rooms were built expressly for Buddhist dance, and contemporaneous (often critical) accounts depict it as uninhibited.[70]

Illustrations of ludic ways of dispensing with or at least alleviating the suffering involved in transmigration could be greatly multiplied. Moreover, as we will explore later on, there was a deep connection between the notion of salvation as play and Buddhism's justification of the playfulness of the literary and dramatic arts. This connection was expressed in a variety of ways in medieval Japanese culture.

The preceding sketch of four basic types of rokudō-bakku is far from exhaustive. It is meant to suggest the intellectual spectrum within which conceptions and symbols of salvation had their places and roles. From the historian's point of view, each of these as well as the philosophy of the *Nihon ryōi-ki* is equal in its claim to be traditional and authentically Buddhist. To favor one would be to participate in the polemics of the medieval debate; it would involve sacrificing the opportunity to observe the range of intellectual possibilities that comprise the medieval episteme.

This analysis also suggests that the significance of the various cults, schools, and movements within medieval Japanese Buddhism is not fully accounted for by sociological and psychological explanations. More useful is to recognize the sustained intellectual struggle that took place to arrive at a satisfying conception of the world. The attempt to find an intelligible and satisfying portrait of reality involved not only the labor of literati and intellectuals but also the cognitive participation of commoners. Of course, in any such effort social and personal processes play a significant role.

This has implications for our interpretation of the conspicuous rivalries among charismatic Buddhist leaders and among the various schools in medieval Japan. Without denying that each was searching for power and for a following, it must be recognized that each thinker and each school was also attempting to provide answers to intellectual and existential problems posed by the rokudō taxonomy and the notion of transmigration. Each was looking for the most adequate way to cover all gaps, inequities, and anomalies in the received paradigm of reality. Moreover, each claimed to have found within the received canon and through the transmission process some specific single text, phrase, symbol, vow, ritual, or concept that, raised to central importance, reduced or completely dissolved the most vexing problems. The history of the period is replete with examples.

The sheer proliferation of such solutions as well as the intensity of the rivalries among schools and leaders, especially in the Kamakura period, tends to disguise the degree to which they shared a common episteme. Though they disagreed, they converged on a common set of problems for this disagreement.[71] Thus, they had a shared vocabulary, shared procedures for appeal to authority (both textual and institutional), and a shared consensus that a specific constellation of qualities made Buddhism deserving of intellectual and social hegemony. Moreover, the rokudō taxonomy was the underlying component in a common episteme that was the shared universe of discourse not only of literati and intellectuals but also of unlettered peasants. Eventually accepted as a priori truth, it had the credence of people in every stratum of society. For the epoch it was, to use Watsuji's phrase, the "common sense."

Through the analysis of a work such as the *Nihon ryōi-ki*, it is possible to witness the opening of the medieval epoch in Japan. The close of that era is much more difficult to describe, and perhaps this problem is best addressed by suggesting the usefulness of distinguishing between the *presence* and the *hegemony* of the Buddhist paradigm. A residual presence of the rokudō cosmology and the concept of transmigration continues to exist in twentieth-century Japan although contemporary literati and apologists for Buddhism tend to emphasize the psychological rather than the literal truth of concepts such as the six courses and transmigration. And, among traditionalists and pious Buddhists in less educated parts of Japanese society, it is possible that transmigration and the rokudō continue to retain their medieval status as common sense in need of no defense. Nevertheless, the fact that an apologetic for Buddhism has had to be launched in twentieth-century Japan is proof that somewhere it lost its viability as the unquestioned a priori truth about reality. Among intellectuals and literati this slippage of the Buddhist paradigm to a place where it could be questioned and attacked undoubtedly occurred during the Tokugawa era. Buddhism's loss of intellectual hegemony is clearly evidenced in the rejection by Motoori Norinaga (1730–1801) and the Kokugaku movement of both Buddhism and Confucianism as alien impositions upon Japan. This nativism represents what H. D. Harootunian has called "the invention or 'eruption' of a new mode of discourse."[72] While it is true that for both Motoori Norinaga and Hirata Atsutane (1776–1843) "the question of death and the afterlife seemed urgent,"[73] they derived their cosmological views from archaic, non-Buddhist sources and had no cognitive use for the notions of karma and transmigration. Theirs was thus a clear rival to the long-held Buddhist schema, and it signals that the rokudō paradigm, whatever its continuing presence might be, could no longer retain its medieval position as a priori truth, the common sense of the time.

3

INNS AND HERMITAGES: THE STRUCTURE OF IMPERMANENCE

quid ultra?
concumbunt docte;
—*Juvenal* VI, 189
as misquoted by Montaigne

T HE BUDDHIST TEACHING THAT nothing lies outside the law of *anitya* or "necessary change," seems, when we survey the literature of traditional Japan, to be ubiquitous. It was referred to by the Japanese as *mujō*, and since, as Ivan Morris noted, it was even the theme of the *ABCs* learned by young pupils in school, we should not be surprised to discover that this " . . . Buddhist stress on evanescence has had a major influence on the literature of the Heian period and later."[1] The richness and variety that existed within this notion, however, have not been much explored by Western scholars. This chapter is an attempt to investigate some of this wealth—chiefly by making a few distinctions and noting a few interrelationships. The principal objective is a clarification of the structure of mujō as it was expressed in the literary topoi of the hermit's hut and the traveler's inn.

Since it is the treasure of the *structure* which we hope to glimpse as it lies beneath the ocean of individual instances, the emphasis in this chapter is on the logical relationships within these two topoi taken more or less synchronically, rather than on those developments that would be salient from a diachronic perspective.[2] This stress on the continuity within the convention should not, however, rule out a few initial observations about changes that occurred in the notion of pervasive change.

Helen Craig McCullough describes the contrast between China and Japan with respect to mujō: "In most respects Heian Buddhism did not differ strikingly from the Buddhism of the Six Dynasties and early T'ang, but one does find in it an unusual preoccupation with the concept of impermanence in nature and in human affairs."[3] In classic works such as the *The Tale of Genji*, this is precisely the case, especially when "nature" is understood as the round of the seasons and "human affairs" is taken to mean the ever-changing love relationships among the leisured elite. Together they reiterate and reinforce the theme of evanescence. By the end of the Heian period, however—that is, by the twelfth century—a particular emphasis on the mujō of dwellings and habitations becomes manifest in the literature.[4] This suggests that, from this point on, mujō was conceived of not only as *impermanence*—that is, as a temporal category—but also as *instability*, a spatial one. This spatial connotation, the matrix out of which the literary topoi of the inn and the hermitage arise, is also an extension of the range of mujō's sway. Its appearance coincides with a change in the scope and character of mujō in nature as well. It is no longer limited to the more or less predictable sequence of the seasons; through earthquake, flood, and fire, impermanence/instability takes a totally unpredictable route.

In its new connotation mujō was often publicly and collectively experienced; no longer was it merely the private experience of those whose mutual love had dissolved. And, as the literature responsive to the historical events of the latter half of the twelfth century makes clear, the warfare of those years was viewed as not only a signal of the end of Heian peace but also a powerful surfacing of mujō in public life, the result of man's own implication in ignorance.

Mujō eventually came to apply to everything. All things move in time and space. Nothing stands still or abides. A much used symbol for mujō in the literature of the period was the human dwelling place—as expressed especially in the conventional topoi of the hermit's hut and the traveler's inn. The late classical and medieval Japanese found in these images an expression of mujō that gave them currency for centuries, and possibly even a latent presence in the fiction of twentieth-century Japan. The hermitage and the inn are immediately sensed by the reader of Japanese literature to be potent symbols of impermanence/instability. The two images function in sophisticated ways and are finally best understood not in isolation from one another but as the two halves of a single Janus-faced structure. Their analysis provides some unique insights into the mind of medieval Japan. This chapter will consider them first in isolation and then as two parts of a whole.

THE HERMIT'S HUT

During the twelfth century in Japan there was a sudden, radical shift in the perspective from which the best poetry and prose was written. Women in palaces and sumptuous homes no longer wrote the literature that has lasted; most of the best work was composed by men who thought of themselves as monks, or as at least semiretired from society.[5] The reasons for this are complex and involve changing social situations as well as new continental influences. What is significant to our specific concerns is that the writing brush had passed from the hand of the court lady to that of the monk (*inja*), that is, to a person either in retirement from the world or at least adopting such a pose. Thus it happened that the hermit's hut, *io* or *iori*—often alternatively rendered as *sōan*, "grass hut"—became not only the real or postured locus for literary composition but also one of literature's central topoi.[6] As demonstrated by the examples that follow, it was both a convention and a structure.

Kamo no Chōmei (1153−1216) was influenced in part by the descriptions of Taoist and Buddhist hermitages in Chinese literature and by the *Chitei no ki* of the tenth century in Japan; yet, his own "Hōjō-ki," or "Account of My Hut," ranks as probably the best prose description of a habitation intentionally modeled after the mujō that shaped all of reality. Ishida Yoshisada, a noted scholar of this literature, sees Chōmei's work as the most representative of the medieval view of the hermitage.[7] The following are some key sections of the "Hōjō-ki":

> The flow of the river is ceaseless and its water is never the same. The bubbles that float in the pools, now vanishing, now forming, are not of long duration: so in the world are man and his dwellings. It might be imagined that the houses, great and small, which vie roof against proud roof in the capital remain unchanged from one generation to the next, but when we examine whether this is true, how few are the houses that were there of old. Some were burnt last year and only since rebuilt; great houses have crumbled into hovels and those who dwell in them have fallen no less. The city is the same, the people are as numerous as ever, but of those I used to know, a bare one or two in twenty remain. They die in the morning, they are born in the evening, like foam on the water.

Of all the follies of human endeavor, none is more pointless than expending treasures and spirit to build houses in so dangerous a place as the capital.

Now that I have reached the age of sixty, and my life seems about to evaporate like the dew, I have fashioned a lodging for the last leaves of my years. It is a hut where, perhaps, a traveler might spend a single night; it is like the cocoon spun by an aged silkworm. This hut is not even a hundredth the size of the cottage where I spent my middle years.

Before I was aware, I had become heavy with years, and with each remove my dwelling grew smaller. The present hut is of no ordinary appearance. It is a bare ten feet square and less than seven feet high. I did not choose this particular spot rather than another, and I built my house without consulting any diviners. I laid a foundation and roughly thatched a roof. I fastened hinges to the joints of the beams, the easier to move elsewhere should anything displease me. What difficulty would there be in changing my dwelling? A bare two carts would suffice to carry off the whole house, and except for the carter's fee there would be no expenses at all.

Only in a small hut built for the moment can one live without fears. It is very small but it holds a bed where I may lie at night and a seat for me in the day; it lacks nothing as a place for me to dwell. The hermit crab chooses to live in little shells because it knows the size of its body. The osprey stays on deserted shores because it fears human beings. I am like them. Knowing myself and the world, I have no ambitions and do not mix in the world. I seek only tranquility; I rejoice in the absence of grief.[8]

On the basis of this selection we can surmise the following. First, the mujō to which Chōmei calls attention clearly extends beyond nature's seasonal rhythm and the private lives of individuals. Mujō was by this point in history seen in natural calamities and in society as a whole. Chōmei could, of course, point to the multiple disruptions of the latter half of the twelfth century as clear evidence that the things mentioned in continental sources eventually occurred on the Japanese archipelago as well. Second, Chōmei's focus on what happens to man's habitations seems especially important; he singles out man's dwellings for special consideration—"not of long duration: so in the world are man and his dwellings." The habitation becomes not merely another instance among many where mujō is demonstrated but a context of particular importance, a precise mediator between the large context, the world as a whole, and the small one, the individual. All are shot through and through with mujō; it pervades all.

There is much more that deserves attention in the "Hōjō-ki," however. We can learn more about what Chōmei intends to say about the hermitage if we elicit the particulars of the hermit's hut from this description and set them against those of another type of dwelling, the ordinary house. For, even though some of the particulars are only adumbrated or implied, Chōmei is clearly stating his preference; and a preference implies a contrast. The following seem to be the salient features of the comparison:

Ordinary house	Hermit's hut
1. in the capital city	away from the capital; in mountains
2. as large as possible	as small as possible ("with each remove . . . smaller")
3. exposed to danger ("dangerous . . . capital")	free from danger, unexposed ("like osprey on deserted shore")
4. immobile, in fixed location ("unchanged from one generation to the next")	intentionally mobile, able to be set up at another location ("two carts carry it off")

Chōmei takes pains to make his dwelling mobile but is insouciant about site selection. In setting up his hut, he gives no heed to the customary considerations of geomancy in the Chinese tradition of *feng shui*: "I built my house without consulting any diviners." In addition, he puts the hut together with what were probably metal hooks-and-eyes,[9] a type of construction eminently suited to disassembly and reassembly elsewhere. "What difficulty would there be in changing my dwelling?" he asks.

Chōmei's rhetorical question is extremely important, especially since he explicitly mentions that diviners are unnecessary or useless. At this point the self-consciously Buddhist character of the work becomes quite obvious. Chōmei implies that the careful practice of geomancy—an important element in traditional Chinese thought and one that had also been of great importance for the Japanese (in locating, for instance, the best place to found the capital of Heian-kyō and also the best sites for Buddhist monasteries)—has become for him irrelevant or of only peripheral importance. Chōmei's degree of sensitivity on this matter may be somewhat special; he suggests that geomancy cannot really be effective in preventing radical dislocation and disruption. By contrast, he finds mujō, a *specifically* Buddhist notion, intellectually and personally compelling. Here the hegemony of Buddhist ideas in medieval Japan is very clear. Chōmei sees that entire conceptual systems are involved in even such an ordinary and mundane matter as how one goes about positioning one's habitation on the soil of the earth; and he sees the difference between the philosophy of Chinese geomancy and that of Buddhism. Rather than a loose amalgam of ideas and systems in such a context, there is for him a precise ordering of priorities, in which a distinctly Buddhist idea has preeminence.

This is reinforced by Chōmei's acceptance of mujō as a fact of existence with which he ought to place himself in harmony. Thus, when he rhetorically asks, "What difficulty would there be in changing my dwelling?" the secondary level of implication pertains to changing one's position or location in the sequence of lives envisioned in the Buddhist scheme of things. Changing one's habitation with ease in the empirical world is analogous to moving with facility through a series of incarnations toward the goal of nirvana. Since the metaphysical moves ought ideally to be made as readily as possible, the effortless moving about of a collapsible hut on the ordinary soil of earth points to ease in making the more profound moves from one lifetime to another. Ideally, both kinds of transposition would be managed with maximum ease. Moreover, moving one's hut here and now is unparalleled practice for dying and being reborn. Chōmei's point is that one ought to learn to live a kind of existence that is in harmony on all levels with the law of impermanence/instability. The corollary is that one ought to abandon all positions and constructions intended as fortresses against mujō, those vain and ignorance-spawned great houses with "proud roofs" which succumb quickly to fire and water.

The difference between the ordinary house and the hermit's hut is thus not only one of physical construction but also one of religious symbolism; the phenomenological contrasts already outlined are expressive of the following personal and religious ones:

Ordinary house	*Hermit's hut*
5. arising from ignorance ("follies of human endeavor")	arising from knowledge ("Now . . . sixty [and] . . . aware") ("Knowing myself and the world . . . ")
6. producing suffering, fear, anguish, grief	resulting in tranquility ("I rejoice in the absence of grief")

Yet the didactic element never seems obtrusive in the "Hōjō-ki" but lies concealed within what would otherwise be a pure form of belles lettres.

In the case of the monk Saigyō (1118–1190), the celebrations of his hermitage are in verse rather than prose. Antedating the writing of Chōmei slightly, Saigyō's descriptions of his hermitage also portray its essential transitoriness but in terms of the hut's porousness and permeability rather than its mobility:

abaretaru	This leaky, tumbledown
kusa no iori ni	Grass hut left opening for the moon,
moru tsuki o	And I gazed at it
sode ni utsushite	All the while it was mirrored
nagametsuru kana	In a teardrop fallen on my sleeve.[10]

It may be Saigyō's characteristic insistence on a direct relationship with the world of nature that leads to his preference for imagery such as this, in which the habitation is seen as coming apart and thus removing a barrier between the poet and nature.[11] But in addition to Saigyō's own particular reasons for depicting the hut as he does, it is certain that he also portrays it as it was generally understood: that is, namely as a construction that is leaky, labile, and coming apart at the seams. In this verse, the hut or "iori" is introduced as in disarray ("abaretaru") and as having perhaps been ravaged by the elements. The water image that pervades the poem is latent already in the first word; *abaretaru* suggests that a rather violent storm may have just passed. In its dilapidated condition, the hut allows the moonlight to drip or leak ("moru") inside, and the reflection of the moon is captured in a teardrop that, although not explicitly mentioned, is understood to be present on the sleeve of the poet's robe. Rain, moonlight that leaks inside, and tears spilling from the poet's eyes—these are three mutually reinforcing associations of porousness and permeability that all reiterate the image of the dilapidated state of the hut.

This depiction of the hut as literally falling apart seems basic; the hut must be thought of as in transition. Here, however, the change is one of natural dissolution rather than anticipated disassembly and removal. According to Ishida: "In addition to having been put together very simply, many of these hermit's huts have been damaged but never repaired. Therefore, because they are left in this dilapidated condition, it happens that we associate the 'grass hut' with something that has fallen apart. Also in literature the invariable depiction of it is as something in a state of ruin."[12] It is thus with justification that we think of the topos of the hermit's hut as one that presents it as porous and in disrepair. Saigyō's poem, moreover, has such rich imagery of wetness and liquidity that we perceive the hut as almost liquid, or at any rate, much less than solid.

The following poem by Saigyō makes the same point by using a different poetic technique:

izuku ni mo	Nowhere is there place
sumarezuba tada	To stop and live, so only

sumade aran	Everywhere will do:
shiba no iori no	Each and every grass-made hut soon leaves
shibashi naru yo ni	Its place within this withering world.[13]

The poet takes full advantage of the homophonic potential of two words in the last two lines: "shiba" ("grass") and "shibashi" ("temporary"). Both function grammatically as modifiers. They sound nearly alike. In addition, there is a conceptual similarity in that what is constructed of grass is, of necessity, temporary. Therefore, we cannot be far wrong in seeing a coalescence of the nouns modified and inferring that the poet suggests a nexus between "iori" ("hermitage") and "yo" ("world").

The use of the word *yo* gives the poem latitude for skillful equivocation, since it shuttles back and forth between being as wide and collective as this "world" or this "society," on the one hand, or as narrow and personal as one's present "incarnation," on the other. No matter what its signification, however, it is qualified by "shibashi naru," "temporary"; to presume permanence would be self-deception. The hermitage, falling apart in a manner the eye can witness, serves as a transparency, a concrete illustration of the way all things really are.

Yoshida Kenkō (1283–1350) wrote his *Tsurezure-gusa*, usually known in English as *Essays in Idleness*, between 1330 and 1332. He, too, is generally considered to be a writer whose perspective is that of the inja, or recluse, though his attitude and approach are considerably more urbane than either Chōmei's or Saigyō's. In Kenkō, simplicity is still highly valued, but it tends to be a matter of good taste. Excess and abundance are repugnant to the developed sensibility. Kenkō's tastes and his ideal are expressed in this section of the *Tsurezure-gusa*:

About the tenth month I had the occasion to visit a village beyond the place called Kurusuno. I made my way far down a moss-covered path until I reached a lonely-looking hut. Not a sound could be heard, except for the dripping of a water pipe buried in fallen leaves. Sprays of chrysanthemum and red maple leaves had been carelessly arranged on the holy-water shelf. Evidently somebody was living here. Moved, I was thinking, "One can live even in such a place," when I noticed in the garden beyond a great tangerine tree, its branches bent with fruit, that had been enclosed by a forbidding fence. Rather disillusioned, I thought now, "If only the tree had not been there!"[14]

The hut would have met all Kenkō's standards if only there had not been a surfeit of tangerines on the tree in the garden. Although elsewhere in his work he makes it clear that he likes the amenities of life, his ideal hermitage is nearly perfectly expressed in the one described above; it is lonely, quiet, hidden, hardly different from the natural setting in which it is found. It is far from the crossroads of civilization and commerce.

Although he lived much later, the poet Matsuo Bashō (1644–1694) adopted the topos of the hermitage, using it often in his writing of essays and *haikai*. An encapsulation of the convention and of his own ideal may be seen in the following, a translation of his brief essay "Rakushisha no ki," "Record of the House of Fallen Persimmons":

> The person named Kyorai has his retreat just outside Kyoto in the middle of the bamboo grove at Shimo Saga, near where the Oi River flows at the foot of Mount Arashi. Filled with quiet, it is a good place for meditation. The fellow Kyorai who lives in it is so lazy that the grass has grown up high enough to cover the windows and the all too numerous branches of persimmon trees hang down over everything. During the long rains of May the house leaks all over the place; the straw mats and paper screens get so moldy that a body cannot find a place to lie down in comfort. Peculiar as it may seem, what the host would offer his guest as a token of hospitality would be a bit of sunlight inside.

samidare ya   May's long rains:
shikishi egitaru   Wallpaper snatched for a poem
kabe no ato   Leaves a gap.[15]

When we read Bashō we realize that over the centuries certain things changed, especially aesthetic taste. Also, befitting the *haikai*/haiku mode, there is a levity in Bashō's portrait of Kyorai's charming indolence which is far removed from Chōmei's description of a city ravaged by various kinds of calamities. However, the underlying sine qua non of the hermitage still remains; it is in a condition of dilapidation and located at considerable distance from the crossroads of civilization. The intention seems invariably to be to depict a condition that is the *inversion* of values ordinarily held in the city centers. In addition, the hermit's hut, as Gaston Bachelard accurately described it in his *Poetics of Space*, "immediately becomes centralized solitude, for in the land of legend there exists no adjoining hut. . . . And there radiates about this centralized solitude a universe of meditation and prayer, a universe outside the universe. The hut can receive none of the riches 'of this world.' It possesses the facility of intense poverty; indeed, it is one of the glories of poverty; as destitution increases it gives us access to absolute refuge."[16] Bachelard has European examples in mind, but the same general things mutatis mutandis characterize the *iori* in the traditional literature of Japan.

Bashō, as Donald Shively has amply documented, identified himself closely with the Buddhist principle of impermanence. This identification extended to the literary name he used for himself. For *bashō* means "banana plant," a specimen of which grew near the famous poet's hut.[17] An important Mahayana text, the *Vimalakīrti-nirdeśa-sūtra*, had cited the banana plant as an exemplar of impermanence with the line "This body is like a banana plant; inside it has no solid part." The motif was transmitted through nō dramas and then picked up by Bashō.[18] Summarizing the reasons for the poet's attraction to the plant, Shively notes: "He could feel a special affinity to the banana plant, which like himself was lonely and defenseless, torn by the storms of this world. It symbolized the frailty, the transiency, of his own life—as he liked to picture it."[19] Again there is a set of mutually reinforcing images: plant, poet, and hermitage are all alike in their fragility and impermanence.

THE TRAVELER'S INN

One's first impression might be that the inn is simply the opposite of the hermitage—both in its particulars and its fundamental conception. Whereas the recluse or hermit—even when only an adopted persona—was understood to have left the world and drastically reduced the level of his social interaction by choosing a life of what Bachelard called "centralized solitude," the traveler stopping at an inn was, at least in the literature of traditional Japan, able to enjoy more than the usual amount of social interaction. The inn was conceived to be a place of meeting and association. In addition, because it was a place where one purchased quarters, it was often depicted as a place where men could buy the sexual favors of courtesans or prostitutes (*yūjo*, "play-women"). In this, the inn appears to contrast sharply with the hermitage: the expectation was that, as a result of a move to a hermitage, one's social interaction would decrease dramatically, but as a result of a move to one of the various inns along a circuit, one's social interaction would greatly increase. If the hut housed one who, at least for a time, thought of himself as a monk, the inn housed one who, again, for a time, thought of himself as a playboy. If the hermitage had in it someone who had left the world in some sense, the inn had in it someone probably thinking himself more worldly than usual. In sum, the person moving into a hermitage appeared to be following a religious or quasireligious pursuit; whereas someone taking up residence in an inn appeared unqualifiedly secular.

These differences can be shown to be comparatively superficial, however. They camouflage both more fundamental differences and very basic conceptual continuities. When analyzed, the texts considered in this chapter disclose a subtle structure of interrelationships between these two topoi of habitation.

The symbol of the inn had religious associations for the Japanese as a result of an interesting episode in the intellectual history of Japan. Indian forms of astrology were part and parcel of the Buddhist texts (especially those of the esoteric tradition) introduced into Japan by way of China in the eighth century. According to Shigeru Nakayama, the Indian astrology absorbed into Japan was "unquestionably horoscopic astrology for individual use, as opposed to the traditional Chinese portent astrology."[20] The Japanese called it *sukuyō-dō*, the "way of lunar mansions and planets." The fascinating feature of this is that, along with the other bodies moving through the night sky, the moon follows a course that had been plotted in a round of twenty-eight different "stopping places." The Sanskrit term for these stopping places (*nakṣatra*) had been rendered into Chinese as *hsiu* and into Japanese as *suku* (*shuku*). The same Chinese character was also used to write *yado*, which in its widest usage might mean "house" but very frequently more specifically designated an "inn."[21]

Nurtured within the ambit of esoteric Buddhism, horoscopic astrology gained a permanent foothold in Japanese society. At the same time, other cognates of *suku/yado* entered the national vocabulary. Words such as *shukuse*, "one's previous life," *shukumei*, "destiny," and *shukugō*, "karma from the past," all derive from the analogy according to which the heavenly bodies take up different lodging places in the sky—positions that influence human destinies. The analogy seems to have worked both ways. The projection of the notion of a lodging place or inn onto the cosmos had a boomerang effect inasmuch as inns in the everyday, empirical world came to be considered symbols of the chain of incarnations. The movement of planets and the moon through a sequence of mansions or inns in the sky seemed to be an apt parallel to the series of lives or incarnations through which terrestrial beings pass. This, when given urgency by the notion of *mujō*, became a lucid way of representing the transiency and ephemeral nature of existence. Its development into a literary topos was natural. In the words of the critic Mezaki Tokue: "Because the Buddhist notion that 'this life is a one-night's stopover' held sway over the minds of medieval people and seemed to be virtually self-evident, all the literature and drama of the period came to have this as its most dominant motif."[22] The investigation of the topos of yado, or inn, in traditional Japanese literature is, perhaps, best begun with a pair of poems by Saigyō. He included these in his own collection of his verse, the *Sanka-shū*. The headnotes and first poem are supposed to be by the monk Saigyō himself and the second poem by an unnamed woman he met in the following circumstances:

On the way to the temple called Tennō-ji, I got caught in the rain. In the area known as Eguchi I asked at one place for a night's lodging. When refused, I replied as follows:

yo no naka o   It is hard, perhaps,
itou made koso   To hate and part with the world;

katakarame	But you are stingy
kari no yadori o	Even with the night I ask of you,
oshimu kimi kana	A place in your soon-left inn.

The response by a "woman-of-play":

ie o izuru	It's because I heard
hito to shi kikeba	You're no longer bound to life
kari no yado ni	As a householder
kokoro tomuna to	That I'm loath to let you get attached
omou bakari zo	To this inn of brief, bought, stays.[23]

The poet takes full advantage of the ambiguities in the situation. He leaves it unspecified whether he was driven to Eguchi, a port area now part of Osaka and known then for its prostitutes, by the weather alone.[24] Whether or not there was play at that inn, there is much of it in the poetry, and it revolves around the double signification of "kari no," a modifier that may mean "temporary" but can also suggest "rented" or "borrowed."

The poem Saigyō presents as his own turns on the notion of relinquishment: he, as a monk, has relinquished the world, so the woman ought quite readily to relinquish him a room and (implicitly) herself for the night. The woman's riposte is a classic of its kind. She turns all the double entendre inside out, emphasizing the religious rather than the ribald possibilities in the phrases. Her point is that her refusal of the monk is not due to a lack of liberality but because she is concerned for his long-range welfare. Since he has adopted a vocation understood to be in harmony with mujō—that is, has left off being a householder—she doesn't wish to see him lose his freedom by becoming "attached" to her house. The keen edge of her retort lies in the implication that, although all houses are temporary and cannot ultimately be "held" by anyone, hers, as an inn (brothel), is especially a place of brief stays.

The understanding of the inn is thus based on the double signification of the homophone *kari no*. The pun relies on the two alternative readings of "kari no yado," with characters that in the one case mean "a rented inn" and, in the other, "a temporary inn." The idea is that the inn (brothel) makes manifest the truth about *all* houses—the "ie" with which the woman's poem begins. It divulges the truth of the fundamental impermanence/instability that is, in reality, characteristic of them all. The paradigmatic significance of the inn is the unambiguous point of the richly ambiguous situation and language.

It is revealing to look at the way this work and the courtesan appearing in the two poems were used later by the dramatist Kan'ami (1333–1384) in his nō play *Eguchi*. Great currency was given these two poems when they appeared in the imperial collection of 1206, the *Shinkokin-shū*.[25] By the time of Kan'ami's

composition of *Eguchi* there had developed a legend that the woman met by
Saigyō at the inn was, in fact, an incarnation of Bodhisattva Samantabhadra
(Fugen Bosatsu). The progressive revelation on stage of a "real" personage
lying behind the one presented initially is, of course, the kind of thing for which
the structure of nō is eminently suited. Furthermore, in *Eguchi* the courtesan
bodhisattva does not demonstrate her comprehension of religious truth by
refusing monks at her door; rather, she teaches men the meaning of mujō while
entertaining them in her bedroom. She turns her pillow into a pulpit of sorts.
The following translation of a key section of the play will suffice to show how
the inn's role is understood:

Lady:	Though being born human
	Is for us something rare,
	Difficult to achieve,
Chorus:	Karma causes us to be born
	Women, shaped by our sins—
	Especially in our case,
	Women floating along through life
	Loosely, like bits of bamboo
	Bobbing on a river's surface.
	We grieve in thinking back on
	The many misdeeds of former lives,
	The acts that brought us to this:
(*kuse*)	How in the morning the spring
	Time of crimson blossoms
	Transformed the hillsides into
	Crimson brocade before our eyes,
	But by evening already lured
	Off and away by the breeze,
	The autumn, its gold
	Leaves making the forest into
	Tie-dyed golden pieces
	Rich with color . . .
	Which too slips away
	Under the cold morning frosts;
	While wind whispered softly
	Through the pines and the moon
	Peeped through the vines
	Hanging by the lattice,
	Ladies exchanging quiet words
	With their night-guests who,
	Once gone, come no more!
	For even those locked in love
	With their pillows together
	Behind verdant curtains

In a crimson chamber
Must separate sometime;
For is there any, any among
The insentient plants or among
Humans graced with feelings
Who will be bypassed
By change, by sorrow?
We know all this . . . and yet . . .

Lady: We get sometimes captured
                    By color that holds us long
                    In its fascination,

Chorus: And sometimes the sound
                    Of a voice captures us
                    Till the mind and the mouth
                    Connive in deceptions—
                    In the way it goes for man:
                    Six organs of perceptions
                    Sinfully taking in all
                    Six fields of the perceived . . .
                    A hearing, a seeing,
                    And a mind gone astray.[26]

This is followed by a dance performed by the Lady of Eguchi, appropriate statements about the fact that man's vain attachment to a temporary lodging ("kari no yado") is the root of his problem, and a final denouement in which it becomes clear that the Lady is in truth the Bodhisattva Samantabhadra in disguise. After this, she is said to fly off to the Western Skies in her boat, which has become a milk-white elephant.

In some ways this depiction is reminiscent of the women's literature of the Heian period: the sumptuous settings, the thin line of distinction between the beauties of nature and the decor of the pleasure barge (here depicted as an inn), and the representation of mujō as the ephemerality of human affairs, the perfect analogue to the cadence of the seasons. But this is not the only understanding of mujō in the drama, in which things have actually gotten considerably more complex. In *Eguchi*, the understanding of role identity unfolds kaleidoscopically. That is, the central female character is first understood to be the prostitute Saigyō met in the Eguchi district, then an aristocrat known as the Lady of Eguchi, and later the Bodhisattva Samantabhadra. As the play moves forward, a progressively more "true" personage emerges from the sequence of conceptual chrysalises.

Although there is an immense social chasm between the court women loved by Prince Genji and the prostitute met by Saigyō, it is the latter who is eventually presented as a religious teacher. Such a progression is common to a number of cultures.[27] But the particularity of facts in this case is that the woman of Eguchi resides in an inn, a place imbued with mujō. Not only her life as a prostitute but also her habitation is understood to articulate the truth of impermanence. The ladies of the Heian court may have suffered in their private lives, but in the medieval development of Japanese literature the prostitute increasingly takes on the role of tutor of men—particularly for the Buddhist teaching of mujō.[28] Whether their boudoirs become settings for homilies on the six organs of perception and the six fields of the perceived or simply places where note is taken of the ephemerality of love, the point is invariably that such women encourage their clients to comprehend the Buddhist dharma.

The role of the courtesan and the topos of the inn are interdependent. The inn functions as a lucid symbol for reality as a whole. When, for instance, in *Eguchi* there is an exchange of the type "Once gone, come no more" between courtesans and their client-guests, this happens because both parties understand that the inn is by definition a place where people can only stay temporarily. If this were not so, it would tend to become a "home" and would no longer serve as a transparent symbol of the pervasive mujō that characterizes all things. It is because she comprehends the deep structure of reality that the courtesan in the inn matches her profession with her place of residence; both articulate impermanence/instability.

Matsuo Bashō, when a poet on a pilgrimage, recorded his experiences at a number of inns, but few are more interesting than his account of what happened to him at a stopover in Ichiburi in Etchū province. He recorded the following in *Oku no hosomichi* (*Narrow Road to the Deep North*):

> We got exhausted crossing a number of dangerous places up here in the North, places with fitting names such as Not-Knowing Parents, Not-Knowing Children, Rejected Dog, Sent-Back Horse, and the like. But in retiring for the night at a place [at the Ichiburi border], we overheard voices in the front room next door to our own room—apparently the voices of two young women. An older man's voice mingled in with theirs and I gathered from things said that the women were courtesans from Niigata in Echigo province, now on their way to Ise Shrine. The old man had, apparently, accompanied them this far but would now leave them here at the barrier and return the next morning to their hometown with all the usual messages to family and friends. I overheard them refer to themselves as "Drifting ones, like so much white froth bubbling at the end of waves hitting the shoreline, made wretched by life, by a karma that keeps their love-lives unsettled, different every day. . . ." I fell asleep, but the next morning, as my companion and I were taking leave of the place, the two women came over to us with tears in their eyes and this request on their lips: "We are at a loss to know which way to go on these roads. We are desperate, in fact. May we

follow you at a pace just beyond the range of your sight? Please give us the chance to follow your clerical robes, to know your great mercy, and to have the hope of release someday from our karma!'' We responded this way: ''Unfortunately, our plans will make things inconvenient for you. We have a lot of places en route where we must make stopovers. But you can simply put yourselves in the charge of anyone who happens to be going your way. Amaterasu will certainly take care of you and see you safely through to your goal.'' With these words, we left them . . . but a deep sense of pity for them stayed with us for some time.

hitotsu ya ni	Under one roof
yūjo mo netari	Play-girls too slept the night:
hagi to tsuki	Bushclover and moon.

When I recited this verse, Sora immediately put it down in his notebook.[29]

This is a rather puzzling story, one Bashō has clothed in abundant ambiguity. One's first impression, especially because of the way Bashō excuses himself from giving assistance to the women, is that here (as elsewhere)[30] Bashō's religious vestments cloak a bad case of pusillanimity. But analysis reveals more. In her book *Natural Symbols*, anthropologist Mary Douglas reminds us that a structural analysis insists especially on ''a familiar principle of aesthetics. The style appropriate to any message will coordinate all the channels along which it is given.''[31] Thus, the recital of place names at the beginning of Bashō's account is more than incidental; rather, it indicates the theme itself. ''Not-Knowing Parents, Not-Knowing Children, Rejected Dog, Sent-Back Horse'' are, to say the least, rather unusual as place names in Japan. Their common denominator, other than a generally unpleasant connotation, is that each suggests a dissolution of a relationship. Even the discarded animals are domestic animals. Thus, from the very first words, the theme is one of impermanent relationships. When a few lines later Bashō tells us that he overheard the courtesans refer to themselves as ''drifting ones . . . made wretched by . . . a karma that keeps their love-lives unsettled, different every day,'' we have a reinforcement of the theme introduced implicitly at the beginning. The poet's refusal to take up with the women even to the extent of letting them follow his trail is consonant with the theme of unavoidable and pervasive mujō.

In this episode, the events, diction, details of narrative, and the location itself all reiterate the major theme. Though their karma had brought the play-women and the pilgrim-poet under the same roof for one night, it was the most brief and casual of relationships. Bashō captures the pathos of this in the

poem: the inn is construed to be what it is by definition, the place of a one-night
stopover. As a place that houses transients, it articulates transience.

BETWEEN HUT AND INN

For the purposes of eliciting the contour of logical relationships between the
hermitage and the inn, the preceding has been a representative selection of
materials and one that illustrates well the center of the medieval tradition in
Japan. Although the examples from the vast corpus of Japanese literature may
introduce some variation in the presentation of the topoi of the hermitage and
the inn, the characteristics already outlined and the structure that follows hold
true generally.

As we have noted, it is at first the disparity between the hermit's hut and the
traveler's inn which captures our attention. In many ways the two topoi appear
to be opposites. We might schematize this polarity as follows:

Hermit's hut	*Traveler's inn*
located off main routes of commerce and transportation (*Hōjō-ki*; *Tsurezure-gusa*)	located at a transportation nexus or place of commerce (Eguchi; the "Ichiburi barrier")
diminished social interaction; solitude	increased social interaction; "chance" meetings
no sexual relationships	sexual dalliance

Moreover, because the inhabitant of the hermitage defines himself as an actual
or potential monk whereas it is the play-woman who is usually identified with
the inn, we might think of the hut as symbolic of world-denial and the inn as the
opposite, a locus for greater worldliness.

The preceding examples lead us to suspect, however, that the problem of
world-denial versus world-affirmation is actually rather complex. If we pursue
the implications of the consistent presentation of both hermitage and inn as
deeply symbolic of Buddhist teachings concerning mujō, then the differences
between them yield to a greater commonality. This commonality derives from
the way both types of ephemeral habitation are implicitly contrasted with a
third: the easily overlooked pole of the "ordinary," the habitation of the
householder.

The contrast between the householding life (*zaike*) and the renunciate or
out-of-household life (*shukke*) was basic for the introduction of Buddhism into
Japan. Much of the discussion and debate of the medieval period centered

around the understanding of these two apparent options. It was customarily assumed that a so-called religious vocation as a monk or nun was the way of realizing the shukke, or world/household-renouncing, goal; the ordinary person remaining among his or her family was, by contrast, following the way of zaike, world/household affirmation.[32]

An intriguing aspect of this is the discrepancy between the rules set down for monks and nuns in the *vinaya* (Japanese *ritsu*) and the presentation of the relationship between monks and courtesans in the various genres of literature. For, although the rules proscribed contact between them, the poetry and prose offer repeated examples of affinity between monks and courtesans. Moreover, the intimated affinity is more than the fascination of the forbidden.[33] Here there seems to be basis for noting that in the traditional literature, the courtesan, like the monk, is someone who has renounced the "household" way of life. She too has taken up a shukke position outside ordinary society, even though this is only implicitly understood. Since both are liminal figures in some sense, the monk and the prostitute share a surprisingly similar position vis-à-vis the ordinary householder; this may be why a figure such as the Lady of Eguchi is presented as understanding the deep meaning of mujō and teaching it in her boudoir.

This is also the reason Bashō felt an affinity for the traveling courtesans he met at the inn in Ichiburi, an affinity the laconic form of the haiku gave him a way of expressing:

> hitotsu ya ni   Under one roof
> yūjo mo netari   Play-girls too slept the night:
> hagi to tsuki   Bush clover and moon

Things are left in a comfortable and comforting ambiguity. No simple allegory, according to which bush clover and moon would refer respectively to play-girls and monks, will do. The reverse would be equally appropriate and that seems to be the point. The unexpected affinity impresses the poet and provides the matrix for his poem.

The same implicit understanding of the courtesan makes her an articulator of mujō in the fiction of Saikaku (1642–1693). It helps us understand the convention that shaped the characterization of the women in his *Kōshoku gonin onna*, "*Five Women Who Loved Love*," a work often compared to Boccaccio's *Decameron*. In this context we can appreciate an astute observation by Wm. Theodore de Bary:

> Saikaku's heroines, forsaking the security of their homes and the "good things of life" to pursue some ill-fated affair, impress us less with their lusty relish for life than with their final unworldliness.

It is in this sense that we see a profound connection between the two seemingly disparate meanings of the word *ukiyo*—the Buddhist "world of sadness" and the "floating world" of fashion and pleasure inhabited by Saikaku and his friends.[34]

DeBary's insight into the "profound connection" seems, in view of the materials examined previously, profoundly right. Thus, Saikaku and his world represent no radical departure from the structure implicit in earlier works.

Viewing the topoi of the hermitage and the inn in contrast to the mutual opposition image of the domestic household or home makes it possible to see their conceptual affinities. Although the actual social understanding of the meaning of *household* undoubtedly underwent considerable change during the medieval period,[35] we can assume that it remained a symbol of constancy throughout; and it therefore functioned as the logical opposite of both the hermitage and the inn. To emphasize the affinity of the two topoi does not preclude contrasts between them, however. These contrasts deserve some attention.

We noted earlier the hermitage that is presented as intentionally mobile in the case of Chōmei's hook-and-eye hut. Saigyō's hermitage is dilapidated, leaky, and almost more liquid than solid. Likewise, the "house of fallen persimmons" is in a state of charming disrepair. The feature that all of these have in common is a perceptible instability. Even if the hermit himself functions as a kind of anchor, his habitation falls apart and "moves" by changing even while he is inside. It embodies mujō by its very mode of existence in the world; it is inherently unstable.

The inn demonstrates none of these characteristics. It is a symbol of mujō because by definition it is where the *tabibito*, "traveler" or "moving person," stays. Descriptions of it need make no reference to permeability or instability in its physical existence. It serves as a symbol of mujō because temporariness is built into its function. Even when it does house someone for an extended period of time, that someone is invariably a play-woman, or yūjo, whose life is an articulation of the principle of impermanence. Brevity is by definition part of stopping over at an inn.

The topoi of hermitage and inn seem to have the power they do in traditional Japanese literature because they suggest a pattern of identities and nonidentities, similarities and contrasts.[36] Mobility and instability characterize the hermit's hut: even if the hermit himself remains more or less fixed, his hut disappears from around him. By contrast, the inn is where a moving inhabitant, a traveler, briefly resides. Both of these, the loci of mujō, are in contrast to another possibility often only implicitly present, that of the householder in his

"home." "Home" is the social and physical situation in which there sup-
posedly is a stable inhabitant in a stable habitation. The hut and the inn are both
like and unlike it—but in opposite ways.

In order to expose the underlying logical structure, we might schematize the
possibilities as follows:

A. Home — stable inhabitant   in   stable habitation
B. Hut   — stable inhabitant   in   moving habitation
C. Inn   — moving inhabitant   in   stable habitation

According to Buddhist teaching, however, home offers only a fraudulent
stability; it has the appearance but not the reality of truth. Japanese literature
shaped by Confucian values or even pre-Buddhist values may celebrate the
overwhelmingly attractive sense of security provided by one's own domicile,
but an orthodox Buddhist position would be that both inn and hermitage are
more closely in harmony with the real structure of the universe. Though that
structure itself has no adequate symbol, the didactic thrust of the literature
suggests it would be:

D. X   — moving inhabitant   in   moving habitation

This is the situation from which all semblance of the futile search for perma-
nence/stability (*ujō*) has been removed. In the parlance of Buddhism, *A* and *D*
are thus opposite poles: one is illusion and the other reality.

Since movement along the series A to D is movement on a scale of value, the
two topoi of hut and inn are concrete mediators of this value. Each in its own
way has broken with the spurious security offered by the image of the household—the hermitage by its articulation of the truth that any world (*yo*) in which
we find ourselves is bound to collapse and come apart, and the inn by its
reminder that we are beings quickly passing through the present existence, one
in a series of incarnations.

An intriguing aspect of this body of literature is the extent to which didactic
purposes are wed to splendid verbal combinations to produce literature in which
the didactic element is never obtrusive or causes us to doubt that we are dealing
with belles lettres. We owe this to the literary artists of traditional Japan, who
through many centuries accepted, refined, and explored the multiple variations
possible within these two topoi.

4

SYMBOL AND YŪGEN: SHUNZEI'S USE OF TENDAI BUDDHISM

The beauty of holiness
> the beauty of a man's anger
reflecting his sex
> or a woman's either,
>> mountainous,
or a little stone church
> from a height
>> or
close to the camera
> the apple tree in blossom
>> or the far lake
below
> in the distance
>> are equal
as they are unsurpassed.

> —William Carlos Williams
> "View by Color Photography on a Commercial Calendar"[1]
> *Pictures from Brueghel*

T HERE IS GENERAL AGREEMENT among both Japanese and Western literary historians that much of the verse of twelfth-century Japan is strikingly different from that written earlier and that this change is best summarized as the presence of a new depth ("fukasa") in the new poetry. According to Robert H. Brower and Earl Miner:[2]

To some degree the depth derives from a complexity of technique, but the subjectivity lent poetry by the preceding period is absorbed by the new techniques, and charges them with a kind of resonance often belied by what on the surface is an easy intelligibility. When a poem seems to present us with description, we are apt to take the imagistic beauty of the poem at face value and to miss the deeper implications.

These "resonances" and "deeper implications" certainly included a multi-layered sequence of allusions—not only to earlier Japanese verse but also to the literature of China. A great deal of earlier literary history could now be compressed into a single poem. In this way, an individual poem often reflected a variety and wealth of earlier poetic worlds. Brower and Miner are justified in concluding that "such allusive depth shows the extent to which a poem of this age is often neoclassical, since it may be fully appreciated and understood only through a knowledge of earlier portions of the Sino-Japanese literary tradition."[3]

There is, however, another important ingredient that went into the development of the detectable "depth" in the poetry of this era, an element clearly drawn into poetry from moves and processes in the intellectual and religious world of the time. Noting its importance for poets such as Fujiwara Shunzei (1114–1204) and his son Teika (1162–1241), Brower and Miner write:[4]

The adaptation of a religious ideal to poetic practice may seem remarkable, yet it is hardly surprising in this strongly religious age, when the art of poetry was regarded as a way of life and just as surely a means to the ultimate truth as the sermons of the Buddha.

The truth contained in this apt observation deserves more attention than it has been given in literary histories of Japan. To explore its significance in some detail will help to clarify some of the intellectual issues behind the major developments in medieval Japanese literary aesthetics.

The twelfth century was one of great social and political upheaval in Japan—a circumstance probably not unrelated to the achievement of a new depth in the verse of poets such as Shunzei, Saigyō, and Teika. This century was also one in which the problems and propositions of Tendai philosophy had a direct impact on an emerging literary aesthetic, and this was clearly of fundamental importance for the new depth in poetry. Though the beginning of the Buddhist and medieval episteme was probably as early as the Nara period, in the late Heian and early Kamakura period the framework of transmigration through the rokudō was complemented and complicated by new intellectual strategies and dialectics in East Asian Buddhism. These new strategies might accurately be described as constituting the entry into a high medieval period.

The effect on aesthetics was profound. Sen'ichi Hisamatsu, one of Japan's most important literary scholars, has described it as the key to understanding not only certain poems of the era but also the shape and particular character of the era as a whole:

> The literary concept known as *yūgen* is an important criterion in judging whether or not a thing is "medieval." *Yūgen* as an aesthetic quality was esteemed throughout the medieval period. In the subtle overtones of its symbolic statements, one discerns the influence of Buddhist philosophy, to which men turned for solace during the tremendous social upheavals of the late ancient and medieval period. Buddhism is the basic element in medieval literature.[5]

This chapter will focus on the Buddhist component in the "high" medieval aesthetic and attempt to clarify some aspects of the much praised but always elusive aesthetic quality called *yūgen*.

Understanding *yūgen* involves entering a world whose intellectual presuppositions and values differ considerably from those of the modern West and also, in important and interesting ways, from those of the medieval West. In order to identify and clarify some of these values, we must take seriously the claim by poets such as Shunzei, Teika, Saigyō, and Jien that their minds and their literary ideals were shaped by certain texts and religious practices. It is important to read and interpret works they read, works such as the *Lotus Sutra* and the *Mo-ho chih-kuan* (*Makashikan*). By so doing we may be able to reconstruct the intellectual and religious structure of this era; and by knowing better the mind of the era we will need to rely less on a host of separate, unrelated bits of information in our reading of ancient texts. The intention of this kind of study is to prevent rather than contribute to that dire state of affairs in which, according to George Steiner: " . . . the 'text' is receding from immediacy, from vital personal recognition on stilts of footnotes, ever more rudimentary, ever more unashamed in their conveyance of information which was once the alphabet of reading."[6] The kind of exercise undertaken in this chapter should make the texts of the era—both scriptures and poems—more accessible and immediate even though they represent a considerable departure from Western modes of thought.

We are well aided in this by the superb scholarship of the Japanese. Konishi Jin'ichi, for example, has reminded us that there is a good deal of continuity between the Tendai Buddhism of the Heian period and the much more famous Zen Buddhism of the Kamakura and Muromachi periods.[7] The point is significant since our very periodization of history places the accent on change and discontinuity, with the direct consequence that we tend to attribute to Zen the aspects of the medieval aesthetic that we find most fascinating and culturally distinctive. Nevertheless, the crucial aesthetic value yūgen really had its matrix in the Heian period—that is, before the end of the twelfth century—and in the Buddhism of the Tendai school. It was already a part of the Japanese experience before the institutional implanting of Zen and the massive impact of Sung culture on Japan during the Kamakura and Muromachi periods. Konishi has called special attention to Shunzei's and Teika's use of a Chinese text, the *Mo-ho chih-kuan* by Chih-i, for the forging of their contributions to the evolving medieval aesthetic.[8] A number of scholars concur with this judgment;[9] the thought and practice of Tendai, especially as expressed in this major treatise, cannot be dismissed or regarded lightly in any attempt to grasp the flowering of the arts in medieval Japan.

The Tendai school has been among the least studied by Western scholars[10] and seems to have a special degree of imprecision and obscurity in our knowledge of the spectrum of Buddhist schools. It is often thought of as merely eclectic and amorphous. We tend to portray it as a matrix, frequently by the metaphor of a mother known chiefly through her sons—the dynamic and much more sharply etched historical personalities of Dōgen, Hōnen, Shinran, and Nichiren. For a variety of reasons, these "sons" of Tendai and the "new" forms of Buddhism they established—forms that had their growth in the Kamakura era—have much more readily captured the attention of Western scholars and have been the subject of extensive research and study. The result has been that the Tendai "mother" out of which they all emerged has remained in relative obscurity, a figure whose role as genetrix is acknowledged but whose own specific character has elicited little serious attention. The following discussion will not, to be sure, entirely redress this imbalance, but it should help to bring this very important school of Buddhism into somewhat sharper focus, as we attempt to understand the evolution of the medieval Japanese literary aesthetic.

The texts to be considered in this chapter are first, the *Lotus Sutra*, the foundation of the Tendai school and the most important Buddhist scripture for the people of the Heian period; second, the *Mo-ho chih-kuan*, the major treatise of the Chinese thinker Chih-i (538−597); third, a key section of the *Korai fūteishō*, the only full-length treatise on poetry by Fujiwara Shunzei; and finally, a number of specific poems in which the new depth, the yūgen, of later Heian and early Kamakura verse is detectable. By demonstrating the interpretative continuity throughout these texts, perhaps both Tendai philosophy and the medieval Japanese aesthetic will be brought more clearly into view.

It is not difficult to understand why the literate people of the Heian period cherished the *Lotus Sutra*. It is still commonly regarded as a literary gem[11] and it was the stimulus for much later literature. Rich and varied, it functions on what Umehara Takeshi calls a level of high drama.[12] A number of its extended metaphors and parables are widely admired for their vividness of narrative and finesse of detail. The work is, in fact, so colorful and picturesque that modern readers have occasionally wondered if it is not mostly froth, with really no substantial or philosophical dimension.[13] Though the question is a valid one, the suspicion is, I think, unfounded. This sutra is both a literary tour de force and expressive of a fundamental philosophical perspective in Mahayana Buddhism.

In both its original intention and its subsequent uses, the *Lotus Sutra* was a harmonizing text; that is, it was useful in bringing unity and order into situations that were rife with conflict or in danger of disjunction. The text's origins in India seem to have been in an attempt to unite and pacify the Buddhist community at a time when there was serious disagreement over which of three "vehicles," or saintly ideals, was to be pursued.[14] That is, it addresses itself to a situation in which some Buddhists claim to follow the path of the bodhisattva by aiming both at one's own and others' salvation; a second group pursues the way of the *pratyekabuddha* by trying to save oneself solely through one's own efforts; and a third group holds to the ideal of the *śrāvaka*, according to which one listens to the Buddha's sermons and, on the strength of these, works for self-salvation. Each recognizably different vehicle must have had its defenders as well as its detractors at the time the *Lotus* was composed in India—probably sometime during the first century C.E. In this context, the *Lotus* unhesitatingly declares the underlying unity of all three vehicles; it argues that all are variants of the one way, the way of Buddhahood. It was thus probably intended to serve a broadly ecumenical purpose by bringing greater unity to the Buddhist community. Later on, and in a very different way, it again served a harmonizing purpose when it was taken as the text that alone could bring order to the vast array of sutras in T'ang China, sutras that, at least in their modes of discourse, often seemed incompatible and contradictory.[15]

The reason for the sutra's ready utility in situations of disunity or disparity is that, from its opening sections, it directly addresses the problem of the relationship of the one to the many—that is, the relationship of unity to diversity. Its primary proposal, offered early in the text, is the notion of *upāya*, which the Chinese call *fang pien* and the Japanese, in their reading of the Chinese text, call *hōben*. This term has usually been translated into English as "skillful devices" or "expedient means," although it might be better, in order to disallow the notion of a duality, to translate it as "modes."[16] The core idea is present in the following excerpt from the chapter on hōben; these words are supposed to have been spoken by the World Honored One to his disciple: "Śāriputra, since becoming a Buddha, I, in a variety of modes and through many kinds of metaphors, have been conversing and preaching very widely, thus in countless ways leading living beings and helping them abandon their attachments."[17] The idea is that the various vehicles, even when they have resulted in sectarian developments, are compatible and fundamentally united on a deeper level. The different modes are the consequence of a genius for adaptability that translates the dharma into a variety of forms for a variety of people.

What follows in the sutra is perhaps its most exciting, unique, and interesting development. The brief statement about hōben is followed by a sequence of chapters that exfoliate with parables and allegories, each purporting to be another way the sutra's message can be concretely and dramatically grasped. The most famous example is the third chapter, on parable (hiyu). It narrates the story of a rich man who, seeing his children trapped in a burning house but so enchanted by their toys that they are oblivious to their own danger, promises them even more extravagant toys—of three types (corresponding to the three vehicles); these successfully entice the children out of the house and into safety. In a later chapter, another, almost equally famous, simile compares the three different vehicles to shrubs, plants, and trees of different heights, all of which receive equally of the rain.

> A dense cloud, spreading over and everywhere covering the whole three-thouand-great-thousandfold world, pours down its rain equally at the same time. From the rain of one cloud each according to the nature of its kind acquires its development, opening its blossoms and bearing its fruit. Though produced in one soil and moistened by the same rain, yet these plants and trees are all different.
>
> Know, Kāśyapa! The Tathāgata is also like this; he appears in the world like the rising of that great cloud.[18]

Thus the point about a single message mediated through a variety of modes is made again and again in the text.

All this seems quite straightforward; and for that reason, it is tempting to interpret the role and purpose of the parables and allegories in the Lotus as similar to those of rhetorical forms in Western sacred and secular literatures. But to do so is to miss the main point of the Lotus, as well as the opportunity to see how the text is both a literary and religious tour de force.

A direct comparison with the role and use of literary allegory in medieval Europe serves to highlight the difference. In recent decades scholars have produced some excellent studies of the history of intepretation and the use of literary modes in Europe. In his brilliant study *Mimesis*, Erich Auerbach called attention to the fact that "figural interpretation," while completely alien to what had been the literary norm in classical antiquity, was the principal mode in medieval Christendom. In figural interpretation, "sensory occurrence pales before the power of figural meaning" and there occurs " . . . an antagonism between sensory appearance and meaning, an antagonism which permeates the early, and indeed the whole, Christian view of reality."[19] In his lucid discussion of the importance of allegory in the aethetics of medieval Europe, D.W. Robertson, Jr. cites and approves the succinct definition of allegory given by Isidore of Seville, according to whom, it is "the art of saying one thing to mean another."[20] For the medieval Christians, the important thing was to be able to decode literal and historical messages because these represented "a shadow of something else more real or more significant."[21] This decoding was thought to be possible through the faculty of reason; Robertson notes that in this context "to eat the chaff is to be a beast of burden; to eat the grain is to be human. He who uses human reason, therefore, will cast off the chaff and hasten to eat the grain of the spirit."[22] As mediated through the hermeneutics of Augustine, the influence of Plato—especially of Plato's *Republic*—was deep.[23] And since, according to Iris Murdoch, it is in the *Republic* that "the forms are transcendent and the objects of opinion diminish near the lower end of the scale from 'being' toward 'not being,' "[24] we can understand how it happened that in medieval Europe there was "an *hierarchical* mode of thought which emphasizes the reality of abstract values."[25]

The result was a rich and creative use of symbol and allegory in medieval European literature, in which allegories, like parables, were understood to be "earthly stories with heavenly meanings." That is, the narrative was a *means* for indicating or pointing to its "meanings." In the implicit hierarchy, the relationship between what I.A. Richards has called "vehicle" and "tenor" was one of lower to higher or of servant to master.[26] The directional flow was from the literal, earthly, and temporary to the spiritual, heavenly, and eternal.

This may help us see how different and, from this point of view, eccentric the *Lotus Sutra* really is. Western readers have overlooked the structure of the text and have thereby missed the critically important fact that the so-called parables or allegories all follow immediately upon, and actually continue, the discussion begun in the upāya, or hōben, chapter about the relationship of means to ends. If we think in terms of the problem of the relationship of means to ends in language, we can see the chapter as concerned with the relationship of vehicle to tenor. It then becomes immediately apparent that the parables in the *Lotus* function in a far different, and in some ways a more sophisticated, fashion than parables do in the allegorical literature of the West. For, the surprising feature of those in the *Lotus* is that they are simultaneously the vehicle and the tenor of that vehicle. In a very important sense, the parables of the *Lotus* are about the role and status of parabolic speech itself. They are what I would call self-reflexive allegory; that is, their trajectory of discourse behaves like a boomerang. Much like the dharmas described in a crucial section of the hōben chapter, they are characterized by "the absolute identity [or equality] of their beginning and end."[27]

Recognizing this makes it possible to see the sutra as much more sophisticated and philosophical than we had been led to think; we can also see why it had such profound implications for subsequent literary and aesthetic expression. By being self-reflexive, the sutra twists the reader's attention into unexpected areas, areas that seem calculated to help him jettison his ordinary expectations about reading and interpretation. The parables (chapters three to seven) of the *Lotus* are presented as if they are going to illustrate what is meant by upaya (*hōben*) (chapter two); but it is equally true that the chapter on hōben explains, and is a means for understanding, the parabolic narratives. Thus, the illustration is in no way subordinate to what it illustrates. Unlike the Platonic allegory in the medieval Christian West—"a shadow of something else more real or more significant"—the narratives of the *Lotus* are not a means to an end beyond themselves. Their concrete mode of expression is not "chaff" to be dispensed with in order to attain a more abstract, rational, or spiritual truth. The *Lotus* is unequivocal on this point: "One may seek in every one of the ten directions but will find no mode [*hōben*] other than the Buddha's."[28] This accounts for what may seem to be an inordinate amount of praise directed by the sutra toward itself. It also implies that within the sutra there is an unmistakable philosophical move opposite to that in Plato's *Republic*, a move to affirm the complete reality of the world of concrete phenomena in spite of the fact that they are impermanent.

As long as the *Lotus* is misread as merely a sequence of elegant pictures without much real substance[29] or as dealing with religious practice at the expense of philosophical theory,[30] the connection between it and the thought of Chih-i seems either tenuous or forced. In my reading of the *Lotus*, the sutra radically *relativizes* our customary projection of an implicit hierarchy of value onto the relationship of means to ends. Fujita Kōtatsu has made the point in a different way by stressing the teaching of śunyatā, "emptiness," in the

Lotus,[31] a teaching best understood through the Nāgārjunic interpretation of *emptiness* as the codependence of all phenomena. Emptiness disallows an ontological hierarchy and makes the abstract just as dependent on the concrete as the concrete is dependent on the abstract.

It was, of course, the Chinese thinker Chih-i who elaborated the implications of these matters.[32] Although he wrote treatises giving a direct exposition of the *Lotus*, his major work, the *Mo-ho chih-kuan*, is intrinsically more important and served historically as a direct link between the *Lotus* and the aesthetics of the later Heian poets of Japan. *Chih-kuan*, or what the Japanese called *shikan*, is at the center of Chih-i's major treatise, which is devoted expressly to the exposition of that topic. The *Mo-ho chih-kuan* describes it as the quintessence of Buddhism, both in theory and practice. The term *shikan* is a rendering of two Sanskrit terms, *śamatha* (*shi*) and *vipaśyanā* (*kan*).[33] These are recognized as two distinct phases or modes that are also united into one process. *Śamatha*, the first aspect of shikan, could be rendered as "standstill," the philosophical/meditational act through which the random and confused perceptions and cognitions of ordinary experience are brought to a stop and remain in a tranquil state. This stoppage makes possible (and is also made possible by) the second aspect of shikan. This is *vipaśyanā*, which could be rendered as "contemplation." This contemplation is directed toward objects of ordinary perception. It does not attempt to locate the essences of phenomena. The contemplator, in accord with the fundamental impermanence of all things (himself included), regards them without obstruction (*muge*), that is, without the sort of discriminating mind that would seek to arrange phenomena into hierarchies of relative importance and select out some—primarily himself or some part of himself—as deserving of exemption from the rule of impartial impermanence (mujō).

On a number of levels, shikan involves a rejection and refutation of ontological dualism. It explores and discloses the fact that there are no exceptions to the change that characterizes all things. There are no "essences" that are impervious to alteration. Likewise, there are no beings that have existence in and of themselves and are therefore independent of all other things. In addition, the very process of recognizing this principle insists that the subject of contemplation is not ultimately separate from its objects. This insistence on "radical nondualism" (*funi*) is very strong in Tendai and makes it fundamentally different from the majority of the philosophies and religious practices that have had their origin in the West.

The association in the West between religious philosophies and Platonic or semi-Platonic modes of thought has been long and deep. Perhaps this has led some Western scholars to project it onto the thought and practices of Buddhism;

they have assumed that, since Tendai is "religious" thought, it will be roughly comparable to Platonism. This, for instance, seems to be what went wrong in the most important Western study of the Japanese poet Fujiwara Shunzei: Clifton W. Royston seems to assume that, since Shunzei practiced the shikan meditation and was immersed in the thought of Tendai, his view of reality was a variety of Platonism. He writes, for instance, of Shunzei's "quasi-platonic, quasi-religious views of poetry,"[34] and in a discussion of the Buddhist component in Shunzei's literary criticism, he maintains: "There is a sufficient resemblance between Tendai philosophy and Platonism to allow the substitution of the term 'noumenon' for the Void. In Buddhism as in Plato, phenomena related to the senses are illusory, unsubstantial, subject to decay, and the products of ignorance. Plato conceives of noumenal forms that are eternal, unchanging ideal forms or absolutes. . . ."[35] On the basis of what we have noted previously about the structure and direction of Tendai thought, it should be apparent that this is misconceived. Royston may have realized there were problems with such a comparison, as he appended the following qualification (which, because it misconstrues the meaning of the emptiness of phenomena, only further confuses the situation): " . . . these noumena, perhaps, strictly speaking, do not exist in Buddhism; what is 'real' is the Void, the antithesis of 'reality.' "[36] The problem is that, once Platonism is imported into Buddhist thought as though it were a useful tool for getting a handle on things, it begins to act like a philosophical equivalent of the sorcerer's apprentice, fomenting misconceptions all over the place.

My intention is not to quibble but rather to isolate and expose a conceptual difficulty that is particularly troublesome. It seems to have made both Buddhist thought and the aesthetic of medieval Japan extremely opaque to many Westerners. Since we are here interested in certain poets for whom the thought of Tendai was an *acknowledged* base for their own aesthetic, it would seem important to get as accurate as possible a portrait of Tendai. In this connection we can profitably follow the lead of Manaka Fujiko, a nun immersed in the Tendai tradition and one of Japan's most erudite students of the literature of this period. Manaka notes that what was philosophically important for Shunzei and Teika in the *Mo-ho chih-kuan* was the teaching of *genshō-zoku-jissō*, literally, "the identity of the phenomenon with the real."[37] What is clear, then, is that Tendai thought entertained something like Platonism as a philosophical option and emphatically rejected it.

Though this leaves a number of aspects of Tendai to be explored further, we can at least conclude that the new depth in the verse and aesthetic taste of the end of the Heian period did not arise out of a dualist distinction between insubstantial phenomena and substantial, absolute noumena. The parallel with Platonism turns out to have been completely misleading. With it out of the way, we can now more directly ask what constituted the depth that came into the medieval Japanese aesthetic. Before returning to the thought of Chih-i, let us consider another key treatise, the *Korai fūteishō*. Completed in 1197, it was Shunzei's only full-length work on poetry. The section that is usually regarded as having crucial importance is one I translate as follows:

> The *Mo-ho chih-kuan* of the Tendai school opens with these words by Kuan-ting [Chih-i's amanuensis]:
> "Calm-and-contemplation [*shikan*] has in itself a clarity and tranquil-
> ity beyond anything known to earlier generations."
> Now, if we pay attention to this at the outset, a dimension of infinite depth as well as profound meaning will be discovered. It will be like listening to something sublime and exalted while trying to understand the poetic sensi-bility—its fine points, weak points, and its depths. This is to say that things that otherwise are incapable of being expressed in words will be understood precisely when they are likened to calm-and-contemplation [*shikan*].
>
> It is worthy of note that in the text of the *Mo-ho chih-kuan* the very first thing related is the process of transmission of the Holy Dharma of the Buddha—that is, the way it was handed down from one man to another. The great enlightened one, Śākyamuni, transmitted it to Kāśyapa who, in turn, passed it on to Ānanda; so it went from master to disciple down through twenty-three persons. When we [Japanese] hear about this process of the transmission of the Holy Dharma, we cannot have anything but great reverence for it. But in a similar way we cannot but be impressed by the fact that our own Japanese verse-form, the *uta*, has from antiquity been handed down to us in precisely the same fashion—taking the shape of a series of anthologies, a sequence that began with the *Man'yō-shū* and then continued on through its successors, the *Kokin-shū*, the *Gosen-shū*, the *Shūi-shū*, and so on.
>
> But someone might charge that, whereas in the case of the *Mo-ho chih-kuan* it is a matter of transmitting the deep truth by holy men known as the "golden-mouthed ones," what I have brought up for consideration is nothing more than those verbal games known as "floating phrases and fictive utterances" ["kyōgen-kigo"]. However, quite on the contrary, it is exactly here that the profundity of things is demonstrated. This is because there exists a reciprocal flow of meaning between such things [as poetry] and the way of Buddhism, a way that maintains the interdependence of all things. This is found in the teaching that:[38]
> "Enlightenment is nowhere other than in the worldly passions."
> Again, it is as in that passage of the *Lotus Sutra* that says:
> "The Bodhisattva Mahāsattva interprets even the secular classics . . .
> to show how they can benefit life and can be reconciled with the
> perfect Buddhist dharma."

Moreover, the matter is explained as follows in the *Samantabhadra-bodhi-sattva-sūtra*:

"Of one thing it is said 'that is bad' and of another it is said 'that is good.' But there is nothing inherent in things that make them good or bad. For each thing's 'self' is empty [of independent existence]."

Thus, for all these reasons I can now for the record state that the Japanese lyric called the *uta* has a dimension of depth, one that has affinity with the three stages of truth in Tendai, namely, the void [*kū*], the provisional [*ke*], and the middle [*chū*].[39]

Though on first reading this passage might appear to be little more than a blatant and facile rationalization, it is actually fairly sophisticated both in what it sets out to do and how it accomplishes it. I propose, first, to make a few observations that may help to clarify Shunzei's argument, and then, by an analysis of specific poems, to show the continuity between Shunzei's theory and his practice.

Shunzei's comparison of the transmission of the dharma with the handing down of Japanese verse form in a sequence of anthologies is more than a naive claim that parallel processes imply equivalent contents. He is not merely claiming that the Japanese need not feel outdone by historic events on the Asian mainland, where Buddhist teachings passed from Śākyamuni Buddha down through a long line of Indian and Chinese masters. He is not merely making a naive claim that the Japanese on their archipelago have, in the form of poetry collections, something tantamount to the dharmic transmission.

Shunzei's argument proceeds quite differently. He is fully aware that some devout Buddhists in China and Japan have given up the practice of poetry in order to give themselves unequivocally to the pursuit of more holy or religious vocations; they have even sometimes dismissed secular prose and poetry as mere "floating phrases and fictive utterances" ("kyōgen kigo").[40] The Japanese courtly conventions, according to which it was necessary to write amorous verse, had been especially troublesome to these more puritanical members of the Buddhist community. Shunzei's response to these Buddhists is an adroit citation of the sacred sutras to demonstrate that a clear, rigorous distinction between sacred and secular is itself problematic according to Mahayana doctrine. The crux of his argument is that the composition and collection of secular verse *must be a Buddhist activity*[41] because the dialectic of the Mahayana (eminently, in the section Shunzei cites of the *Samantabhadra-bodhisattva-sūtra*) demands a rejection of any bifurcation of the holy and the profane.

Shunzei then brings in Tendai's three "stages" of truth (*santai*), the void, the provisional, and the middle. An aspect of Chih-i's thought, the three stages are crucial to the linkage Shunzei sees between poetry and Buddhism. The initial stage of the santai is the doctrine of the fundamental emptiness or voidness (*kū*) of all phenomena. Emptiness is a classic Buddhist teaching and in no way peculiar to the Tendai school. The Buddhist claim of the emptiness of phenomena is not the positing of a nihil but simply the insistence that nowhere can there be found an entity that has existence in and of itself. This is to say that the ancient Buddhists found no evidence of any being or phenomenon having what in Western philosophy was once called *aseity*, the status of being unconditioned and beyond influence or causation by any other thing. The Buddhists insisted that even things or beings imagined or said to have independent existence really do not, for their existence depends on the imagination or speech of the person thinking or speaking of them. For the Buddhist, there are no beings with aseity, no exceptions to the rule that all phenomena are void of self-existence (*muga*). (In fact, to the extent that aseity would be viewed as an attribute of deity, Buddhists have traditionally had some difficulty accepting the notion of a ''god'' in this sense.) The corollary of the doctrine of the void is that all things are radically related. In the third chapter of his *Mo-ho chih-kuan* Chih-i referred to this, the first move in the santai, as ''juke-nyūkū,'' ''leaving the provisional and entering into empty'';[42] this means forsaking our ordinary way of perceiving phenomena as having independent being and accepting the correct view of them as void of such independence.

The establishment of the doctrine of the void is fraught with hazards, however. Chief among these is the danger of reifying or hypostatizing the void itself. Tamura Yoshirō notes: ''It will not do to think of having gone from the provisional to the emptiness of things as if one had somehow now reached some *entity* called 'the void.' ''[43] For this reason, it was sometimes maintained in the Mahayana that ''emptiness itself is emptied'' (''kū kū''). Thus, to regard phenomena as empty is itself an activity that needs to be relativized and seen as dependent. In the *Mo-ho chih-kuan* this is accomplished by a reaffirmation of the reality of provisional phenomena (*ke*). This was the second stage of the santai. Chih-i called it ''jukū-nyūke,'' ''leaving the empty and entering into the provisional.''[44] The term is diametrically opposite to *juke-nyūkū* but the intention is not to establish two mutually negating propositions; rather, it is to hold that both propositions describe reality and both are necessary in order to describe reality accurately.

The recognition of the perfectly balanced codependence of the void (*kū*) and the provisional (*ke*) was Tendai's third stage, that of the middle (*chū*). The middle is not a position midway between the other two but the holding of both in a state of dynamic and equalized tension. Each way of looking at things is valid but only because the other is also true; each side gives existence and function to the other. The classic Mahayana account of the bodhisattva figure makes the same point in more narrative, less philosophical, language. According to it, the bodhisattva recognizes the phenomenal world as empty, without abiding entities, and therefore worthy of being forsaken for nirvana; nevertheless, in order to rescue others, he returns to the world of samsara.[45] Moreover, since "enlightenment is nowhere other than in the worldly passions" ("bonnō soku bodai"), even for the bodhisattva himself there is no other world in which to be, or to be saved. This is the conceptual basis for the Boddhisattva Samantabhadra's realization in the person of the Lady of Eguchi.

Shunzei's cryptic statement quoted earlier may now be easier to understand: "Thus, for all these reasons I can now for the record state that the Japanese lyric called the *uta* has a dimension of depth, one that has affinity with the three stages of truth in Tendai, namely, the void (*kū*), the provisional (*ke*), and the middle (*chū*)." Shunzei has in mind the entire corpus of Japanese verse, not merely a category of poems said to have yūgen. Based on this we can, however, anticipate what he means by yūgen; by linking the uta with the three stages of Tendai, he places the composition, reading, and appreciation of poetry in a context of complete open-endedness.

It is clear that Shunzei's view of poetry included what has recently been called "the indeterminacy of meaning."[46] For him, the "dimension of depth" in poetry had nothing to do with a determinate "meaning" that had been coded into a poem by the poet to then be decoded by the sensitive hearer or listener. According to him, a Japanese poem, or uta, though it may be a thing of wonder, cannot really be recondite. The interpretation of depth is not the discovery of hermetic elements, the supposed meaning under the surface of words.

This is in part because the santai process in Tendai aims at a kind of ontological egalitarianism. The abstract is no more and no less real than the concrete. Surfaces are never merely superficial. Vehicles cannot be subordinate to tenors. Shin'ichi Hisamatsu, recognizing that our ordinary rubrics of understanding tend to attribute more weight and value to what is "inside" and at the "core" and implicitly denigrate the outside as superficial, has astutely observed that Buddhism handles this by saying that "the true inside of the inside is not having inside or outside."[47] In this extremely valuable formulation, Hisamatsu suggests that to dig to the core of the core is to discover the invalidity of such distinctions and also to discover that, seen from inside, the surface is deep. The terms are completely relative. The Zen poet Shinkei (d. 1544) wrote of this in his classic work, the *Sasamegoto*: "The beginner enters from the shallow to the deep; and once he has attained the depths, he emerges again into the shallow: this is the essential rule of all disciplines. Cause produces effect; effect in turn leads to cause."[48]

The open-endedness of both phenomena and interpretation are very important for understanding Shunzei. In accordance with the movement through three stages of truth (santai) in Tendai, in Shunzei's view the depth of poetry is not a place but a process.[49] It is not a determinate point at which the interpreter arrives after doing a certain amount of linguistic homework to solve conundrums built into the poem by its author. It is much closer to what George Steiner calls the "rich undecidability" aimed at by a poet.[50]

In a number of essays Konishi Jin'ichi has focused on the medieval aesthetic's roots in Tendai, though we often associate it exclusively with Zen; citing the importance of Chih-i, Konishi reminds us that the "content of *shikan* is equivalent to the content of Zen."[51] He pursues the implications of this, using the distinction between vehicle and tenor, signifier and signified: " . . . the Zennist strives for the cessation of understanding arrived at through processes of judgment; this means, therefore, that there is no substantive element that can serve as tenor. This leads to the conclusion that imagery in Zen is tantamount to tenorless symbolism."[52]

Imagery in Tendai seems to have been no different, especially as informed by notions of shikan and the three-stage process of truth. The effect was a tendency to *reject* symbolism rather than affirm it. The following poem by Shunzei is illustrative:

harusame wa	Spring's fine rain
konomo kanomo no	both in the distance and right here
kusa mo ki mo	both on grasses and trees
wakezu midori ni	is evenly dyeing everything
somuru nariken	everywhere in its new green.[53]

No literate reader in medieval Japan would fail to recognize that on one level this poem is a thirty-one syllable encapsulation of the "yakusō-yu," or "plant parable," chapter of the *Lotus Sutra*,[54] a favorite of the courtiers. Shunzei's poem uses the fairly common ambiguity of the verb *somuru*, which can mean both "to commence" (as in the beginning of spring) and "to dye with color." But the poem's brilliance lies in the way it draws the reader or listener into an extended visualization of the gently falling rain. It does so first on a horizontal plane: "konomo kanomo" is a sequence that refers both to the "far distance" and to the "near at hand." Then it does so vertically: "kusa mo ki mo" refers to the lowliest of grasses and the loftiest of trees. Thus, in very simple but precise language the poet draws attention to the fact that wherever one looks one sees the falling spring rain (''harusame''), a rain always thought of as light, gentle, and nourishing. The poem moves on to depict the rain as evenly and indiscriminately (''wakezu'') serving as the dye (''somuru'') that brings out the color green (''midori'') in everything. Since ''somuru,'' also means ''to commence'' or ''to begin,'' it reinforces the idea that at this moment spring has come. Thus the poem has not only a vivid spatial sense but a temporal one as well; the present moment is itself a perfection.

This poem is almost an open invitation to symbolic or allegorical interpretation.[55] Not only does it recapitulate the imagery of the ''plant parable'' chapter of the *Lotus* but, in the strategic location of the word *wakezu* (meaning ''without discrimination,'' or ''evenly''), it also captures the motif of that chapter of the sutra, the undiscriminating and undifferentiating beneficence of the Buddhist dharma. This beneficence, like the rain, falls on all and on all equally. Certainly Shunzei would have expected his contemporaries to recognize the allusions and allegorical possibilities in this poem. Nevertheless, the poem becomes more fascinating when viewed in the context of the preceding discussion. For then it is not a simple restatement of the imagery of a chapter in the *Lotus* but an expression in verse, and through the sophisticated structuring of verse, of something very important concerning the nature of allusion itself. The relationship between the poem and the sutra is not merely a matter of the poem alluding to the scripture and so being dependent in a unidirectional way upon it. On the contrary, because the theme of both the sutra and the poem is the fundamental absence of discrimination (*wakezu*) or hierarchy in the dharma, any sense of the poem as derivative or subordinate is itself subverted and disallowed. Since we know that Shunzei was intensely concerned to demonstrate and justify the uta as a form of religious discourse, we can now see how he thought through the implications of the act of allusion. For Shunzei, the classic to which a given poem alludes is neither to be enshrined nor to be bested; in that sense it is neither Parnassus nor father. For the relationship of the classics or scriptures to poems currently being written is the same as that of large trees (''ki'') to lowly grasses (''kusa''); it is fundamentally nonhierarchical (''wakezu''). This is articulated both in the *Lotus* scripture and in the poem.

This fits in precisely with what Shunzei says in the *Korai fūteishō* concerning the status of the Japanese poem. Shunzei's position was that, though it is a form some of the pious call ''floating phrases and fictive utterances'' (''kyōgen-kigo''), the uta is a context in which: ''. . . the profundity of things is demonstrated. This is because there exists a reciprocal flow of meaning between such things [as poetry] and the way of Buddhism, a way that maintains the interdependence of all things.'' In Shunzei's view, a poem is Buddhist not because it has hidden within it an allusion to a scripture or an unambiguously sacred source, but because the trajectory back to that source itself produces a rejection of the distinction between sacred and profane literatures.

This rejection results in a strong reaffirmation of the phenomena of the empirical world. In the doctrinal discussions carried out in Chinese and Japanese Tendai, it led to the conclusion that the plants and trees referred to in the *Lotus Sutra* do not merely symbolize truths beyond themselves but actually have Buddha-nature in their own phenomenal existence ("sōmoku jōbutsu").[56] In the final analysis, Shunzei's poem is not a literary utterance that uses the rain, grasses, and trees to refer to the sutra and, through the sutra, to the universal and abstract Buddhist dharma: in its structure and diction it finally disallows a merely symbolic or allegorical interpretation. The orbit of its concern returns inevitably to concrete particulars; it affirms the existence and the beauty of the rain, the grasses, and the trees as they are.

This does much to explain the concrete and vivid qualities prized in the poetry of this era. Thus, for a poet such as Shunzei, there was ultimately not the slightest discord or gap between the requirements of poetry and those of Buddhism; the rejection of allegory and the return to the immediacy of trees and plants as the locus of reality is the aspect of shikan called "jukū-nyūke," "leaving the empty and entering into the provisional." As a literary act, it is tantamount to a collapse of what Auerbach has called "the antagonism between sensory appearance and meaning," because such antagonism, although entertained by the Buddhists as a possibility, is discordant with the motif of the undiscriminating and even (wakezu). Poetic depth involves more than the use of symbolism; it is not as much a move away from surfaces to seek inner essences and meanings as a move away from such inner "meanings" to reaffirm the reality of the so-called surface.

The poems themselves make the point more clearly and interestingly. The following is also by Shunzei:

ima zo kore	Right here and now!
irihi no mite mo	I watch the sun slip away,
omoikoshi	thoughts gone to the west
mida no mikuni no	paradise of Amida, where
yūgure no sora	this is the sky of nightfall.[57]

There is an intended strangeness and tension in this verse.[58] The whole poem is, in fact, a structured oxymoron; *here* and *there* seem to be categories in total confusion. It begins with an emphatic declaration that everything that follows depicts something in the immediate present and in the poet's exact spatial location. It is this insistence that makes what follows puzzling, since all the succeeding images are of things usually associated with the idea of being distant or removed. Most especially, the Western Paradise of Amida was popularly conceived to be disjunct from the present world, the so-called *shaba* world of suffering and darkness. The world of Amida was referred to as "the other shore," a place of perpetual light and felicity.

There were, however, Amidist thinkers who insisted that such a dualism was ultimately untenable within Buddhism and that "this shore," our world, is really identical with the perfect world of Amida. The phrase "shaba-soku-jakkō" ("this world is none other than the one of tranquil light") expresses the point exactly. It is undoubtedly the conceptual background for Shunzei's composition of this poem. It provides the philosophical grounding for the oxymoron in the poem; and it also links up directly with Shunzei's use of the phrase "enlightenment is nowhere other than in the worldly passions" in the crucial section of the *Korai fūteishō*.

To disregard these points would be to dismiss things that were of utmost intellectual, religious and aesthetic importance to Shunzei. Thus, they were also important for his verse. Yet they do not necessarily vitiate even a complex poem such as this: Shunzei's poem is, after all, in concrete language. The final line vividly portrays the sky in which night is falling so the reader is compelled to acknowledge the poet's claim that a nightfall in this world is really one in Amida's paradise, where, at least according to dualist projections, there was supposedly no place for "negative" things such as night and darkness. The natural implication is the attribution of both beauty and positivity to the fall of night in the empirical world.

This attribution of positivity to the negative is directly related to the depth and the yūgen of the best poems of the epoch—as, for instance, in the following, a superb poem by Fujiwara Teika:

miwataseba	Gaze out far enough,
hana mo momiji mo	beyond all cherry blossoms
nakarikeri	and scarlet maples,
ura no tomaya no	to those huts by the harbor
aki no yūgure	fading in the autumn dusk.[59]

For very good reasons, this poem has been highly praised. Many have noted that it deftly moves the eye of the mind over various landscapes—implicit definitions of beauty—to a place where, through the negation of the usual canons of beauty, something beyond them all is discovered in the most mundane, even the most drab, of contexts. For centuries, the literature of China and Japan had depicted the beauties of the various seasons and offered reasons for preferring one or the other; the court poets of Heian Japan often saw the cherry blossom as the quintessence of spring's beauty and the brilliantly colored maple as that of fall. Teika, however, here envisions a beauty "beyond" all these.

It would not do, however, to characterize yūgen simply as a preference for the faded and colorless. And since this term was first used in Japan by Shunzei as a concept in aesthetic criticism, his view of it deserves consideration. Though Brower and Miner are correct in stating that Shunzei left us "nothing in the way of a detailed poetic of yūgen,"[60] we can infer what he meant by the term from a few of the era's classic poems that he said embodied it. We should keep in mind Konishi Jin'ichi's interpretation of yūgen through the theory and practice of shikan in Tendai Buddhism. In addition to the preceding poem, let us consider a few others, such as this one by Shunzei himself:

> yū sareba   Night and fall close in:
> nobe no akikaze   winds from the wide heath
> mi ni shimite   howl into me
> uzura naku nari   along with the muffled moans
> fukakusa no sato   of grass-hidden quail.[61]

These by Saigyō are often cited as examples of yūgen:

> kokoro naki   Thought I was free
> mi ni mo aware wa   of passions, so this melancholy
> shirarekeri   comes as surprise:
> shigi tatsu sawa no   a woodcock shoots up from marsh
> aki no yūgure   where autumn's twilight falls.[62]

> tsu no kuni no   Famed for its springtime,
> naniwa no haru wa   Naniwa in Tsu, seen today at last:
> yume nare ya   a field of withered weeds
> ashi no kareba ni   bent down by harsh winds—my dream
> kaze wataruru nari   to see it come false . . . . come true.[63]

Though many other verses could be cited, these four are considered classic examples of the yūgen of this period.

We can begin by noting the obvious. Each of these poems focuses on things in nature usually associated with darkness or cold. The reader, in projecting himself or herself into the setting of each poem, has, initially at least, a sense of discomfort, perhaps even displeasure. Peasant huts disappearing in the dusk, winds on a heath at nightfall, the moans of quail, marshes and fields getting progressively colder and darker—such are the poems' settings and materials. It is not a coincidence that the two Chinese characters used to write the term yūgen both refer to something that is dark and opaque. Nevertheless, the sense of unpleasantness is quickly, even simultaneously, replaced by a sense of the extraordinary dignity and beauty of the phenomena depicted in the verse.

In view of this, it would be tempting to interpret Shunzei's idea of yūgen through sentences written in the *Mumyō-shō* by Kamo no Chōmei between the years 1211 and 1216, or some time after Shunzei's death. Chōmei wrote the following concerning *yūgen*:

> Since I do not understand it very well myself, I am at a loss as to how to describe it in a satisfactory manner, but according to the views of those who have penetrated into the realm of *yūgen*, the importance lies in *yojō*, which is not stated in words and an atmosphere that is not revealed through the form of the poem. When the content rests on a sound basis and the diction excels in lavish beauty, these other virtues will be supplied naturally. On an autumn evening, for example, there is no color in the sky, nor any sound, and although we cannot give a definite reason for it, we are somehow moved to tears. A person lacking in sensitivity finds nothing particular in such a sight, he just admires the cherry blossoms and scarlet autumn leaves that he can see with his own eyes.[64]

Konishi Jin'ichi has warned, however, against interpreting Shunzei's view through that of Chōmei—especially since, in contrast to those who like white blossoms or scarlet leaves, Chōmei has a decided preference of his own, namely, for the colorless "color." Konishi contrasts Shunzei and Chōmei as follows:

> When Shunzei himself expresses the sense of yūgen, it is of course something that is supported by the intentions of shikan, and it simply will not do to remove this factor. However, there is a difference between this and the specific chromatic which Dr. Nose [Nose Asaji in his *Yūgen-ron*] has demonstrated. The intentionality of shikan itself embraces no definite chromatic. Shikan expresses the mutual permeation of what is grasped and what is doing the grasping, and as such it can materialize in any one of various colors: sometimes that of splendor, sometimes sadness, sometimes simplicity, sometimes subtlety—each is allowable. This is where there is a difference between Shunzei's own idea of yūgen and a view of it such as Chōmei articulated.[65]

The significance of this observation lies not only in the way it helps us differentiate between the views of two medieval Japanese literati but also in its potential for disclosing and articulating more of the basic structure of yūgen. Konishi has done this with considerable success. There is a difference between seeing yūgen in Chōmei's terms—where it is primarily an ineffable and inexplicable preference for certain emotions evoked by scenes and actions that are faint and thin to the point of being almost without color or definite character—and seeing yūgen in Shunzei's terms, where we must draw upon the structure of shikan in order to begin to comprehend it.

Konishi's is a good lead to follow. In an early essay on the origins of yūgen, he lavishly documented his claim that, before its usage by Shunzei and others as a term in literary aesthetics, it was used in Buddhist texts, especially those of the Prajñāpāramitā (Hannya) and Mādhyamika (Sanron) literatures. This placed it squarely within literatures concerned to demonstrate that the nature of all phenomena is *śūnya* (*kū*), "emptiness."[66] The Prajñāpāramitā literature was especially concerned to demonstrate that all things were empty of self-existence. Its unyielding dialectic at the same time refused to allow emptiness to congeal or reify into an absolute or independent principle; it demanded, as we have seen, that emptiness too be emptied. The operation of this ongoing process of emptying implied a vastness and richness in the universe as explored in its interrelatedness. Since nothing anywhere could be found to have independent existence, there were no stopping places or barriers within reality as investigated by the Prajñāpāramitā. And it is this, according to Konishi, which is directly linked to the depth, density, distance and wondrous quality that seems to be so much a part of yūgen. Reality is boundless in the most precise sense; since there are no hard, absolute, or independent entities, there are no boundaries or limits to the deep and mutual interpenetration of all existent things. Yūgen acknowledges and discloses this.

In both the shikan of Tendai and the arts of yūgen there is a definite quiescence and tranquility. In shikan this is undoubtedly related to the practice of seated meditation, basically the seated *zen*, or *zazen*, that was a part of most Buddhist practice but received special emphasis in the Zen Buddhist school. In zazen the body (through quiet sitting in the lotus posture), the speech (through silence and the quiet chanting of the name of a Buddha), and the mind (through focused concentration rather than random thoughts) penetrate in a united fashion to the realization that: ". . . there is an absolute rejection and dismissal of existence conceived of as a confrontational relationship between the perceiver and perceived."[67] This is basically consonant with those practices in earliest Buddhism which focused on the cessation of random and disturbed perceptions (*śamatha*/*shi*) and the quiescent observation of the constellations of things (*dharmas*) as they come into being and pass away without obstruction (*vipaśyanā*/*kan*).

Except for the fact that its expression is in poetry and drama, the structure of yūgen is not fundamentally different. That is why the poems we have cited, in spite of their initial presentation of uncomfortable phenomena, succeed in conveying a far from ordinary sense of tranquility and dignity. The phenomena presented in these poems are observed in such a way that both their coming into being and their dissolution are observed with equanimity. There is a clear sense that they are characterized by impermanence (mujō), an impermanence that is greeted and treated not as tragic but as right and ultimately acceptable because it is simply "the way things are" (*tathāgata, nyorai*).

Perhaps what is most important is the collapse of the distance between observer and observed noted by Konishi. This implies that in the yūgen aesthetic as conceived by Shunzei there is a crucial move whereby initially the poet or actor, and then also the reader or audience, are fundamentally implicated and involved in the process whereby entities come into being and pass away. Both the poet and the reader are drawn into or implicated in this impermanence not on some secondary philosophical level but in and through the mechanics of the poem as a poem.

Let us look more closely at the classic example by Teika:

<table>
<tr><td>miwataseba</td><td>Gaze out far enough,</td></tr>
<tr><td>hana mo momiji mo</td><td>beyond all cherry blossoms</td></tr>
<tr><td>nakarikeri</td><td>and scarlet maples,</td></tr>
<tr><td>ura no tomaya no</td><td>to those huts by the harbor</td></tr>
<tr><td>aki no yūgure</td><td>fading in the autumn dusk.</td></tr>
</table>

In the poetry of Japan prior to the twelfth century it was a commonplace for verses to be written about the quickly disappearing blossoms of the cherry tree in spring or about the ephemeral beauty of maples in the fall. These were also so associated with the Buddhist teaching of mujō that they began to serve as the easily recognized synecdoche for all other things and the impermanence that is necessarily a part of every individual existence; the emotion engendered by such poems was inevitably sadness. By comparison, the poems of the late twelfth century which began to evidence the quality of yūgen are considerably more sophisticated. Teika's is no ordinary evocation of mujō—though in part, the genius of this verse lies in the way it has enfolded within it a traditional but ordinary statement of impermanence with the accompanying conventional emotion of sadness. The second and third lines of the poem could be independently read as: "hana mo momiji mo nakarikere" ("the cherry blossoms and maple leaves have disappeared"). But by the end of the twelfth century these had become hackneyed lines and trite emotions; and they are transformed into something quite different and much richer by Teika's incorporating them into a complex and dynamic poetic action. He prefaces them with the verb *miwatasu*, referring to the act of looking or gazing out, over, and beyond things lying close at hand toward a place much farther in the distance. This perceptual act drops, discards, and in a sense negates the cherry blossoms and maple leaves; Brower and Miner rightly note that Teika "uses the old symbols of the beauty of spring and autumn, cherry blossoms and colored leaves, as negative comparisons for praising something else.''[68]

Teika is not merely expressing an unconventional preference for the detection of beauty in things ordinarily dismissed as drab, however. The voice adopted in the poem is of someone engaged in a perceptual act much more ambitious than usual, an attempt to look over and beyond things that by convention signify the ephemeral and transient—that is, everything expressed in the now hackneyed image of the phrase "cherry blossoms and maple leaves have disappeared." Perhaps the speaker wants to see not only beyond conventional notions of beauty and transience but also beyond all impermanent things. If so, it is ironic, that, as he fixes his vision on things far off in the distance—the peasant huts by the harbor ("ura no tomaya")—they have already begun to disappear from sight in the autumn dusk ("aki no yūgure"). The wonderful irony lies in the fact that what is seen in the distance is quickly and presently disappearing. Although not conventional images of mujō, the huts are no less characterized by the radical impermanence of all existent things.

Perhaps the most magnificent aspect of this verse is its sophisticated way of handling the relationship of the perceiver to the perceived. At the very moment when the speaker/perceiver is attempting to carry out his almost Promethean attempt to transcend impermanence, dusk cuts him off from the object of his observation. This means that his observational activity comes to an end; as observer, he is negated with the object of his observation. This is a concrete example of what Konishi claims is essential for yūgen, namely, the negation of "existence conceived of as a confrontational [*tairitsuteki*] relationship between the perceiver and the perceived." The poem is an adroit execution of this negation. The act of observation comes to an end at the same moment that it begins—in the unit of time the Buddhists called *kṣaṇa* (*setsuna*);[69] thus, the observer is no more permanent than what he or she observes. Implicit in the perceptual process of the poem is an exact parallel: just as the particular that lies in the distance (huts by the harbor) is not fundamentally different from that lying close at hand (cherry blossoms and scarlet maples), so the general class of things always thought to lie in the distance (the objects of one's perception and observation) is not fundamentally different from the class of things always assumed to lie close at hand (the subject or self that engages in perception and observation). This is the collapse of the distance between object and subject. Ōnishi Yoshinori, in his classic study *Yūgen to aware*, depicts the process that occurs in such a context:

. . . when all of one's "ego" has been transformed into the datum of nature and when one has penetrated into the arena of shikan—that is, into the locus of absorption into the vision of pure tranquility—then nature and mind or object and subject will have become one and the same. At this point we should say that all aspects of existence (German: *Sein*) seem to be directly and simultaneously present in a split second of time, and the individual's existence is the same as the totality's, and the microcosm is amplified in the macrocosm. This is the unique aspect of this aesthetic experience.[70]

Ōnishi also suggests here that, as an aesthetic experience, yūgen recapitulates and participates in the structure of shikan thought and meditation.

It should be apparent that poems of this sort are much more intellectually sophisticated than any that had preceded them in the history of Japanese verse. This sophistication led Teika's contemporaries to denigrate such poems by referring to them as "daruma-uta," meaning that they were equally abstruse as the Zen of Bodhidharma, the Indian who was reputed to have brought Zen from India to China.[71] In more recent centuries some Japanese critics have also found them less than completely palatable, either because they seemed far removed from the pure, direct feeling communicated in poems of an earlier collection such as the *Man'yō-shū*, or because they seemed too contrived for the tastes of critics such as Saitō Mōkichi (1882–1953), for whom modern "realism" was the single most important criterion.[72]

Poems such as this will probably continue to bear whatever opprobrium attaches to the labels "intellectual" and "Buddhist." Konishi and other recent scholars have acknowledged this and gone on to research those very aspects of the ambience within which such poems, and the aesthetic or yūgen, came into being. At the same time, they have insisted on the value of these poems as literature, that is, as poetry that is probably unequalled in medieval Japan.

The value of such poetry is reinforced by a brief look at a verse quoted previously, a justly famous poem by Saigyō:

kokoro naki	Thought I was free
mi ni mo aware wa	of passions, so this melancholy
shirarekeri	comes as surprise:
shigi tatsu sawa no	a woodcock shoots up from marsh
aki no yūgure	where autumn's twilight falls.

The poet initially presents himself as courting either pretense or self-deception. Perhaps because he is a monk, he thinks of himself as having transcended the ordinary person's vulnerability; he portrays himself as having gone beyond any susceptibility to being moved, swayed, or thrown into disarray by emotions, beauty, and the like. His attitude is that of a "body without a heart" ("kokoro naki mi"), or a person free of passions. But this pretentious posture collapses when a powerful feeling (*aware*), undoubtedly of melancholy, rises within him at the moment when, very unexpectedly, he happens to see a woodcock or a flock of woodcocks take flight "shigi tatsu" from the surface of a marsh "sawa"—a marsh that was at exactly that time being encompassed by both nightfall and autumn "aki no yūgure."

Many critics have pointed out that the linguistic and conceptual break (*kire*) in this poem comes, as it often does in Saigyō's verse,[73] at the end of the third line, breaking the poem into two distinct halves. This sets up a juxtaposition between the first and second parts of the poem. Moreover, this decisive break also makes for an implicit parallelism: just as the woodcock rises suddenly from the midst of the darkening marsh, so the emotion of melancholy seems suddenly to well up within the body and experience "*mi*" of the poet. We assume that the poet has created an effective and moving parallel between an event outside himself, in nature, and one inside himself as the subject and observer.

Yet the poem is neither so static nor so simply symbolic—if it were so, it would have nothing of the yūgen that Saigyō's contemporaries detected in it. A much more useful approach to it is through Konishi's dictum about "tenorless symbolism," which I have suggested is fully harmonious with the mutual reciprocity of tenors and vehicles we noted in the hermeneutics of the *Lotus Sutra*. Taking this approach, the *kire*, or "break," between the two halves of the poem becomes a fulcrum upon which the point of view "moves" in a quite remarkable way. As the poem begins, the observational point is the poet himself:

> kokoro naki
> mi ni mo aware wa
> shirarekeri

> Thought I was free
> of passions, so this melancholy
> comes as surprise:

Then, at the break, the observational point switches abruptly and completely to the natural scene before the poet's eyes:

> shigi tatsu sawa no
> aki no yūgure

> a woodcock shoots up from marsh
> where autumn's twilight falls.

The vividly depicted scene is of a bird suddenly lifting off the surface of the swamp and just as quickly becoming a mere speck before disappearing entirely into the night.[74]

This scene turns the attention of the listener or reader *back again* to the first half of the poem; the swamp, bird, and nightfall now *become* the point of view from which the poet and his experience are seen. What had been the locus of the observed now becomes that of the observer, and the original subject becomes an object. The result is that the irruption of emotion that had initially seemed a disruption of the poet-priest's tranquility now comes to be viewed *sub specie naturae*, or at any rate, from the perspective of nature interpreted in Buddhist terms.[75] This makes the ''disruption'' like any other phenomenon of existence—it necessarily comes into being and passes away; thus, the ''melancholy that comes as surprise'' lasts no longer and is really no more significant than the bird that lifts off the surface of the swamp and disappears into the night.

The result is a poem in which there is a complete collapse of what Konishi calls the view of observer and observed as in a ''confrontational relationship.'' This is not because observer and observed have now been fused into one undifferentiated entity but because the poem has disclosed the fundamental *interdependence* of the two. Through the mechanics and concrete language of a classical Japanese *waka*, Saigyō achieves something fundamentally in accord with Nāgārjuna's dismantlement of epistemological atomism, his demonstration that every act of seeing is one in which the seer and the seen not only depend on one another but also bring each other into being.

The ''calm darkness'' that Shin'ichi Hisamatsu detects in this type of art[76] is undoubtedly related to its embodiment of an awareness that ultimately even ''being'' is fully interdependent with what Western languages call *nonbeing*. The languages of China and Japan have a greater facility for expressing the mutuality and balance between what is and what is not; they are not as intrinsically tilted toward defining being as real and nonbeing as a privation. As languages they do not give the benefit to the being side of things.[77] On this point, though, maybe the language of poetry—even perhaps in translation— can communicate more immediately and directly what is essential. Certainly both the imagery and the emotional range of the poem by Saigyō encompass the two poles of all our usual dichotomies—light and darkness, life and death, being and nonbeing, joy and sadness. One always implies and elicits the other.

This is why it would be a complete misunderstanding to classify Saigyō's poem as a sad poem, even though its final lines depict autumn and twilight and imply a coming death: ''Shigi tatsu sawa no / aki no yūgure'' (''a woodcock shoots up from marsh / where autumn's twilight falls''). The tranquility that is so clearly a part of this poem contravenes any attempt to classify the poem according to conventional rubrics; the twilight and death that are present are a twilight and death that refuse to be bound by our customary ways of understanding and reacting to them. Thus, even in the *emotions* engendered by a poem expressive of yūgen, there is an indeterminacy.

It is no wonder that poets such as Shunzei maintained that in such poems there was a ''surplus of emotion'' ''yojō.'' I think they meant by this that the poem's world was somehow larger than its words. This was so because the poems were composed in a manner that rejected any real satisfaction with the conventional linkages between phenomena and emotions. Just as being implies nonbeing, so an image that had conventionally been associated with sadness must be made to imply its opposite as well. So, too—beginning with this poetry but extending into nō drama and at least as far as the haiku of Bashō—certain sounds were evocative of silence and certain motions brought stillness in their wake. The world of such poetry and such drama was one in which determinate emotions or ideas were no longer fixed to determinate images or actions. Simple symbols no longer seemed adequate; their portrait was deemed naive because it had too severely limited the relationship among phenomena. The Buddhists of medieval Japan, nurtured as they were in Tendai, held that the universe was such that even "in one thought there are three thousand worlds" ("ichinen sanzen"). This implied the boundlessness of the interpenetration of phenomena with one another. To the dimension of depth in the universe itself these Buddhists reacted with a sense of awe (*myō*). And, to poets such as Shunzei, a universe of this depth deserved a degree and a mode of appreciation beyond that given it by the traditional aesthetic; something new and more adequate was needed. The arts of yūgen were their response.

5

CHŌMEI AS HERMIT: VIMALAKĪRTI IN THE "HŌJŌ-KI"

Should storms, as may well happen,
　Drive you to anchor a week
In some old harbour-city
　Of Ionia, then speak
With her witty scholars, men
Who have proved there cannot be
　Such a place as Atlantis:
　Learn their logic, but notice
How its subtlety betrays
　Their enormous simple grief;
Thus they shall teach you the ways
　To doubt that you may believe.
　　　　　—W. H. Auden, *Atlantis*

T HERE IS MUCH MORE than meets the eye in the concluding section of the great classic the "Hōjō-ki" when its author, Kamo no Chōmei, says of his hermitage that it may be no more than a "poor imitation of that of Jōmyō Koji," a figure known throughout Buddhist Asia—as Vimalakīrti in India, as Wei-mo in China, and as Yuima in Japan. This chapter will attempt to explicate this reference in the "Hōjō-ki," demonstrate why it is fundamental to an understanding of the work as a whole, and draw out its implications for a deepened understanding of the role of Buddhism in the literature of medieval Japan.

On the simplest level, an effort will be made to provide basic information about the *Vimalakīrti-nirdeśa-sūtra*, which the Japanese usually abbreviated and referred to as the *Yuima-gyō*. It is a key text of the Mahayana and one that was well known to literate Buddhists of East Asia. A brief recapitulation of its contents will be made to compensate in part for a grievance I voiced earlier about the all-too-common practice among scholars of making footnote references to the religious and philosophical texts alluded to in literary works without actually becoming familiar with the texts themselves. These texts often provide insight into the basic structure and meaning of the very literature we attempt to understand. A knowledge of the basics of the *Vimalakīrti Sutra* is essential because the "Hōjō-ki" cannot be adequately grasped without an appreciation of the degree to which Chōmei relies on the sutra—not merely to sprinkle his text with arcane or gratuitous allusions but to fit his work into a received tradition that is at once both literary and philosophical.

The intent of the present chapter is ambitious in a further sense: I wish through the analysis of the nexus between the *Vimalakīrti Sutra* and the "Hōjō-ki" to demonstrate the lineaments of what I earlier called the emergence of the high medieval in Japanese thought and letters. This emergence, which took place during the twelfth and thirteenth centuries, marks a distinct development, deepening, and complication of the Buddhist episteme that commenced some centuries earlier and can be witnessed in the pages of the *Nihon ryōi-ki*. While this high medieval period evidences a deepening of the penetration of Buddhism into the intellectual and religious experience of the Japanese, it also shows the existence of two somewhat divergent versions of Buddhism in Japan, with all the characteristics of a tension between the two. The following chapter continues this discussion in the context of Zeami's thought and describes the tension in terms of the differences between Buddhism as hierarchy and Buddhism as dialectic. In this chapter, my purpose is only to show that the "Hōjō-ki" is a complete heir to discussions and intellectual moves that had long before, on the Asian continent, been part of the development of Mahayana Buddhism—moves almost paradigmatically present in the much-acclaimed *Vimalakīrti Sutra*.

Earlier, when we considered the "Hōjō-ki" as a prime source for an understanding of the literary topos of the hermit's hut in Japanese literature, a strictly synchronic framework was adopted, eliminating all concern for diachronic and historical development. That was for the purposes of a strictly structuralist kind of analysis. Here that method will be complemented with a much more historical analysis, which considers the "Hōjō-ki" not in an atemporal context but as a work that reveals its author as dealing seriously with questions, concepts, and formulations characteristic of the high medieval in Japanese history. In contrast to some traditional accounts that tended to view the "Hōjō-ki" as the major index to the *inception* of the medieval period in Japan, my view is that it must be seen as evidence that the Buddhist episteme in Japan had entered a new level of sophistication and complexity—a level of complexity that also reflected the influence of developments in Mahayana Buddhism more generally in East Asia.

The figure of the Buddhist layman Vimalakīrti had been a model for Buddhist literati since the Six dynasties period in China.[1] It was thus quite natural that, as a literatus, Kamo no Chōmei found the image of Vimalakīrti sitting in his ten-foot-square hut (*hōjō*) a fitting exemplar for himself and his aspirations as a man of belles lettres and of religion.

Taken from Mahayana texts of which there are Tibetan and Chinese translations and from the extant fragments of the Sanskrit original,[2] the basics of the text are as follows: Vimalakīrti is portrayed as a layman who lived contemporaneously with Śākyamuni Buddha in India. He was a bodhisattva though he was not a monk. To summarize a key section describing Vimalakīrti's *upāya*, the sutra says that, although he was a layman, he was free from all attachments to the three worlds. Although married, he lived purely. Although possessing family and retinue, he lived continually as if in a hermitage. Although he ate and drank like others, he delighted really in the taste of meditation. Although he made much money, he took no delight in it. Although he went into the inner palaces to meet the women there, he took his delight in converting them to the Buddha dharma.[3]

That is the context. The narrative begins when the sutra tells us that Vimalakīrti, in order to use his upāya to teach others, has taken on an appearance of illness. This illness and the news concerning it has brought kings, ministers, officials, and others, numbering thousands, into his hermitage and to his sick-bed. When they come he teaches them about suffering and pain, *duḥkha* (*ku*). Śākyamuni Buddha has also heard about his illness, and he wishes to dispatch one of his disciples to inquire after Vimalakīrti's health. One after another he addresses the most revered arhats, monks, and bodhisattvas in his retinue, asking them to visit the pious layman. In wonderful, often humorous, passages of prose each of the famous arhats begs off, recalling how once in the past he was bested by the layman Vimalakīrti in the forensics of Buddhist debate. None feels equal to the task; each is rather pathetically eager to avoid another confrontation with the sagacious, overwhelming layman. In each case it is largely Vimalakīrti's unparalleled way with words—that is, his locutionary, and by extension literary, skill—that intimidates the disciples of

Śākyamuni. Finally, however, the Buddha turns to Manjuśri, the one of superior wisdom; Manjuśri agrees to go to visit Vimalakīrti. He is accompanied by 8,000 bodhisattvas, 500 śravakas, and hundreds of thousands of devas.

Vimalakīrti, with his uncanny powers, learns of Manjuśri's visit in advance and does something significant to his dwelling (a hermitage tradition later came to refer to as the original hōjō): he dismisses all his own servants and gets rid of all the furniture except for his sick-bed. With everything gone, he is ready to entertain Manjuśri and the latter's vast retinue. What follows is a command performance, an ongoing dialogue between the two masters of doctrine and dialectic that continues quite delightfully for several chapters. Sickness is, of course, an index to the impermanence of all things. Scholars generally agree, however, that the sutra reaches a climax in the chapter on the nondual. After some of the guests offer their comparatively feeble definitions of nonduality, Manjuśri makes his attempt:

> "In my opinion, when all things are no longer within the province of either word or speech, and of either indication or knowledge, and are beyond questions and answers, this is initiation into the non-dual dharma."[4]

He says then that since all the guests have offered their views, Vimalakīrti's definition is what they all most wish to hear. How does the great layman view the initiation into the nondual?

Vimalakīrti kept silence, saying not a word.

Manjuśri exclaims:

> "Excellent, excellent; can there be true initiation into the non-dual dharma until words and speech are no longer written or spoken?"[5]

This is the famed "silence of Vimalakīrti," the perfect retort, the response that combines form and content so that silence itself ends the duality always implicit in the forensic and dialogic situation. It is a response that has not only wisdom but also wit.

These points were not lost on the sophisticated Buddhist gentry and literati of the Six dynasties in China. They noted that, although in the end Vimalakīrti went beyond words and speech, the move was cleverly made and there was much enjoyable wordplay engaged in on the way to that point. It was not unlike the so-called ch'ing t'an (seidan), or "pure conversation," so loved by the literati of the period[6] (conversation described by Arthur Waley as very much like that of "clever undergraduates at our own universities").[7] So the Vimalakīrti Sutra had a deep and long-standing appeal to literary people. It was a text in which a layman, not a monk, turned out to be more profound than the

Buddhist clergy, all the while turning phrases and making conversational moves that were simultaneously witty and wise.

Nevertheless, the reasons for the sutra's appeal to Kamo no Chōmei may be significantly different from those that explain its appeal to the Chinese. The overwhelming appeal to the Buddhist gentry of China lay in the fact that Vimalakīrti was not a monk but an ordinary householder who, nevertheless, possessed all the virtues and attainments of the best of the monks and, in fact, surpassed them. As both Richard Mather and James D. Whitehead have pointed out, this *internalizes* the household-departure (*ch'u chia, shukke*) and makes the *Vimalakīrti Sutra* an Indian text that legitimizes being a good Confucian householder while "leaving" home mentally—a very convenient mode of being Buddhist for those who do not wish to cease being Confucian.[8] Interesting in this connection are interpolations into the Chinese text of references to filial piety as among the virtues possessed by Vimalakīrti. The reason for the appeal of this sutra in China is undoubtedly related to its portrayal of Vimalakīrti as a pious layman, a man still in his household.

Kamo no Chōmei, I would argue, read the sutra quite differently; he was, after all, more interested in reclusion than householding. The point in the narrative which kindled his interest was not early on where Vimalakīrti is presented as holy while in the household, in gambling houses, in government offices, and in the chambers of beautiful women. On the contrary, for Kamo no Chōmei the story of Vimalakīrti began to fascinate and become meaningful at the point where Vimalakīrti demonstrates the impermanence of all things by manifesting (even if as an *upāya*) illness in his own body, and then moves into a habitation from which he eventually dismisses all his servants and companions and reduces what he needs for life to the very barest of essentials. The Vimalakīrti admired by Chōmei is not the householder who has inner detachment but the one who moves deliberately and emphatically out of society and into isolation and solitude. It is not Vimalakīrti as householder but as recluse (inja) that Chōmei chooses as his model. He admires not the layman's mansions but his hōjō. His reading of the sutra is strikingly different from that of the Six dynasties literati, and he puts it to a very different though equally sophisticated use.

An important essay on the "Hōjō-ki" was published in 1974 in the Japanese literary journal *Bungaku*. Professor Imanari's Motoaki's essay is entitled "Ren-in Hōjō-ki no ron."[9] This is an intentionally provocative title since Professor Imanari insists that the "Hōjō-ki" is a profoundly Buddhist work by an author who preferred to be called Ren-in rather than Kamo no Chōmei since the final words of the "Hōjō-ki" are, "[This was written] by the śramana named Ren-in in his hermitage on Toyama Hill'' (''Sōmon no Ren-in, Toyama no iori ni shite, kore o shirushu''). Needless to say, not all the critics have agreed with Professor Imanari that we need to drop our references to Kamo no Chōmei and call him by his clerical name instead.[10]

The point of the essay is more than the ''Hōjō-ki's'' authorship, however; it is that the structural affinities between the ''Hōjō-ki'' and the *Vimalakīrti* are deep. I have some reservations about the extent to which Imanari pushes the similarities and so will discuss only those I find especially convincing. I do agree with him that the reference to the sutra is more than an allusion; it provides the key to the intentionality and the structure of the ''Hōjō-ki.''[11]

Imanari finds the theme of the ''Hōjō-ki,'' namely that of mujō, especially well articulated in the following section of the sutra, although the metaphors are found throughout Buddhist literature:

> This body is like a mass of foam which is intangible. It is like a bubble which does not last long. It is like a flame, the product of love's thirst. It is like the banana plant [*bashō*] which has a hollow center. It is like an illusion produced by inverted thoughts. It is like a dream . . . a shadow . . . an echo . . . a floating cloud . . . lightning.[12]

Not in itself convincing, this is immediately followed by something more important according to Imanari:

> [This body] is ownerless for it is like the earth. It is egoless since it is like fire. It is transient like the wind. It is not human for it is like water. It is unreal and depends on the four elements for its existence. It is empty, being neither ego nor its object.[13]

Imanari finds this immediate reference in the ''Hōjō-ki'' to the four elements (*shidai*) (earth, fire, wind, and water) significant, and he concludes: ''The first half of the ''Hōjō-ki'' is a context in which Ren-in (Kamo no Chōmei) vividly describes the way humans are afflicted by the four elements in and through the concrete phenomena of the era in which Chōmei himself lived.''[14] Thus, the gale and fire of the third year of the Angen, the typhoon of the fourth year of the Jisho, the famines and pestilences of the Yōwa, and the earthquake of the second year of the Genryaku era are all not only vividly described in the ''Hōjō-ki'' but also lead Chōmei to state overtly the theme that is the organizing principle of the first half of the work: ''Of the four great elements, three— water, fire, and wind—are continually causing disasters, but the fourth element, the earth, does not normally afflict man.''[15]

The second half of the ''Hōjō-ki'' stands in stark contrast to the first: in it Chōmei depicts in intimate detail his small hermitage, the joys he knows while living in it, and the solitude that is so deep, he says, that "even without intending to keep the Buddhist precepts, they are not easily broken when one lives so far from society."[16] Here, he claims, is a life worth living, and it is possible because his hermitage or hut is designed to be impermanent and is therefore totally unlike the habitations built by men dwelling in illusion in the city.

Professor Imanari, however, does not stop with a neat division of the "Hōjō-ki" into two parts—life in society contrasted with life in reclusion, the calamities in society contrasted with the peace in the mountains, the great houses of the wealthy contrasted with the small hut of the priest or hermit. Using the *Vimalakīrti Sutra* as the key to the work, he calls attention to the last paragraphs of the "Hōjō-ki":

> Now the moon of my life has reached its last phase and my remaining years draw near to their close. When I soon approach the three ways of the hereafter what shall I have to regret? The Law of Buddha teaches that we should shun all clinging to the world of phenomena, so that *the affection I have for this hut* is some sort a sin, and *my attachment to this solitary life* may be a hindrance to enlightenment. Thus I have been babbling, it may be, of useless pleasures, and spending my precious hours in vain.
>
> In the still hours of dawn I think of these things, and to myself I put these questions: Thus to forsake the world and dwell in the woods, has it been to discipline my mind and practice the Law of Buddha or not? Have I put on the form of a recluse while yet my heart has remained impure? Is my dwelling but a poor imitation of that of the Saint Vimalakīrti while my merit is not even equal to that of Suddhipanthaka, the most stupid of the followers of Buddha?[17]

Professor Imanari sees as significant Chōmei's recognition that his attachment to his hut and to his solitude may be a new version of illusion. Moreover, he holds that at this point in his narrative Chōmei is very much aware that his decision to lead a life of reclusion has divided the world into two parts, secular society and the life of religious reclusion. "Have I put on the form of a recluse while yet my heart has remained impure? Is my dwelling but a poor imitation of that of Vimalakīrti . . . ?"[18] Chōmei's awareness that he has divided the world into two is significant according to Imanari because the question of entry into nonduality (*funi hōmon*) is the doctrinal and narrative climax of the *Vimalakīrti Sūtra*, the point at which the sagacious layman answers with his long-remembered silence.

It is important to note the adroit harmony in the *Vimalakīrti Sutra* between the fact that Vimalakīrti is a layman and a bodhisattva—rather than a monk— and the fact that the central doctrine discussed is the entry into the nondual. This harmony comes about because the Mahayana had early made the point (against the so-called Hinayanists) that the idealization of the life of the monk (*śramaṇa*) or arhat had led both to an unnecessary separation of Buddhism from society and to an unfortunate bifurcation of reality into secular and sacred zones. The way into the nondual, in Mahayanist terms, involved more than just a critique of the world-separated life of the reclusive arhat; in philosophical terms, however, this critique arose because of the Mahayana impulse and drive to overcome all dualisms. Vimalakīrti symbolizes success on both counts: he has enlightenment while still in the world as a layman, and he has the sagacity to counter the discriminating, dualizing intellect's questions with a profound silence. The sutra demonstrates the nondual not only by Vimalakīrti's silence but also by his leading of a lay life. There is great literary skill in the composition of the sutra, a subtle reinforcement of points in various ways.

Much of the literary finesse of the final section of the "Hōjō-ki" lies in the way it handles a central paradox. Chōmei explicitly compares his own situation in life with that of Vimalakīrti and bemoans the fact that his very attachment to his reclusive life in his hut may be a "hindrance to enlightenment." At least in print, he identifies himself with the foolish arhat Suddhipanthaka rather than with the wise bodhisattva Vimalakīrti. It is as if he has slipped back onto the lower level of the Hinayana, with its blind insensitivity to the fact that even *homo religiosus* can be very attached to his own specifically religious ways and so lose the whole point of the Buddhist teaching. After having spent many pages to portray in vivid contrast the difference between the worldly life of the householder in the city and the life of the recluse on the mountainside, in the final section of his work Chōmei suggests that he is nothing more than a rather miserable and unenlightened *śramana* on Toyama hill, someone who personally had not been able to advance beyond the rather limited and naive insights of the Hinayanist tradition.

There is obviously something tongue-in-cheek about all this. After all, Chōmei is implying that, although he has not been able to escape the Hinayanist attachment to the eremitic life, he really has no problem understanding the meaning and the implications of the Mahayanist principle of nonduality. Therefore, although his attachment to his hut is a "hindrance to enlightenment," he is perfectly lucid about what it is that differentiates his mode of life from that of the great Vimalakīrti. His way of life is different from that of the sagacious bodhisattva, but, when it comes to an understanding of the meaning of nonduality, Chomei really makes no apologies for himself. Perhaps in his posture there is even the idea that he is so knowledgeable about the nondual that he has been able to pass beyond the bodhisattva's hackneyed rejection of the reclusive life and find the freedom once again to lead such a life. This time, however, it is not on the basis of a naive "Hinayanist" rejection of the world but, rather, on the basis of a Mahayanist realization that an understanding of the nondual ought to imply the possibility of a negation of the usual bodhisattva's negation of the arhat ideal. Chōmei has returned to the eremitic life but suggests that he has done so for very subtle reasons and with an understanding that is deeply grounded in the basic direction of Mahayana thought.

The "Hōjō-ki" is a very sophisticated work not only in its literary execution but also in the understanding of the Mahayana that it demonstrates by subtle twists and turns. The Buddhism in it is not really parallel to the simple reclusive ideal of the early Buddhist sangha in India; it has been developed and refined through centuries of Indian and Chinese Mahayanist thinking about the relationship of Buddhist ideals to worldly realities, of nirvana to samsara, and of religious to mundane vocations. Chōmei's move into, and depiction of, his hermitage is not a simple act of world-flight based on a perception of society as doomed and corrupt. Rather, it evidences a very dialectical understanding of Buddhism, one that is based on critiques and strategies that had arisen earlier in the Mahayana. In this way it is a clear example of a type of literature that I have called the high medieval in Japanese history.

6

ZEAMI'S BUDDHISM: COSMOLOGY AND DIALECTIC IN NŌ DRAMA

Virtuous monks, what are you seeking as you
go around hither and yon, walking until the
soles of your feet are flat? There is no Buddha to
seek, no Way to attain, no Dharma to obtain.
The Record of Lin-chi

T HE PLAYS OF the Japanese nō theater comprise a repertory comparable
to that of ancient Greece or seventeenth-century Europe. Written and
then produced over the past six hundred years, the 230 extant plays of
nō have even earlier roots and precursors; their view of man and the world is
decidedly medieval. The fact that they are shaped and framed by the medieval
religious perspective—the perspective of Mahayana Buddhism—is well summarized by Makoto Ueda: "The Nō is religious drama; it is ritual. The
implications of the Nō are predominantly Buddhist; they point toward a
Buddhist scheme of salvation."[1] What is it, however, about nō that causes
people to sense that it is shaped and informed by Mahayana Buddhism? The
present chapter will attempt to give this question a modicum of specificity and a
possible answer. In doing so, it should articulate things intuitively recognized
and understood by many people—both Japanese and non-Japanese—who have
at one time or another been part of nō's audience.

This chapter assumes some familiarity with nō as a theatrical experience and some acquaintance with its range and typical types of plays. Though the discussion builds on earlier chapters, I am here especially interested to demonstrate that an answer to our question concerning nō may be best obtained by attention to the treatises on nō written by Zeami Motokiyo (1363-1443). Konishi Jin'ichi, in a statement that deserves greater attention than it has received in the West, has insisted that in Zeami we have not only probably the most important of nō playwrights but also one of the major thinkers in Japanese history. Konishi maintains that as a systematic thinker Zeami can easily be put alongside Dōgen, Itō Jinsai, and Motoori Norinaga.[2] This claim may strike some as excessive, since it is not uncommon for readers of Zeami's treatises on the theater to conclude that they are scarcely systematic and perhaps even contradictory. Konishi and others disagree, holding that Zeami is a complex, rather than confused, thinker. I share this judgment and argue that there is a striking internal consistency within Zeami's thought and a remarkable correspondence between his mode of thinking and the plot structure of a typical nō drama.

At the outset, I wish to point out that it is the *general* Mahayana viewpoint in nō that will be the focus of this discussion. Whether nō has a special debt to one Buddhist school or another is, of course, an interesting problem. The late Hisamatsu Shin'ichi, a great philosopher and, to anyone who had met him, a redoubtable man of Zen, stated categorically: "The unique feature of our experience of Nō is not something having to do with Shinto or with any of the other schools of Buddhism; it is entirely something of Zen."[3] However Arthur Waley, also redoubtable in the eyes of many who knew him, wrote: " . . . it was in a style tinged with Zen that Zeami wrote of his own art. But the religion of the Nō plays is predominantly Amidist; it is the common, average Buddhism of medieval Japan."[4] The two statements are flatly contradictory and not easily reconciled; but it is more than temerity before the prospect of being caught between two opposing "redoubtables" that prompts me to avoid the question in this form. It is the desire to propose another possibility, one that might suggest why on one level nō drama presents the "common, average Buddhism" of Japan and on another it is informed by a mode of thought often associated with Zen. This chapter will therefore procede in two stages: first, a consideration of the Buddhist cosmology in nō, and second, a consideration of the Buddhist dialectic. The movement from one to the other is an important aspect of nō.

BUDDHISM IN NŌ: THE COSMOLOGY

One of the areas most neglected in Western studies of Japanese Buddhism is the cosmology that was basic to the mind of medieval Japan. We have already investigated it in some detail in chapter two, where we noted that it was very effectively articulated in the eighth century by Kyōkai, the author of the *Nihon ryōi-ki*. The point made in chapter two was that this cosmology appealed to the Japanese on all levels of society as a basic outline for the workings of the universe. In this chapter we shall explore one of the most creative *reworkings* of this cosmology under the aegis of the artistic imagination of the Japanese—although the Buddhist cosmology must be recognized as the single most important framework for all the great literary works of medieval Japan. It was a surprisingly resilient cosmology; although challenged by different views of the universe offered to the Japanese since the Tokugawa era, the cosmology that accompanied Buddhism provided cognitive satisfaction and had psychological persuasiveness for centuries. It still retains a certain power.

Although there is no need to recapitulate all the details of the rokudō system of transmigration (*rinne*) through the six realms, its importance for nō drama is so great that a brief summary might be useful before turning to the ways nō creatively reworked the medieval system using it to give dynamic thrust to one of the world's great theatrical traditions. It is important to recall that the rokudō scheme provided not only a simple taxonomy for the classification of all things met by man's experience and imagination but also gave a teleological thrust to all forms of existence. They were seen as moving up and down on a scale of existences. Karma out of past acts determined the direction of travel, the rate of travel, and the specifics of one's next rebirth. There were six basic rubrics, called *gati* in Sanskrit, *tao* in Chinese, and *dō* in Japanese. Because movement was intrinsic to their meaning, they might best be termed "courses" in English. In order of descending value, they were as follows:

1. divine ones   (*deva-gati*)
2. human ones   (*manusya-gati*)
3. warring ones   (*aśura-gati*)
4. animal ones   (*tiryagyoni-gati*)
5. hungry-ghost ones   (*preta-gati*)
6. hell-abiding ones   (*naraka-gati*)

There are variant versions of the order; an occasional elimination of the *aśura* or incorporation of them into one of the other categories (thus making five courses) can also be found. The basic structure, however, was fairly stable and intelligible. It was a picture of the universe comprehensible to even unlettered people in medieval Japan. To them it was perhaps even the core of Buddhist teaching, more readily grasped than the more subtle teachings of "no-self" and "codependent origination."

The rokudō system establishes a way of understanding a tension between appearance and reality. It asserts that, although we are ordinarily caught in a web of illusion so that we think only in terms of this present life, we are, in fact, beings-in-process, moving up or down through innumerable lives and according to a rigorous law of karma. To see the wider picture, the *system*, behind individual instances is to make an epistemic leap; in Buddhist terms it is to begin to escape from illusion. Although not itself nirvana, this breakthrough is a sine qua non for eventual attainment; it stimulates one to work to move upward along the rungs of the taxonomy. Transcendence of the six ways, which are collectively referred to in some texts as samsara, is the ultimate goal. Though I will suggest later how the dialectical developments in Mahayana Buddhism altered the relationship of nirvana to samsara, for now it is important only to point out that, as commonly understood, the six courses were hierarchically arranged; to move from lower ranks to higher ones was an unquestioned value.

In theory, the universalism central to Mahayana Buddhism made it possible to postulate that even hell was temporary (more like a purgatory in medieval Western cosmologies) and that eventually all beings would reach the upper realms. But "eventually" refers to Buddhist time frames inherited from India, that is, time measured in astronomical numbers. Moreover, ascent is accompanied by many swings downward along the way. Especially when blinded by illusion so that one disregards the system and its implications for morality and religious practice, one is likely to be a slave to the passions and so move steadily downward along the six courses. Even the recognition of the existence of the system of transmigration does not automatically cancel the karma of the past. Thus, even conceived of as only purgatorial, the prospect of being detained at length in realms of suffering is scarcely a pleasant one; it is very Dantesque indeed.

As a form of theater, nō incorporates this basic Buddhist cosmology in two ways. The first is commonly recognized; it consists of an epiphanic event fairly early in most plays in the repertory, a moment in which the main character discloses that he or she is a reincarnation of someone who lived previously. In almost every case this revelation is accompanied by a dramatic narrative that rehearses the events and passions of the former existence which led directly to the sad condition of the present incarnation. At this point there are often overt references to the rokudō and the inevitability of transmigration. This break-through moment signals not only that things are not really what they seem (a characteristic of even the most realistic or psychological forms of modern drama) but also that the explanation for this lies in Buddhist cosmology, the real system lying behind the initially perceived world of appearances. In this double sense the breakthrough represents the fulcrum between illusion and reality (reality defined as the mode of theatrical presentation informed by Buddhist assumptions about man and the universe).

The second manner in which nō embraces and uses the Buddhist cosmology of rokudō is more covert. It is in the way the system of six courses came eventually to be interwoven with the progression of five categories of nō which constitutes the sequence of plays in a typical day's performance. The correspondence is not exact, but the *structure of the progression* is what is important. Discounting the initial *okina* play, a form of ancient ritual opening and not included in any of the five standard categories, the basic rubrics are these (in the order of a typical day's presentation):[5]

Class one: *Waki-no-mono* or *kami-nō*, plays about gods
Class two: *Shura-mono*, plays about *ashura* or martial figures
Class three: *Kazura-mono* or *onna-mono*, plays about women
Class four: *Genzai-mono*, plays about miscellaneous or contemporary figures
Class five: *Kiri-no-mono*, plays about demons.

Since I wish to maintain that this sequence corresponds fundamentally to the taxonomy of the six courses, let us first consider possible objections to that hypothesis.

The first anomalous aspect of the hypothesis is the placement of the plays about *ashura (shura-mono)* immediately after those concerning gods (*kami-nō*). Anyone would concede that these fit nicely into two of the top three *gati* of the six-course system, but in the basic paradigm the ashura occupy the third slot, directly below the human. Though it might legitimately be asked whether this destroys the theory, there are substantial reasons for concluding that it does not. First, as Paul Mus has shown, the location of the ashura in the sequence of gati is strikingly inexact in the texts of the tradition: some place it in the second position because the ashura are thought of as titans, brothers (though rivals) of the gods.[6] In power they rank above human beings. Inasmuch as they are *warring* beings, however, they deserve rather less than great respect in a Buddhist system of values. Thus, if the plays about ashura seem somewhat anomalously placed in the nō progression, it is the reflection of a great deal of ambiguity and vacillation in the received tradition. The irregularity is thoroughly consistent with a pattern of ambivalence concerning their exact location.

An additional reason for maintaining that this irregularity is only apparent is the equally deep ambivalence with respect to martial heroes in medieval Japan. Not only nō but also the great histories and war chronicles testify to this ambivalence. The point of view in all these genres is double, caught between an impulse to honor the valor and loyalty of the military figure and a resistance that is based on the way the samurai's mode of life conflicts with Buddhist morality and brings havoc to society. Nowhere is this ambivalence more poignant than in the great suffering of the ashura who in the course of a nō play are disclosed to be incarnations of great and honored military heroes of the past. These figures emerge as simultaneously worthy of worship and pity. This is a reflection within the affective dimension of nō of the taxonomic dilemma posed by the ashura: are they to be classified next to the gods—above ordinary human beings—or are they to be classified below ordinary men, as creatures consumed by a karmic destiny that keeps them bellicose for the foreseeable future? It is around this ambivalence that the playwrights of nō were able to construct some of the most powerful dramas of the repertory.

The second possible objection to the hypothesized correspondence between the nō sequence and the six courses might arise from an apparent imprecision in the correlation between the categories of hungry ghosts and animals in the traditional taxonomy and the third and fourth categories of nō, the plays about women and about miscellaneous or contemporary figures. Here, too, the disparity may be much less than it appears. A content analysis of the plays of the third and fourth rubrics shows that many initially present the main character as crazed or tortured ghosts of historical figures, reincarnations in the realm of *preta (gaki)*. In fact, three of the major subdivisions of the fourth rubric are: (a) *kyōran-mono*, crazed and frenzied ones, (b) *shūshin-mono*, infatuated and attached ones, and (c) *onryō-mono*, revengeful ghosts. The two distinguishing characteristics of the preta, namely, its shadelike mode of existence and its passions that bring it into delirium, are present in characters in the great majority of plays in the third and fourth categories. Although nō gives only limited opportunities for the representation of animals on stage, they are not totally absent; moreover, the consuming, sometimes bestial, passions of the pretas often make the division between them and animals indistinct.

Even in these middle categories of nō there exists an approximation to the middle rubrics of the Buddhist cosmology, though the matching of categories is less precise than it is in the case of the top and bottom ranks. Represented on a graph, the correspondence looks like this:

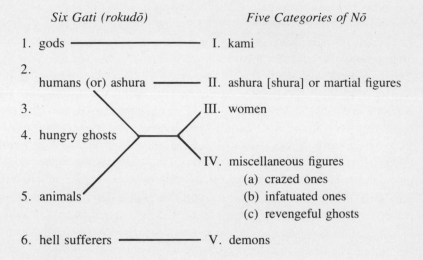

Six Gati (rokudō)	*Five Categories of Nō*
1. gods	I. kami
2. humans (or) ashura	II. ashura [shura] or martial figures
3.	III. women
4. hungry ghosts	
	IV. miscellaneous figures
	(a) crazed ones
5. animals	(b) infatuated ones
	(c) revengeful ghosts
6. hell sufferers	V. demons

This suggests that the rokudō, or at least the basics of its structure, is the underlying framework of a day's repertory of nō; a day at the theater adumbrates microcosmically the basic world order of Buddhism.

It is commonly agreed that the third, fourth, and fifth categories of nō are the most interesting. In them the drama is most highly charged. The opening plays about kami, or godlike figures (*Takasago, Hakurakuten,* etc.), are celebratory; they are pleasant but not captivating. Likewise, the plays of the final category, though they include some popular ones such as *Funa Benkei* and some excellent ones such as *Yamamba,* are for the most part less fascinating; detractors have been known to call these plays "confections," desserts at the end of the day's menu of nō.

It would seem natural that the plays in the three middle categories, which present dilemmas closest to those actually experienced by human beings in their daily lives, would most fully absorb the audience and have the most potential for being great drama. It is of crucial importance, however, that these dramas (for example, *Michimori, Matsukaze, Kinuta*) are built around a great tension between the values and teleology implicit in the rokudō system and another set of values at variance with it. For, according to the official hierarchy of Buddhist values, the principal characters in these plays have done things deserving of karmic retribution: they have shed blood as warriors, burned with infatuated longing for absent lovers, or sought revenge for wrongs suffered. The lines of the chorus never fail to remind all hearers that sins like these necessitate transmigration in a downward direction and the prospect of great suffering. On other moral criteria, however, warriors, infatuated lovers, and revenge seekers can be seen as loyal, devoted, even self-sacrificing. Above all, they have given themselves single-mindedly to something. Thus, there exists a point of view that finds in them a heroic quality. The tension comes at the point when they have committed a sin that propels them downward along the gati.

The dilemma of position that is posed by the ashura, or fighting spirit—that is, Is he *less* than others because consumed by bellicosity, or *more* than the ordinary man because heroic and a titan?—is a dilemma posed more generally by all the major characters in the middle categories of nō. Their pathos derives from their apparently tragic situation; that is, although we find in them something heroic and eminently moral, they have done things that necessitate cosmic punishment. This is the tragic component Northrop Frye calls the "epiphany of law, of that which is and must be."[7] On this level, nō does not deviate from the pattern of the tragedies of ancient Greece or seventeenth-century Europe. Frye's analysis is apropos: "The tragic hero is very great as compared with us, but there is something else, something on the side of him opposite the audience, compared to which he is small. This something else may be called God, gods, fate, accident, fortune, necessity, circumstance, or any combination of these, but whatever it is the tragic hero is our mediator with it."

To this list we can add the inexorable law of karmic effect. In the early sections of the great dramas of nō, karma is invariably disclosed as having brought the principal actor to his pitiable plight. Karmic retribution is, in theory at least, a totally rationale and knowable system of justice. The hero in nō is portrayed as someone who should have known the implications of his deeds. Nevertheless, for reasons that were "good," he acted in such a way that the incurring of karmic punishment was inevitable. The revelation of this is the first major disclosure in the plays of nō. It fits Frye's formula: "Tragedy seems to move up to an *Augenblick* or crucial moment from which point the road to what might have been and the road to what will be can be simultaneously seen."[8] This moment of wider—double—sight and the tragic dimension it reveals is critically important in nō.

The fact that the moment of revelation occurs early in the course of a play is, however, interesting and significant. It suggests that, unlike the drama of ancient Greece or seventeenth-century Europe, nō does not stop with the disclosure of a tragic dimension. It is the movement *beyond the tragic* which gives nō its specificity as a form of drama. In order to consider what this involves, it is necessary to go beyond the conception of Buddhism as a cosmology and think of it in terms of certain philosophical moves made within the Mahayana tradition.

BUDDHISM IN NŌ: THE DIALECTIC

In the preceding analysis of the elements that make nō a powerful and moving form of drama, I have suggested that much of the tension arises because the *shite*, or "protagonist," is caught between two very different versions of moral responsibility, or between what students of ethics often refer to as conflicting codes of the moral ought. In warrior plays, for instance, a figure of almost titanic strength will be caught in the dilemma of having to take the lives of others in battle in order to fulfill the responsibility to protect the innocent or avenge a wrong. In a similar way, the passion of a woman for a man long absent will drive her to frenzy—representing a clear example of what was regarded by the classical Buddhists as passion's deepening of delusion—but also provide her with an unparalleled capacity for fidelity and single-mindedness. What seems right according to one code is wrong according to the other.

The question of how to interpret this dilemma and how to locate a passable course of action through it has for centuries attracted the attention of Japanese (and much more recently, Western) thinkers involved in reconstructing the course of Japan's intellectual history. One strategem frequently employed has been to see a deep disparity between Buddhist moral imperatives and the values and ethical objectives of Shinto or Confucianism. The roots of this schematization go back several centuries, but in the twentieth century it has become widely accepted and has crystallized into probably the most commonly held theory. According to this theory, Buddhism presented to the Japanese a set of life ideals and ethical objectives that required a vast amount of self-privation, asceticism, and rejection of things deemed "natural," for the sake of goals—especially the elusive and nebulous nirvana—that seemed distinctly otherworldly. Shinto and Confucianism, by contrast, in spite of the great differences between them, were alike in that they tended to affirm the things of this world. Shinto seemed to affirm the naturalness of ordinary human emotions, sexuality, and passions; and Confucianism, in a somewhat complementary role, seemed to affirm the social structures—especially the family and institutions modeled on the family—which might also be called this-worldly and natural. According to this conceptual framework, much of Japanese intellectual history can be viewed in terms of a long period during which "otherworldliness" and "unnaturalness" of Buddhism were presented to the Japanese in a variety of ways but were constantly undermined by the older, indigenous, "natural" values of Shinto and by Confucian or Neo-Confucian emphases on success in this world and on the naturalness of social frameworks.

It is quite easy to see how nō could be interpreted in such terms. In accord with the otherworldly, nirvanic goal of Buddhism, for the sake of which all killing must be avoided and all passion expunged, the shite can hope for nothing but inevitable karmic entrapment in the round of samsara because he or she remains attached to sinful acts. But, at least according to the usual theory, there is something unnatural and unbearable about such a vision of reality and such a vision of the fate of a titanic or heroic figure. That is, the Shinto values of naturalness and the Confucian approval of virtues such as loyalty and fidelity are even in the context of nō sufficient to frustrate the Buddhist view of karma; they are enough to introduce elements of hope and the promise of some kind of salvation.

It is thought that because the Buddhist vision of life as merely a system of karmic rewards and punishments is finally an unbearable one, mitigating and optimistic factors and strategies are therefore introduced. The short pieces of kyōgen between the heavily serious nō pieces in a day of theater are thus seen as just bits of comic relief but as moving in philosophical and religious counterpoint to the somber, dire, Buddhist direction of events in the nō pieces themselves. In this view kyōgen brings back not only a note of this-worldliness but also elements of hope and naturalness. Humanity, lightness, and optimism return to the stage and to the mood of the theater when the kyōgen players appear on stage. According to this theory, these qualities are all in counterdistinction to the Buddhist framework of nō; they represent the resurgence of another structure of values and perhaps even an indigenous (Shinto) dimension of protest against the Buddhist vision of reality.

Though the more Shinto and Confucian elements of the experience of the medieval Japanese may have sometimes been restive and dissatisfied with the Buddhist hegemony, it should be clear by this point in our discussion of medieval Japan that the modern portrait of Buddhism as negative, otherworldly, and weighed down by the notion of inexorable karma is only a partial one. It takes a simplistic, reductive approach to the complexities of thought in medieval Japan. In order to provide a more adequate representation of the intellectual and religious environment of the period, I have suggested that there were at least two different versions of Buddhist thought and that to neglect or overlook one of them is to severely reduce or truncate one's vision of the period.

It is the more dialectical, less hierarchical, more subtle form of Buddhist thought which tends to be more affirmative concerning the natural human proclivities and passions. This form of thought resulted from the move in Mahayana that, as we have seen, established that there was "no nirvana apart from samsara"; it held, too, that the compassion, as well as the vocational ethic, of the bodhisattva was best articulated when he or she became identified with the world of suffering, with sentient beings, not as an act of ascetic abnegation but as one of compassionate, beneficent play. This is the conceptual affinity we have seen among the thought of Nāgārjuna, the figure of Vimala-kīrti, Fugen Bosatsu's incarnation in the courtesan of Eguchi, Shunzei's defense in the *Korai fūteishō* of "floating phrases and fictive utterances," and other elements in the literature of this epoch.

Although the old values of indigenous Shinto and the later ones of Confucianism exerted pressure on Japanese Buddhists to adopt more affirmative or natural attitudes than those of a Buddhism defined only through the notions of karma and a distant nirvana, within Buddhism itself, there was an intellectual and religious energy moving in much the same trajectory. It had made some of its basic moves in the Mahayana of continental Asia and entered Japan as part of a double-layered, double-faceted Buddhism. It was the special inspiration and genius of the Japanese to recognize that this energy had deep and wide implications for the artistic and literary life. They certainly pursued these implications in the literary and aesthetic treatises of the medieval period as a whole and especially in those of what I have called the high medieval era.

It is for this reason that the thought of Zeami—not only that implicit in his plays but also that contained in his treatises on nō—is so important and deserving of attention. Because his treatises are written in the format of guides for actors who wish to learn the art of nō, it is easy to suppose that they are less important for people interested only in appreciating nō as members of its audience; but such a supposition is unfortunate. Richard N. McKinnon is correct in stating that Zeami's treatises "serve as a key to an understanding and evaluation of Zeami as an artist, and are fundamental to the appreciation of the Nō as a stage art."[9] Especially in certain statements in Zeami's treatises it seems obvious that he wishes to encapsulate his understanding of nō in pithy, precisely worded phrases. By examining them we can detect the basic mode and structure of Zeami's thought.

One such phrase, an especially well-known one, appears near the conclusion of the third chapter of the *Kadensho*: "The flower is the mind; the seed is the performance" ("Hana wa kokoro; tane wa waza narubeshi").[10] Nishio Minoru took this phrase as the clearest evidence that the arts had undergone a "medieval" development in Japan. Comparing this phrase by Zeami with the one to which it clearly alludes—the statement in Ki no Tsurayuki's (884–946) preface to the tenth-century *Kokin-shū* to the effect that poetry has its seed in the human heart and issues forth in myriad words—Nishio saw Zeami deliberately reversing the image.[11] If he had applied Ki no Tsurayuki's fine sentiments about poetry to the genre of the nō in a straightforward fashion, Zeami would have asserted that the seed planted in the mind of the actor, perhaps in growing through disciplined training, eventually flowers on the stage for all to see. Put this way, it would have been a rather natural simile.

Instead Zeami has twisted the old image inside-out so that it becomes almost a koan, an intended conundrum not at all unrelated to the Zen tradition. We cannot but notice the deliberately strange twist and wonder about its purpose. I wish to suggest an explanation, or put forward a hypothesis, concerning Zeami's peculiar image. The botanical metaphor is a very important one in Japanese intellectual and religious history[12]; it deserves close attention whenever and wherever it appears.

Why did Zeami choose to state things in such a fashion? It seems apparent that Zeami thought of the training of a nō actor as a religious discipline. Words derived from the vocabulary of Zen are found in key places throughout his treatises. He thus conceived of the relationship between the training for nō (*keiko*) and its actual performance as similar to the relationship between practice and the attainment of enlightenment in the Buddhist monastic tradition. That is, for Zeami the training of an actor is to his performance as the disciplined practice of a monk is to his realization.

Recognizing this makes the whole *Kadensho* more fascinating. For Zeami seems to have been aware of the unique formulations of the relationship between practice and realization in the writing of the Zen master Dōgen (1200–1253). One of the most striking things about Dōgen was his use of Nāgārjuna, who much earlier had maintained that the logic of "no-self" demanded the conclusion that there can be no nirvana apart from samsara and, conversely, no samsara apart from nirvana. This, the so-called principle of codependent origination, was applied by Dōgen to the area of Buddhist practice; and he came to an innovative conclusion for which he is well known. It is, as stated in his essay "Bendōwa": "In the Buddha dharma, practice and realization are identical" ("Buppō ni wa, shushō kore ittō nari").[13] Condensed, the phrase becomes "shushō ittō."

It is not unwarranted to say that Zeami applied the principle of codependent origination to nō drama and was either directly or indirectly influenced by Dōgen in this. For one of the things his peculiar statement, that the flower is the mind and the seed the performance, seems to suggest is that our ordinary unidirectional thinking about the relationship between discipline and attainment is faulty. It divorces the practice from the goal; it makes practice only instrumental to an end separate and elsewhere. It is like those formulations of Buddhism that would prize an eventual nirvana apart from the samsaric realm and, as a consequence, see all practice as nothing more than a means to an eventual enlightenment. Zeami's dialectical statement puts him directly in the tradition that runs from Nāgārjuna through the *Daijo-kishin-ron*, the hongaku principle of Tendai, and to Dōgen. He rejects the implicit hierarchical ordering: practice is *not merely a means* to something higher, namely, performance on the stage. The flower exists in the mind of the actor as well. By deliberately reversing the direction of the simile to which he alludes, Zeami holds to the identity of practice and performance. Dependence is always mutual; it works both ways.

The conceptual fulcrum of Zeami's thought is the notion of *soku*, "identity."[14] His specific vocabulary may most closely resemble that of Zen, but the underlying mode of his thought is that of Mahayana more generally. Soku has its classic formulation in the well-known phrases of the *Heart Sutra*: "That which is form is emptiness; that which is emptiness is form" ("Shiki sokuze kū; kū sokuze shiki"). Zeami explicitly uses this text in his essay entitled "Yūgaku shudō kempū" in discussing an ease of mind and performance such that one no longer employs the usual bifurcating, discriminating mind in order to be concerned about "good" or "bad" performances.[15]

The principle of soku pervades Zeami's thought. Sometimes it seems to propel him to conclusions that strike his readers as strange to the point of being unacceptable. For instance, in an important section on miming in the sixth chapter of the *Kadensho*, he has just distinguished performances having that prized quality called yūgen from those characterized by *tsuyoki*, or "strength." The entire section seems concerned to clarify the difference between these two. But then, in a sentence which seems inexplicable, he suddenly concludes: "But looking very seriously at these distinctions, our understanding goes astray when we think of yūgen and of strength as being separate." ("Kono wakame o yokuyoku miru ni, yūgen to tsuyoki to, betchi ni aru mono to kokorouru ue ni mayou nari").[16] To Shidehara and Whitehouse, the translators of this text into English, this seems impossible. They insert words so that their translation will make more sense, but it does so by altering Zeami's intention:

> Adequate consideration of these distinctions shows that our going astray is due to a belief that grade (=yūgen) and strength (=tsuyoki) have an existence separate *from the objects of our miming*. [The underlined words are those interpolated into the text by the translators.][17]

The interpolation is interesting; it arises, I suspect, because it seems absurd that Zeami would have gone to great pains to make a fine distinction only to collapse that distinction by saying, "our understanding goes astray when we think of yūgen and strength as separate."

Yet, the basic mode of Zeami's thinking is characteristically of this type; it makes fine distinctions only to collapse those distinctions with a statement concerning identity. A good example is the opening paragraph of chapter seven ("Besshi no kuden") of the *Kadensho*, which I would translate as follows:

> As for what has been called *hana*, or "flower," in these secret teachings, it is important to understand first of all why the flower that blooms in nature has been used here as a simile for many things. Since every variety of tree and plant comes into bloom in its own time in one of the four seasons, we prize the timeliness and rarity of the blooming of each. So too in nō: our minds take as "interesting" that which we experience as a rare thing. Now what we call *hana* or "flowering," what we call "interesting," and what we call "rarity" are not three separate things but really one and the same. But all flowers eventually are scattered; none stays in bloom. And it is precisely because it blooms and perishes that a flower holds our interest as something rare. So also in nō: to know the flowering is first of all to know that nothing abides. The rare thing exists because it does not stagnate but moves on from one style to another.[18]

Concerning this passage its commentators are generally agreed that Zeami has in mind the Buddhist notion of *mujū*, or "nonfixation," in the phrase "jū suru tokoro naki" ("There is no abiding place").

Zeami's treatises thus do much more than borrow phrases from and make allusions to the classics of Mahayana Buddhism; they go farther by adopting a Mahayana *mode of argument* that proceeds through differentiation into the collapse of the basis for the distinctions made. The dialectic of Nāgārjuna and its subsequent use by Dōgen are never far from Zeami's mind and style. This is why works such as the *Kadensho* can be seen as prime examples of developed Buddhist thought and at the same time manuals for aspiring actors of the nō stage.

Exactly how does this assist our understanding of what happens in a given nō play? This question is best addressed by recognizing that the mode of Zeami's thinking in the treatises and the developmental process of the best nō plays have an identical structure. That is, both consist of a move through differentiation— and the unequal values and ordering it implies—to the collapse of that differentiation and an affirmation of identity. This cannot be a facile or simple identification; it can be successful only when the differentiations have been pushed to the limit and from *within* them there comes an understanding of how and why they contain an identity after all.

The implication of this is that, in nō, salvation is eventually seen to be not separate from suffering and its causes. In the course of a single nō there is a twofold disclosure. The first, the one we considered previously as dependent on the value system of the rokudō cosmology, comes early in the play; through it the hero or heroine is portrayed as suffering his or her retribution for misdeeds in an earlier life. The presentation of Buddhist values at this point in the play is in terms of samsara and nirvana as antipodal. Congruent with this view, the six courses are levels between, but also ultimately separating, the two extremes. The nō play never stops here, however. It moves on, because the real denouement is still to come in the form of a disclosure that the principal character *has found salvation*. This involves a radical relativizing of the hierarchy of values in the rokudō cosmology; and, as I have suggested, the critique of the hierarchy arises not primarily out of values extrinsic to the Mahayana—Shinto or Confucian, for example—but is intrinsic to it. The dialectic according to which there can be no nirvana apart from samsara turns the events in a nō play into something significantly different from what had seemed to be the case early on in the play when the principal character was portrayed as merely moving downward along the cosmic hierarchy of beings.

On occasion this is reflected in the actual libretto of a play. *Kinuta*, for instance, is an intensely moving and poetic play about a woman who pounds her sorrow out on a fuller's block, bewailing her husband's willful separation from her. She is filled with anguish, resentment, and intense love; this itself is the matrix out of which her salvation comes. In a lucid analysis of the play, Frank Hoff notes that, according to the chorus, the reflection on the matter will show the woman's salvation to have come from the sound of her own incessant beating of the fuller's block.[19]

In many plays, however, there is little or no overt verbal reference to the salvation of the suffering, no indication that the principal character is doing anything but making a rapid descent into greater and greater suffering. In this, the texts alone are not representative of the range of events, emotions, and implications in nō. They have no way of capturing those mental and physical actions usually said to be characterized by yūgen, the quality in nō that has proven so elusive that it has never been captured in the definitions of either Japanese or Western scholars. Rather than attempting another definition, I would like to make a few observations concerning it.

The first observation is that, in many nō plays, although the libretto gives no indication that the principal character has gained salvation, the audience has a strong sense of mental and emotional relief as the play comes to a close. This relief seems to derive from a clear sense that the character on the stage, while still theoretically moving downward in the ranks of the cosmology, has in some real way been released from what had seemed sheer tragedy. That is, the actor or actors have communicated a sense of *profound tranquility* even though their apparent modes of existence remain those of beings in samsaric realms, perhaps even of demons. Yūgen moves beyond the text to reveal, through the tranquility it captures, the presence of nirvana in the midst of samsara, not as an abstract principle but in the concrete actions of the characters on the stage.

The second observation is that, in spite of the fact that yūgen involves an epiphany of depth and seems eminently spiritual, this depth and spirituality cannot be attained apart from or in contradistinction to the "superficial" and material. Notions of depth predicated on dualism miss the impact of the Mahayana dialectic on the structure of yūgen; perhaps it is for this reason that something seems slightly askew when, after stating that nō goes beyond duality, Jacob Raz depicts it as "the spiritual level . . . a shapeless, wordless, mindless realm of art."[20] For yūgen does not consist in any way of actions that become adumbrations of something else; the actions in a nō play are not like what Yeats referred to as "a spume that plays / Upon a ghostly paradigm of things."

To avoid construing yūgen and nō in Platonic terms is not enough, however. To put it more positively, through yūgen nō discloses the underlying inter-dependence of things. Nō is a unique form of theater in which the eventual dramatic breakthrough consists of an epistemic, religious contemplation of the free, unhindered movement of beings on the stage. Of course, in this sense the stage is the universe. What opens as a revelation of the tragic, karmically determined "fate" of the principal figure becomes the relativization of the dualistic implications of the rokudō cosmology. The real denouement is one in which all conflicts and oppositions are resolved. The affirmations that come out of this arise from the dialectic of the Mahayana itself; according to Konishi Jin'ichi, in nō they arise out of its foundation in the principle of hongaku, or original enlightenment.[21]

This perhaps explains why, in an attempt to clarify the basic differences between nō and the dramatic traditions of the West, a group of Japanese scholars a few years ago came to the following conclusion: Whereas in the drama of the West the action revolves around a situation of confrontation (tairitsu)—a situation of conflict between at least two actors, a protagonist and a deuteragonist—nō operates quite differently.[22] In Japan's classical drama the second actor (waki) is not really an adversary, and the action proceeds because of a story being told rather than through conflict between personalities.[23]

Given this definition only, we might expect nō to be unrelieved boredom. Of course, it is not. There is a high degree of tension and stress; the tension is not between two characters, however, but between two alternative versions or visions of the situation and destiny of the principal character, the shite. As the play opens, one view of his or her fate is presented, an unrelievedly tragic one of dismal descent along the levels of being. The tension develops because this simplistic reading of karmic retribution is unacceptable to the audience; the audience's empathy is directed toward the character. As the play moves toward its climax, the disparity between what happens on stage and what the audience senses as *just* is overcome. From within the perspective of Mahayana Buddhism comes the justification for recognizing the "tragic" figure as, in fact, enlightened and free. It is no wonder that the audience experiences a great sense of relief. At the same time, it has been moved to contemplate the embodiment of a basic intellectual development in Mahayana Buddhism.

7

SOCIETY UPSIDE-DOWN: KYŌGEN AS SATIRE AND AS RITUAL

> The devil is, of course, quite at home in sacred realms.
> —Susanne Langer[1]

I N RECENT DECADES there has been impressive progress in the study of the theatrical arts largely owing to the recognition of the social context within which forms such as tragedy, farce, comedy, and satire develop.[2] The history of the interaction between theater and society has proven both complex and fascinating; and this is as true of the Japanese case as of any.[3] Donald Shively demonstrated it some years ago in a provocative study of kabuki. With rich documentation, he portrayed "the running duel between the *bakufu* and *kabuki* [which] lasted the entire 250 years of the Tokugawa period, the *bakufu* constantly thrusting with restrictive laws, the *kabuki* parrying with ingenious devices."[4]

This chapter will use a somewhat similar method to look at kyōgen, the form of traditional Japanese theater often classified as comedy. In addition, however, it will explore what happens to religion—and especially Buddhism—in kyōgen. The scope of this exploration will thus include aspects of three things and how they interconnect: the theater, religion, and social hierarchies in the Muromachi and Tokugawa periods.

On the surface, what happens to Buddhism in kyōgen seems fairly clear: it is mercilessly satirized and lampooned. And this happens in what invariably appears to be a direct inversion of all the religious values that inform nō, the serious form of theater. Whereas in nō the Buddhist notions of karma and transmigration through the six realms of being (rokudō) are taken seriously, in kyōgen they are treated with complete frivolity and become the context for farce and humor. The play *Esashi Jūō*, for example, is about a man named Kiyoyori who has just spent a whole lifetime as a snarer and hunter of birds—that is, accumulating an immense amount of bad karma by killing sentient beings. Ordinarily, rebirth in hell would be the certain destiny of one such as he. But the dead Kiyoyori is quite cheeky about the matter. He comes out onto the stage with these lines:[5]

> Without a pang of parting,
> Without a tinge of remorse,
> I forsake the world of impermanence,
> And as I wander about with no guide,
> I have already come to the Meeting of the Six Ways.
> Indeed, this is already the Meeting of the Six Ways
>   of Existence. After due consideration, I wish
>   to go to Heaven.

He is met by Emma, the bureaucrat who is the ruler of Hades, who threatens to send Kiyoyori to hell at once. As it turns out, Emma has never had an opportunity to experience the taste of bird flesh. Kiyoyori gladly offers to give Emma that experience and proceeds, by way of mime, to catch birds for him, the judge of his destiny. Emma declares:

> Well, well! I will have a taste.
> Munch-munch! Crunch-crunch!
> What marvelous flavor!

He then comes to his decision; it is to send Kiyoyori back to the terrestrial realm where he is to continue catching birds. Emma gives his jeweled crown to the bird catcher, who then marches triumphantly offstage.

Esashi Jūō is only one of a number of kyōgen that directly and flagrantly ridicule the seriousness with which religious ideas, functionaries, and values were ordinarily taken. It is as if whatever is sacred in the world of nō becomes the object of ridicule and farce in kyōgen. This is especially so in the many plays that portray the quasi-Buddhist figure of the *yamabushi*. Whereas in nō and in ordinary piety the yamabushi's ascetic life in the mountains brought him magical powers and the reverence of pious folk, in kyōgen he is presented as powerless, bumbling, and ridiculous. In *Kusabira*, for example, a man summons a yamabushi because huge mushrooms have begun growing inside his house and he wishes to have them removed. The yamabushi arrives and chants his formulas but these are of no avail; in fact, the mushrooms only grow larger and eventually fill the man's whole house. Likewise, in *Kani Yamabushi*, a yamabushi out walking with his servant openly brags about the new powers he has gained through meditation and asceticism. On the road they are met by the spirit of a crab, and the yamabushi demands that his servant break the animal's shell with his stick. When the servant is caught in the pincers of the crab, his master proceeds to try to free him through prayers. These prove totally ineffective, and the yamabushi himself gets caught in the pincers. The humiliated pair are released only when the crab deigns to free them.[6]

Satake Akihiro concludes that in kyōgen "the yamabushi is the object of derision through and through."[7] He further notes: "In *Kani Yamabushi* it is the yamabushi's prayers intended to bring salvation from the clutches of the crab which, ironically, bring the matter of his 'powers' to a crisis and get him caught in the claws of the crab. And in *Kusabira* the yamabushi flees in terror from mushrooms that, the more he tries to pray them into stopping, the more they multiply."[8] In some cases, scholars have been able to detect quite accurately the original text of which the kyōgen is an intentional parody. Taguchi Kazuo sees *Kusabira* as an obvious and direct lampoon of events and values articulated in an episode in the *Shaseki-shū*, a thirteenth-century collection of Buddhist tales.[9] Materials originally intended to inspire belief in a world view that attributes to the yamabushi extraordinary powers—because he understands the way of the Buddhist dharma—were used in kyōgen to depict situations in which such faith leads to nothing but fiascoes.

It is not only piety that is the butt of ridicule in this form of drama, however. The pretense of lords and rulers is likewise the object of laughter and derision. It seems that whatever had official sanction—the Buddhist belief-system and clergy, or the enshrined social status of the daimyo and other masters—suffered a comedown in this form of theater. This has, quite understandably, fascinated critics and historians whose perspective is that of Marxism or socialist realism. Within such a framework of interpretation, kyōgen becomes an early example of proletarian literature, a breakthrough in the Muromachi period of an awareness of the necessity and value of class struggle. To these critics, kyōgen is far more fascinating than nō, the officially approved classical theater of Japan. Many kyōgen, taken to be examples of Japanese proletarian literature, have already been translated into modern Chinese. This was done primarily by Chou Tso-jen (1885–1966) (a brother of Lu Shun), who made an extensive study of Japanese literature. Concerning kyōgen's significance Chou wrote:

> The kyōgen described society's injustice and foolishness in the vernacular language of the day. The daimyo who appear in them are all unenlightened, and most of the Buddhist clergy are corrupt—so that both types are made to

look ridiculous by their own subordinates and servants. Even demons and gods are ordinarily the butt of jokes. On these points kyōgen is clearly very different from nō. It shows contempt for and resistance toward the authority of the rulers and is the mainstream of a comic literature of the masses.[10]

According to this interpretation, kyōgen expresses the degree to which persons on a politically and socially oppressed stratum of society saw through the pretense of their masters and recognized the injustice in society.

There are, however, certain problems with this understanding of kyōgen. For two reasons particularly, the Marxist explanation leaves much to be desired. The first of these is the presence of a good deal of black humor in the kyōgen repertoire. No reader or observer of kyōgen can fail to be impressed by the fact that in many of the plays it is not the daimyo and priests who are the object of humor but the most unfortunate members of society, especially the poor, the aged, and the physically disabled. In fact, in one entire category of kyōgen called *zatō* plays, the poor victims of jest are invariably blind persons. An especially well-known play in this rubric is *Sarugae Kōtō*.[11] It is a story of a blind man who goes with his wife to enjoy the cherry blossoms at Kiyomizu temple in Kyoto. While there, the two of them get rather drunk on saké while a man with a monkey comes close enough to admire the beauty of the blind man's wife. He whispers to her in private that it is a pity that someone as pretty as she is married to a blind man who cannot appreciate her properly. He proposes that she run away with him, and she eventually agrees. Unaware of this but conscious that his wife is repeatedly absent from him, the blind man ties her to his belt. Then the clever monkey-man merely substitutes his leashed monkey for the woman on the blind man's belt and runs away with her. After much slapstick, the blind man exclaims:

> "Oh, how terrible! My wife has turned into a monkey with hair all over her body. What can I do about it? Ouch! Don't scratch me like that! Please forgive me, dear wife!"

With this, the play ends.

It is difficult to reconcile the unusual amount of black humor in kyōgen with the hypothesis that this type of theater is illustrative of social consciousness and proletarian drama. Although kyōgen often celebrates individual instances of servants getting the better of their masters and skeptics taking advantage of the foibles of the clergy, there is no sense at all of social solidarity, which ought to be present at least embryonically in a kind of literature identified as proletarian.

The second reason for dissatisfaction with the Marxist interpretation of kyōgen has to do with the success of kyōgen in the Tokugawa era and its official sponsorship by Tokugawa shoguns. Joined as it was with nō, it not only survived but received the patronage of the very rulers whom, according to strict Marxist theory, it would be trying to subvert. This anomaly will be given considerable attention later in this chapter. The point to be emphasized here, however, is that it is indeed strange for the de facto rulers of Japan in the Tokugawa era to have provided official support for a form of theater that, according to Chou Tso-jen, intended to "show contempt for and resistance toward the authority of the rulers. . . ."

Though the perspective of socialist realism does not seem able to account adequately for the evolution of kyōgen, the alternative of seeing such theater as a form of psychological release for the players and their audiences seems equally problematic. That is, it overlooks the fact that kyōgen has not been everywhere and always the same kind of theater. Now that the evolution of kyōgen can be more clearly delineated than it could at an earlier stage of scholarship, one can and ought to be historical in the analysis of kyōgen's literary and social role in Japanese culture. The following highlights of what Japanese scholarship has discovered about the evolution of kyōgen suggest how recent theories concerning "symbolic inversion" in society can explain the patronage of kyōgen by Tokugawa shoguns.

In many ways the evolution of kyōgen provides a superb aperture for the observation of the interaction between high culture and popular culture in Japan—especially if kyōgen's origins are traced back to the Muromachi period. For, though vastly different from nō, kyōgen underwent a similar elevation. Like nō, it originated in a period when some of the most creative developments in Japanese culture were occurring on the more popular level of society and were being conceived and produced by persons of humble origins. The fecund creativity of popular culture in the Muromachi era is now recognized by scholars. John W. Hall sums it up well: " . . . a realization that many of the elements of the Muromachi 'great tradition,' which are considered particularly new, should be attributed less to the creative work of aristocratic artists than to the adoption by the elite of elements from the 'little tradition.' Men of humble origins were intimately involved in the perfection of such genre as nō, poetry, gardens, architecture, and certain styles of painting."[12]

The period was one in which patronage was important, but the very fact that patronage could be gained—or lost—made for a social and cultural mobility not known before in Japan. The growth of urban commerce during this era created conditions in which troupes of players of rural origin could succeed in the city. When a troupe's more rustic qualities had worn off, the serious dimension of its theater became patent, and patronage gave it a social standing it had not had before. This was all part of its elevation to high art. Certainly this was the case with nō; by winning the attention and patronage of the shogun,

Kan'ami (1333—1384) and Zeami (1363—1443) were able to bring this form of theater to perfection.[13] Kyōgen differs from nō in that its rusticity and many other traces of its popular origins were retained even as, by its inclusion in the repertoire of a day's performance of nō, it gained social approval and artistic respectability.

Political and cultural historians have been fascinated by the high incidence of the phrase "gekokujō" ("the below conquers the above") in documents of medieval Japan in general and in those of the Muromachi period in particular.[14] The phrase seems quite certainly to have derived from the explanatory systems of yin-yang and the five elements (*wu hsing*) of China, according to which wood overcomes earth, metal overcomes wood, fire overcomes metal, water overcomes fire, and because the cycle is endless, earth overcomes water, wood again overcomes earth, and so on. The Japanese were captivated by this capacity of "lower" to overcome what had appeared to be "higher." They used it in locating omens and portents. But, more importantly for our purpose here, they also used the notion of gekokujō to account for sudden and drastic social change, such as the quick demise of a strong clan or the sudden rise in fortune and prestige on the part of a previously lowly person or group. It is not incidental in a period such as the Muromachi—when social mobility (and what we might call the upward mobility of artistic and literary forms) was more common than before—that gekokujō provided an explanation for dynamic change.

Fukuo Takeichirō suggests that this notion was often combined with the Buddhist concept of karma in medieval Japan.[15] Especially after the direct application of Buddhist concepts to historical explanation by Jien (1154—1225) in his *Gukan-shō*, the possibility of a fairly sophisticated Buddhist philosophy of history was present. Now, through a combination of the notions of gekokujō and karma, the medieval Japanese had conceptual tools for making sense of general social upheaval as well as sudden changes in personal fortune or status. While we have ample evidence to show that the elite of the Muromachi period used the phrase gekokujō with alarm, the very same notion of below-conquers-above would give pleasure and hope to people on lower strata anticipating or actually experiencing sudden good fortune and upward mobility. There is therefore no reason to assume that talk of karmic necessity was always and everywhere accompanied by pessimism; it also connoted the conditions for improvement in one's own lot or that of one's group.

Viewed as a form of drama that encapsulates the principle of gekokujō, kyōgen becomes especially interesting. Unlike nō, which envisions change only as a slow cosmic process stretched out over the canvas of nearly infinite time, kyōgen presents a world in which servants get the better of their masters and skeptics see through the delusions of religious charlatans in a very short period of time. Whereas in nō change is envisioned as altered status in the cosmic taxonomy (rokudō), which is achieved through eventual rebirth and as the culmination of much religious practice, in kyōgen change occurs in the much more empirical world of ordinary society. The difference in pace between nō and kyōgen is therefore not merely a matter of footwork and bodily movement on the stage; it extends to the world view of each art form.

This is not to say that the world of nō is Buddhist and that of kyōgen is not. As noted previously, the karmic explanation is sufficiently fluid to encompass occurrences of rapid change in man's empirical and social world. And, as we shall see, even the irreverence and impiety of kyōgen is not necessarily inimical to some Buddhist values and beliefs.

Before looking further at this matter, the social role of Muromachi kyōgen needs more precise depiction. It is because kyōgen offers a unique opportunity to see the process whereby popular art forms gain respectability that it has already been carefully scrutinized by Japanese scholars of social history.[16] It appears that kyōgen episodes were conceived and performed by actors who were themselves in the process of enjoying upward social movement, from the countryside to the urban centers and from obscurity to recognition by wealthy patrons. These patrons had only recently made a rapid social ascent and now had more actual power and wealth than the old *kuge*, or Japanese nobility. In different ways, then, both the troupes of players and their urban sponsors had a stake in the experience of upward mobility; the dynamics of gekokujō intrigued them both. Together they could laugh at the expense of the old aristocracy. In plays that portrayed masters as dimwitted or easily duped—that is, in a great number of plays—it was easy for the sponsors of kyōgen to see a lampooning not of themselves, the current holders of power and wealth, but of the now ineffective and virtually displaced older aristocracy of Japan, the class of people called the kuge.

There was still sensitivity on this point, however; and when presented in a setting still close to the aristocracy, kyōgen clearly possessed the character of satire. This is evident from a historical note from the year 1424, an item that has caught the attention of scholars charting the history of kyōgen. The episode is recorded in the *Kammon gyoki* and falls within the year Oei 31.

Eleventh day of the third month. Clear weather. Continuous performances of *sarugaku* yesterday. . . . A problem arose because the kyōgen consisted of various kinds of performances on the theme of the distress of the nobility. This kind of thing was inexcusable and, therefore, the director was dismissed from his post. This happened at the palace. To use the destitute condition of the nobility for performances of kyōgen in the very residences of the nobility is to display a gross insensitivity to old customs and manners. It is the epitome of rudeness. The dismissal of the director was an object lesson for future generations.[17]

This has led scholars to conclude that in its earlier stages kyōgen had a much sharper satirical edge than it came to have later on. Rather than being pure farce or comedy, it was satire in that it had an object of attack. It thus fit Northrop Frye's definition: "Two things . . . are essential to satire; one is wit or humor founded on fantasy or a sense of the grotesque or absurd, the other is an object of attack. Attack without humor, or pure denunciation, forms one of the boundaries of satire."[18] As the *Kammon gyoki* clearly states that some person or group in the aristocracy felt attacked by the kyōgen performed in 1424, an audacity and satirical intent were evidently detected in that performance; it was certainly not light comedy and pure fun for all involved.

The judgment that early kyōgen was considerably more satirical is given further support by the discovery of an old text of kyōgen synopses, the *Tenshō kyōgen-bon*. Made public in 1940, this text could not be published until 1956, but it has interested scholars because it is datable to Tenshō 6, or the year 1578.[19] It therefore gives the outlines of plays performed in the Muromachi era and is the only source that predates the Tokugawa period. This text gives us the chance to compare the kyōgen of the two eras and to notice what had changed over the years. Although it is a book of synopses rather than full texts, the *Tenshō kyōgen-bon* includes twenty plays not available in the extant Tokugawa books, and a number of these have a sharp satirical edge. One, for instance, is concerned with a farmer who brings a protest and then a suit to a ruler because of an injustice done him. For the *history* of kyōgen the existence of plays such as this is especially significant, since it is clear that plays of this more directly satirical nature had largely been dropped from the repertoire of kyōgen in the Tokugawa era. Such a dropping of texts is of extreme interest for the recon-struction of the social history of an artistic or literary form, as is well expressed by Lotman and Uspensky. "Culture constantly excludes specific texts from its particular sphere. The history of the destruction of texts, of their extromission from the collective memory bank, runs parallel to that of the creation of new texts. . . . "[20]

The evolution of kyōgen from the Muromachi to the Tokugawa period thus involves a refinement that is not only aesthetic but also social. With the passage of time, the object of social satire would have no longer been viewed as the impotent and eclipsed aristocratic kuge but as the now equally vulnerable shoguns and other high ranking lords. As they were expected to be the patrons of kyōgen, which accompanied the nō plays loved and promoted by the same Tokugawa rulers, it is not surprising that plays that might be viewed as satirizing the behavior of these patron-rulers were forgotten or expunged from the repertoire. In a most literal way, kyōgen was aesthetically refined by being made more socially presentable.

This elimination of more directly satirical plays was, however, only a *relative* change in kyōgen. Satirical elements remained and helped maintain the clear distinction between kyōgen and nō, a distinction more complex than the usual one between tragedy and comedy. The distinction between nō and kyōgen must be made in terms adequate to embrace the particular range and world view of each form, not simply refer to the rubrics of comedy and tragedy.

Of great assistance in characterizing kyōgen is the work of Satake Akihiro. Satake's essays on kyōgen have been widely read and praised; in 1967 they were republished under the title *Gekokujō no bungaku*.[21] In order to define the specificity of kyōgen, Satake contrasts these plays with a contemporaneous genre called *otogi-zōshi*. Otogi-zōshi is a form of tale notorious for "abrupt and straightforward religious didacticism"[22] and episodes in which, according to Chieko Irie Mulhern, "the difficulties and misfortunes in real life can be completely remedied by, and almost solely by, divine power."[23] Otogi-zōshi envision good fortune and blissful days for the meek and poor of society but do so only through an obviously contrived deus ex machina. In kyōgen, by contrast, the only success for people comes through cleverness and cunning, usually the right ruse at the right time. Satake portrays the contrast quite vividly:

> In *Kagami otoko emaki* [an otogi-zōshi] the hero is a weakling; he is the recipient of divine grace—is granted wealth and happiness—all moving toward a happy, festive ending. But when the same hero appears in kyōgen a complete turnabout takes place; he who in the otogi-zōshi was eventually a winner now turns out to be a miserable loser. The weakling is in the one instance the winner and, in the other, the loser; fate leads one and the same character in diametrically opposite directions, sporting with him in this way. What needs to be understood in this, however, is that this total contrast in the respective fates of the characters is determined by the intrinsic nature of the two different genres, otogi-zōshi and kyōgen.
>
> When the poor underdog is categorized as a good person, basks in all manner of divine grace, and then becomes a success in the end—this way of conceiving of things is one that is completely traditional, in keeping with the essence of the archaic tales. In this sense the *Kagami otoko emaki* is very orthodox, a classic illustration of otogi-zōshi. In it the aspirations of impoverished common people are portrayed in the most lofty terms imaginable. But is this really anything more than a world of the imagination, one with no relation to reality, one that in no way has substance outside the world of the

otogi story itself? The truth of the matter is that this era was anything but one in which someone without power could, as a weakling, achieve easy success. It was a society in which there was absolutely no salvation for weak or stupid people. Gods and Buddhas were unreliable; prayer had no effect. The passport to riches and prosperity was never anything other than one's own talents, wits, agility, cunning, nerve, and power. Practical reason and real power made up the code that was in effect in this turbulent "jungle" of an era. In otogi-zōshi, people turn their backs upon the cruel, real world and make an excursion into vicarious experience, that of dreams. But in kyōgen things are just the opposite: a direct confrontation with the realities of the times, as well as uninhibited, caustic laughter, are directed at those people who had somehow been left behind in this era of outrageous freedom, an era in which the higher could be replaced by the lower [gekokujō]. In kyōgen, cowards are the butt of ridicule; aged people are bamboozled; country folk are treated like fools; the physically disabled are used for sport; and people in trouble are bullied and bandied about.[24]

Satake's analysis appears to be correct and, unlike Chou Tso-jen's interpretation of kyōgen, is able to account for the presence of black humor in this kind of theater. Kyōgen, written by and for people who had gone from a lower position in society to a higher one, celebrated the wit and cunning with which they had made such an advance. Conversely, kyōgen lampooned and satirized all forms of credulity, gullibility, pious naiveté, and impotent submission to fate.

This is the nature of the barb in a play such as *Sarugae kōtō*. The physical blindness of the man whose wife is lured away by the monkey-man is complemented by a psychological and social obtuseness so grave that he naively assumes his wife has been supernaturally transformed into a monkey and that this has happened because of *his own* wrongdoing. Physical blindness becomes in kyōgen a vantage point from which satire is directed at all forms of faith in "the existence of things not seen."

The world of kyōgen is one in which the outlook is uncompromisingly positivist and the regnant notion of power is of an unrelenting realpolitik. Jacqueline Golay is certainly correct in saying that kyōgen ". . . had its origin in the spontaneous expression of popular wit which emerged from the sternness of religious and ritual representations, and which delighted in bringing objects of worship down to earth and to an everyday dimension."[25] The bringing of religious objects down to earth in kyōgen involves an across-the-board skepticism about the validity and viability of the cosmology accepted by the mainstream of Buddhism in medieval Japan. This was the cosmology according to which transmigration through the various levels of the six worlds was taken literally and with utmost seriousness. It was a view that held that beings have their place in the present world owing solely to the karma accumulated in past lives or through past deeds in the present life. Upward mobility in such a view involves kalpas of time, acceptance of the rokudō as the way things really are, and many lives lived in accordance with the requirements of piety and morality.

Whereas in nō the six worlds and transmigration through them are accepted as the proven structure of reality, in kyōgen this entire framework of understanding is treated irreverently and as a fabrication spawned to obfuscate the reality of *this world* and the fact that power, ruse, and cunning are the only ways of achieving success in it. Consequently, in kyōgen, monks and priests who traffic in religious venerabilia are either fools or charlatans; and if they are the latter, it is clear that they too have implicitly adopted an attitude of affirming this world and what they can get out of it, while mouthing pieties about other worlds in order to dupe the naive. As we saw in *Esashi Jūō*, the man who has led a life as a snarer of birds enters death without remorse or compunction; while mouthing phrases about being at the place of the "meeting of the six ways," he treats the whole framework as a joke and says he expects to enter heaven rather than hell. In the end he succeeds in converting the Buddhist ruler of Hades to his own brand of world-affirmation and irreverent disregard for the Buddhist precepts. Crowned and rewarded, he marches offstage.

If it be granted that taking the cosmology seriously constituted the common and popular position of Buddhism in medieval Japan, it is easy to see both why the cosmology was so amenable to the shoguns of the Tokugawa era and why its blatant subversion in kyōgen might be taken as incipient, germinal evidence of what Robert Bellah calls the "early modern" era, an era in which there would eventually be a "collapse of the hierarchical structuring of both this and the other world."[26] This matter goes to the heart of the way in which theater in late medieval Japan played a significant role in the cognitive and social ordering of the world.

It is clear that the Tokugawa shogunate placed its official stamp of approval on the nō theater and promoted it consistently as the preferred form of drama in Japan. Aside from the obvious and indisputable aesthetic superiority of nō, a government such as the Tokugawa shogunate, consistently concerned as it was with the maintenance of order and the hierarchical arrangement of society, would naturally view favorably a form of drama that articulates a world in which *order* is a value. The Tokugawa rulers recognized that the freeze they wished to place on the officially approved hierarchy of social strata in their realm would be reinforced by a form of drama that was informed by a world view of stratified levels, with mobility through the levels projected over vast expanses of time. There could thus be a coalescence between the order seen as normative for society and the cosmic order of mainstream medieval Buddhism—in which mobility was seen in terms of advance through positive rebirth rather than in terms of striving, cunning, or plays for power within this lifetime and this world.

The emergence of kyōgen, especially viewed through the analyses of Satake Akihiro, represents the provision not just of lighthearted playfulness but of an alternative vision of life and society, a vision in which the medieval cosmology is seen as the product of purveyors of blindness. It is a crack in the cognitive world of medieval Japan, although not necessarily the first such questioning of the mainstream cosmology and values. It is legitimate to see kyōgen as the staging of plays in which the values embraced are strictly this-worldly and thus antihierarchical and "modern," in the sense of the term used by Robert N. Bellah and other contemporary thinkers.

If this is so, why did kyōgen accompany nō in receiving the approval and patronage of the shoguns of the Tokugawa period? Why was there support for a form of theater that seemed to condone and endorse ruses whereby inferiors bested their superiors and servants their masters? Was this not incongruous, a strange contradiction for rulers anxious to freeze society and maintain social hierarchy at all costs? Was not the official patronage of kyōgen by the Tokugawa shoguns one of the greatest anomalies of Japanese history?

My hypothesis is that the potential disruptiveness implicit in kyōgen was rendered innocuous, first by the removal of the more blatantly satirical elements when kyōgen was made more "refined" in the Tokugawa era, and second and more importantly, by its ritualization as a *form of symbolic inversion* that was contained within the officially patronized performances of nō. Since the first of these was considered previously, it remains to elaborate on the process of symbolic inversion as the key to grasping how limited affronts to social and cosmic order could receive the support of rulers with a notorious vested interest in the maintenance of that order.

Nō in the Tokugawa era must be viewed not only as theater in the usual sense of the word but also as a type of public social ritual. We do well to recall Donald Keene's description of what happened to nō in the Tokugawa. He sees the construction of Ieyasu's castle in Edo in 1606 as the opening of a new era for nō: "From this time on, Nō served as the official music of the Tokugawa regime. The shoguns, devoted to Confucian doctrines, considered rites and music to be the essential elements of government and just as bugaku had provided the ceremonial music for the emperor's court, the gravity and stately movements of Nō won favor at the shogun's court, which was run according to the decorum imposed by the Confucian code. The performances of Nō, especially at the New Year, were elaborate rituals believed to be capable of effecting the prosperity and welfare of the State."[27] From all the information we have this would seem to be accurate, a description of a form of drama being transformed into rituals of state that articulate and reinforce the themes of social order and national welfare.

This being so, it seems logical that kyōgen could be not only tolerated but also appreciated as a form of symbolic inversion within a day's repertoire of nō. By being enfolded within the extensive program of a single day's performances, kyōgen appeared as both comic interlude and symbolic counterpoint to nō's adumbration of hierarchical values. It was tolerated as the permitted and circumscribed eruption of an alternative, *inverted*, set of values, an eruption that quickly subsided as the kyōgen performers ran offstage and the licet world of nō returned.

Thus, the ritualization of nō included also the ritualization of potential dissent from the values of the Tokugawa regime. Kyōgen's potential for serving social purposes derives, of course, from a period much earlier than the Tokugawa—in fact, from the much earlier association between nō and kyōgen. Zeami had mentioned that kyōgen ought to be kept close to nō and that, if it were, it might even be possible to have an expression of yūgen in kyōgen.[28] Later, Ōkura Toraaki (1597–1662), in his *Waranbe-gusa*, stressed an even more intimate link between the two forms of theater.[29]

By enclosure within the ambit of nō, kyōgen lost the satirical bite it might otherwise have had. It became an art form that gives an officially sanctioned place to the eruption of disorder but at the same time keeps that disorder exactly *in place*. It therefore, paradoxically, reinforces order and regularity. This process has been brilliantly and persuasively demonstrated by Victor Turner in his studies of antistructure, which he shows can really mean "something positive, a generative center."[30] Especially through ritualization, according to Turner, disorder can be accounted for and given its "place" rather than repressed and denied: "Cognitively, nothing underlies regularity so well as absurdity or paradox. Emotionally, nothing satisfies as much as extravagant or temporarily permitted illicit behavior. Rituals of status reversal accomodate both aspects. By making the low high and the high low, they reaffirm the hierarchical principle. By making the low mimic (often to the point of caricature) the behavior of the high, and by restraining the initiatives of the proud, they underline the reasonableness of everyday culturally predictable behavior between the various estates of society."[31]

James L. Peacock has explored the drama of contemporary Java in a similar fashion;[32] he has especially noted that, in drama viewed as a form of public ritual, there is a complex but fascinating interplay between "high" and "low" elements in society.

The audience gets a . . . kick out of interplay between low and high, as when Semar caricatures Prince Ardjuna. The response is not simply delight that the patrician is mocked or bested; an inappropriately gross triumph of a proletarian clown is censored even by a proletarian audience because the aristocrat represents ideals common to all classes. Rather, the opposition between high and low acquires added meaning through the richness of the permutation and combination of the two categories; the clown reduces high to low, transcends the high while adhering to the low, plays a counterpoint to the high, and performs other symbolic manipulations that enliven the basic opposition in the minds of its perceivers while demonstrating its fundamental unity. Though the Javanese enjoy the clown and transvestite partly because they break taboos, release tensions, and permit the disorderly mixing of normally segregated categories, they also appreciate these figures, I would suggest, because they demonstrate the underlying unity of the cosmology, a unity which, through mysticism and other means, the Javanese have traditionally sought with fervor.[33]

Peacock thus agrees with Turner that such a ritualization of the theater is fundamentally a rite of reversal taking place in the public arena; it both says something about society and does something within it. This explanation of the relationship between serious and comic theater goes considerably beyond psychological explanations and sees comic theater as much more than a context for "letting off steam."[34]

Nō and kyōgen have a close connection both in conception and in performance; they are interdependent. If kyōgen is social drama that demonstrates that at bottom there is something terribly arbitrary and unjust about the distinctions and ordering of ordinary society, nō, by virtue of the way it enfolds kyōgen as an interlude within it, for a long time prevented that insight from becoming a bitter or sustained protest against the way society is constituted. In kyōgen, a master may be a fool whose wits would in no way qualify him for his position in society; but in the high mimetic mode of nō, the nobility, especially if they are great personages in history, pay the price for their status with uncommon suffering and grief. The result of boldly interpreting the *combination* of kyōgen and nō as a view of society might be as follows: Indeed, there *is* something arbitrary about the structure of society on one level, but viewed from another perspective, the hierarchy of society has its legitimacy since it is only relative and since, most fundamentally, all sentient beings are moving equally toward the goal of universal Buddhahood.

In medieval Japan Mahayana thought pursued a path of relativizing, and implicitly leveling a critique against, the hierarchical cosmology of Buddhism; but it continued to hold cosmological and dialectical versions of Buddhist teaching in some form of tension. The collapse of the division between samsara and nirvana had potentially devastating implications for certain versions of Karma and the rokudō, and for the hierarchical arrangement of society that could be seen as matched to these concepts. During what I have called the high medieval of Buddhist thought in Japan, conceptual moves were being made to equalize and coordinate unequal and disparate elements of human experience. It was a time when Buddhist thought, following its own dialectic, was moving toward an intellectual and religious egalitarianism. It thus had to regard even the received set of Buddhist symbols with a grain of salt; it had to subject their usual seriousness to a profane consciousness that had itself arisen out of Mahayana thought.

It was in this context that certain monks, with a strong sense that they were standing firm in the tradition, engaged in behavior and entertained thoughts that in an earlier era would have seemed flagrantly impious, unorthodox, and disruptive. Stories abound from both China and Japan about the eccentricities and antics of such monks, especially in the Zen tradition, and they were no doubt exaggerated in the retelling.[35] Nevertheless, they are representative of a Buddhist way of thinking that felt free to criticize the older modes of Buddhist piety and to play with them. It is not difficult to see some of the antics of the shrewder characters in the kyōgen theater as very like those of the humorous, often uninhibited, "crazy" monks.

It was probably in the Muromachi period that this tendency was most readily and freely expressed. A paradigmatic figure in this may have been the Rinzai priest Ikkyū (1394-1581), a monk who tried to fashion a mode of life in keeping with his understanding of the greater depth of Mahayana dialectical thinking. In contrast, the Tokugawa period and its most representative Buddhists seem to have stepped back from the more radical implications—at least in the world of behavior and action—of the Mahayana dialectic.

It may be that the Tokugawa period—for whatever social and political reasons—represented a reversion to the earlier Buddhist paradigm, one that was articulated in the *Wu-men kuan's* account of the advice of Pai-chang to the old monk reborn as a fox: "The enlightened man does not ignore causation." There can be no doubt that the official doctrines of society in the Tokugawa period garnered intellectual and religious support from a renewed respect for the truth of karma and from a fear of the dire effects that might come from ignoring it. The paradigmatic Buddhist thinker of the Tokugawa period may very well have been Bankei (Eitaku) (1622-1693), who, although an articulate monk of Rinzai Zen, was very different from Ikkyū, devoting much of his intellectual energies to demonstrating the internal coherence between the Buddhist dharma and Confucian views such as filial piety.

In such an intellectual and social climate, the role of nō was cast largely in terms of an artistic adumbration of a structured cosmos ruled by notions of order and hierarchy; and kyōgen, the dis-ordered alternative, was given its ludic moment on stage. It told briefly the tale of an idiotic, unorderly world and then was heard no more—or at least this was the object of enfolding it in nō's larger, more important, world of order and established place.

8

THE POET AS SEER:
BASHŌ LOOKS BACK

> . . . the meaning of a poem can only be a
> poem, but *another poem—a poem not itself.*
> —Harold Bloom, *The Anxiety of Influence*

T HIS CHAPTER, WHICH takes a retrospective look at the ideas and issues
of the previous chapters, analyzes a piece of prose that is itself reflective
and retrospective. It is by Matsuo Bashō (1644–1694), widely regarded as Japan's finest poet, from his *Oku no hosomichi*, or *Narrow Road to
the Far North*. Although the work itself is well-known, I think Bashō hid away
in a rather dense section of text some things that, once excavated, help to reveal
how he himself looked back on his literary and Buddhist heritage.

First, however, it might be of benefit to consider again the assumption made
throughout this book that the medieval period of Japan is best viewed in terms
of a strong *conflation* of the religious and literary dimensions of human
experience. Since some might still dispute the justification for this point of
view, insisting that religion and literature occupy separate territories and have
intrinsically different subjects and modes of understanding, I would like for a
moment to defend it both in terms of our present understanding of the history of
the various academic disciplines and in terms of what I perceive to be a quite
special emphasis in Japan regarding this matter.

Until very recently it was an unchallenged assumption in the Western
university that the various intellectual disciplines were separated into spheres of
scrutiny according to lines that were natural, necessary, and rational. Thus,

sociology was, or ought to be, separate from the natural sciences, psychology from philosophy, religion from the arts, and so forth. Although it was granted that there were nodal points where interests merged, the so-called interdisciplinary studies that focused on such academic hyphens were considered to be ad hoc arrangements that in no way disturbed the inevitability of the basic separation of spheres.

Recently, Stephen Toulmin has challenged this. Looking at their historical evolution, he sees the various disciplines as changing "conceptual populations."[1] There is nothing necessary and inherently rational in the divisions that exist; fission and hybridization go on all the time. Social factors—that is, the influence of members of existing professions—rather than intellectual factors, often prevent the creation of new subdisciplines.[2]

The implications of this for the study of non-Western civilizations are quite profound. Toulmin himself suggests how this approach can illuminate the specificity of China's scientific history.[3] Understanding need not proceed according to the intellectual distinctions currently accepted in our own academy. Other paradigms are possible and may carry the weight of tradition in another culture. The study of Japanese civilization provides an interesting case in point. It has already been nicely clarified by Joseph M. Kitagawa; for one of the most valuable insights into Japanese culture is Kitagawa's insistence that in Japanese history there is a tradition of refusal to bifurcate elements that might be thought naturally divisible. Thus, already in early times the Japanese ". . . did not draw a line of demarcation between the sacred and profane dimensions of life, or between *matsuri* (religious rituals) and *matsuri-goto* (political administration), both of which were ultimately under the authority of the emperor who himself was directed by the divine will."[4] In his studies of *kokutai*, the "national community," Kitagawa has richly documented this tradition.[5]

Likewise, aesthetic and religious experience merged easily in Japan from early times. Kūkai (774–835) made this a central aspect of Japanese Buddhism, according to Kitagawa: "Kūkai in presenting religion as art represented the central core of Japanese piety, and in this he may be rightly regarded as a paradigmatic figure of Japanese religious history."[6] The weight of tradition is thus on the side of the assimilation and mergence of the two spheres. And Japan seems to be a civilization in which the new is usually added to the old without greatly displacing it. Watsuji Tetsurō termed this the "stadiality" of Japanese culture, the adding of new levels while retaining earlier ones.[7] Kitagawa's *Religion in Japanese History* richly and systematically demonstrates how all the religious experience of the past is valued in some way rather than jettisoned just because something new appears on the scene.

The refusal to bifurcate spheres is heuristically valuable for understanding the specificity of Japanese intellectual history. The point is that refusal does not imply inability; rather, the possibility of making a separation is understood, envisioned, and *rejected*. For instance, the complex intellectual tools devised in the medieval period to articulate Buddhism and Shinto as the two Janus faces of one phenomenon—tools such as *honji-suijaku* and *ryōbu-shintō*—presuppose a recognition that potentially the two religions were divisible. More than likely, the type of dialectic developed especially in Shingon and Tendai Buddhism, according to which full understanding encompasses an underlying relatedness, shaped these intellectual developments.[8] To Buddhism the notion of *sui generis* would be a conceptual error, implying a "self-existent being" and thus clearly in conflict with the teaching of *anatman* and of *pratīya-samutpāda*. Perhaps this great part of the Japanese tradition that refuses categorical bifurcations is evidence of how deeply the Buddhist style of thinking was integrated into the national experience. The interesting thing is that, according to our evidence, the coexistence between Buddhism and Shinto was not due to a naive inability to make distinctions or an easy-going syncretism that served as a substitute for real thought. This was, on the contrary, a way of viewing things arrived at through historical experience and the development of arguments. The postulation of fundamental oneness and indivisibility was made *after* entertaining the thought of separation and division.

Exactly how nonbifurcation operates in the Japanese context and why it is important for understanding traditional Japan is best understood by looking closely at a specific case in which it can be clearly seen that the Japanese tradition is one of refusal to make an understood distinction. At the nexus of religion and art, called by Kitagawa "the central core of Japanese piety" lies a less than opaque prose passage and one haiku verse by the great poet Bashō (1644–1694). My focus on them will be textual and historical, borrowing some of the techniques of structural analysis in order to understand and comment on the specific character of the *Oku no hosomichi*, especially on how, in this passage of the work, Bashō consciously reflects on his own received tradition.

The passage is short but dense. In the *Oku no hosomichi* the poet on pilgrimage, Bashō, has just passed the barrier at Shirakawa. He has gone through the town of Sukagawa and stands at its edge. I translate the crucial section as follows:

On the edge of this post-town was a great chestnut tree, in the shade of which a world-despising monk had taken his refuge.
I mused that this might be the very mountain where once was written a

poem about "picking up horse-chestnuts." With something in hand to write on, I jotted down the following:

> "The Chinese written character for *chestnut* is comprised of *west* and *tree* and is, therefore, linked up with Amida's Paradise in the West. This is why Gyōgi Bosatsu all throughout his lifetime used the wood of this tree both for his walking stick and for the pillar supports of his house.
>
> Men of the world
> Fail to see its blossoms:
> Chestnut of the eaves."[9]

The passage contains a rich lode of images and ideas, all related to one another through Bashō's literary genius. In explicating it, an initial warning by Makoto Ueda is apropos. Ueda summarized contemporary Japanese scholarship on Bashō by pointing out that Bashō's craft was such that he would often omit materials and change the facts of his experience in order to "present his theme more effectively";[10] therefore, everything counts in a passage by Bashō. There are no throw-aways or gratuitous bits of unassimilated information.

Bashō presents his theme immediately, if implicitly. The setting is not background but rather the introduction of his subject. His statement that he is standing at the edge or outskirts "katawara" of the town announces that the forthcoming passage will be about putting distance between one thing and another. This is followed by the introduction of the "world-despising monk" and the "chestnut tree." At this point all of what will follow is already present in embryo: chestnuts and world-rejection will pervade the passage. Also significant is the mention of the monk as having "taken his refuge" under the tree; dependency and reliance ("tanomu") will be important. And the image of a monk seeking shelter under a tree is thick with associations in the Buddhist tradition. In the classical portrayal, Śākyamuni's enlightenment took place under a protective tree, the so-called bodhi tree, or *ficus religiosa*. No Buddhist would miss the allusion. Furthermore, there is quite likely an association between the coolness sought under the tree and the Buddhist nirvana, which was classically described in terms of coolness. These associations make it clear that the place of refreshment is by implication also one of practice; it is a multiple "refuge."

At this point, as Bashō tells it, a "snippet" of verse enters his mind. And a snippet is precisely what it is; Bashō provides his readers with only two words: "tochi hirou," "picking up [horse] chestnuts." Critical scholarship is generally agreed that the obscure allusion is to a poem by Saigyō. The two words are lifted from a verse that Bashō's readers, steeped in the literary tradition, would have recognized. The original poem by Saigyō and my translation are as follows:

yama fukami	Deep wooded mountain—
iwa ni shitataru	Water dripping off the rocks
mizu tomemu	Gets to be a puddle
katsukatsu otsuru	While I pick up now-and-then
tochi hirou hodo	Falling horse chestnuts.[11]

Bashō lets his prose flow on, taking no notice of the fact that Saigyō had written about horse chestnuts (*tochi*), whereas his own discussion refers to a different variety, the ordinary chestnut (*kuri*). The two species merge into one as a result of poetic license; but perhaps their merging also reinforces the envisioned assimilation of Bashō's location and experience with that of Saigyō, the poet of the twelfth century he most admired and sought to emulate.

Bashō's identification with Saigyō is, as we shall see, much more than sentiment; it will function as the kingpin of the verbal structure of this passage. For Bashō characteristically viewed Saigyō as the monk-poet of an earlier epoch who had mastered the art of world-rejection. This is present in the mere mention of "tochi," "horse chestnuts." Concerning them Makoto Ueda writes:

> These [horse] chestnuts are not of an ordinary variety; they are only found deep in the mountains. . . . Unlike ordinary chestnuts they are not very tasty; in fact, to be edible they have to be cooked. It is obvious, then, that they symbolize wild, untouched nature seldom glimpsed by those who are busy pursuing their pleasures in the "floating world."[12]

The original poem by Saigyō was therefore one in which he portrayed himself in quite straightened circumstances. Deep in the mountains, literally very distant from urban society or the world, he was picking up a less than savory nut. Moreover, the horse chestnuts were falling from the tree only infrequently ("katsukatsu") and the poet meanwhile was likely getting wet from the dripping water. Obviously, the world-despiser knows hardships, cumulative ones. But, in the passage by Bashō, the motif of world-rejection, the note of distance implicit from the very first words, is now greatly reinforced. The theme continues to exfoliate.

Having at this point moved the imagined location far beyond the outskirts of Sukagawa to somewhere "deep in the mountains," Bashō says he felt moved to respond to the situation by writing something down. The remainder of the passage is this bit of prose and one haiku, both internal to the larger piece. What Bashō writes is quite remarkable. It consists of a sustained reverie on the orthography of the Chinese character for *chestnut*, *kuri* in Japanese. It strikes Bashō as terribly significant that *chestnut* is an ideograph composed of two basic radicals. That is, when written, *kuri* is made up of the radical meaning *west* superscribed on the one meaning *tree*. For Bashō, or at least for his literary invention, this is marvelous good fortune. It suits him well—as it later did Ezra Pound and Ernest Fenollosa—to take the written Chinese character as a medium for poetry and to see it as made up of solely semantic elements.[13] He reasons, at least for his literary purposes, as follows: If *chestnut* is comprised of *west* and *tree*, it can legitimately be called the "tree of the west" and is thus linked up with "Amida's Paradise in the West" (Saihō Jōdo). This flagrant non sequitur is a literary find for Bashō. His prose holds that the ideography contains a hidden etiology of the item it represents. Thus, the character reveals the origins of the tree; it tells that it originally derived from the Paradise of Amida. It is then really a sacred tree even when it grows in this, the profane, world. With this suggested, the reason Bashō has found a Buddhist monk taking refuge under such a tree is clear. Characteristic traditional phrases about "taking refuge in Amida's grace" lie in the background of all this.

Though the name *Saigyō* never explicitly appears, it becomes critically important in a similar fashion. Because it is written with two characters, *sai* referring to "west" and *gyō* indicating "go" or "going," Bashō is able to do verbal magic with it. Without ever surfacing explicitly in the text, it is the fulcrum. Moreover, by not making the reference to the name overt, Bashō has crafted an extraordinary device for recapitulating and reinforcing his motif of the hidden ones who are removed from the "world" where they could easily be seen. Bashō has literally hidden Saigyō away in his text. An application of literary skills is required for finding him there, but once he is discovered, it is clear that he is all-important for the text in which he appears only faintly and indirectly.

The architectonics of this passage are so subtle that it is necessary to move forward and backward in it—and repeatedly at that; but before going on with the exegesis, a brief look at the underlying structure of theme and composition is in order. On the assumption that everything counts and there are no throw-aways in Bashō's writing, we can sketch the basic structure in terms of a progressive elaboration on the theme of placing distance between a position *A* and a position *B*. "Placing distance" might also be called "going." Thus, the poet's literal movement from the post-town to the chestnut tree on the edge of town is already an anticipation of the monk discovered there who is described as a rejector of the world, that is, as one who has put distance between himself and society. Chestnuts remind the poet of horse chestnuts and that, in turn, of

Saigyō, a world-renouncing monk. His name means "going west," that is, putting distance between here and there, and in explicitly religious terms, between the secular world and Amida's Western Paradise.

Schematically, the progression of ideas would be as follows—the conceptual affinities run both horizontally and vertically:

A or "here"	distancing/going	B or "there"
1. post-town	[a going]	edge [of town]; chestnut tree
2. world/society	rejecting	[monk under the tree]
3.	[away in mountains]	horse-chestnuts
4. [the world]	going	west = Saigyō
5.		west's tree = chestnut
6. world/society	distance	Western Paradise of Amida

Not only is the movement in the text a many-layered one between the poles A and B but under each of these two rubrics, when considered vertically, each element also has direct links to the others in the set.

We return to the text at the point where the poet has suggested that *chestnut* is rightly written as it is, since it derives from Amida's Paradise in the West. It continues: "This is why Gyōgi Bosatsu all throughout his lifetime used the wood of this tree both for his walking stick and for the pillar supports of his house." The rationale implied in "This is why" is not exactly limpid. To grasp it, some background concerning "Gyōgi Bosatsu" is essential. Gyōgi, encountered previously in our discussion of the *Nihon ryoi-ki*, lived from 670 to 749. He was one of the most fascinating and enigmatic figures of early Japanese history.[14] He was a holy man who lived at a time when Buddhism was still a rather new arrival to Japan from the continent and was still mainly confined to the elite and literate classes. Early in his career, Gyōgi apparently was as much a shaman as a Buddhist—and a preacher among the masses rather than a monastic and scholar. In fact, he was viewed with considerable apprehension and alarm by both the government and the Buddhist hierarchy. In 717, when he was forty-seven years old, he was arrested for his activities.

Old age brought a sudden change in Gyōgi's fortune, however. In 745 he was adopted by the government and made an archbishop (*daisōjō*). By this decision the support of the masses was marshaled for imperial and ecclesiastical projects. Kitagawa notes: "The fact that Gyōgi, who had neither training abroad nor ecclesiastical standing in the Buddhist hierarchy, was suddenly elevated to the position of archbishop, bypassing all ecclesiastical dignitaries, indicates how eager the court was to secure the cooperation and support of the masses for the project of erecting the image of the Lochana Buddha.''[15] Gyōgi assisted actively in the promotion of this project but died three years before the image was dedicated at an ''eye opening'' ceremony in the great temple Tōdaiji, in the capital at Nara.

Exactly what Bashō knew of Gyōgi is impossible to determine. From this brief mention of him, however, we can single out three things of importance. The first is that Bashō was aware of Gyōgi's reputation as a devotee of Amida. Although there may be some historical question concerning to what degree Gyōgi was an Amidist, there is no doubt that later traditions recognized him as such. The phenomenal growth of Amidist pietism in later centuries may have exaggerated Gyōgi's Amidist role due to his fame; but by the time of Bashō no one had any doubt: Gyōgi was the ancient Amidst par excellence. In this section from Bashō's *Oko no hosomichi*, the link is evident; Amida has been mentioned and Gyōgi the archaic Amidist fits in naturally.

The second detectable item is Bashō's awareness of Gyōgi's reputation as a saint who *walked* extensively. Materials at our disposal suggest that Gyōgi walked among the common people, to whom he preached and for whom he constructed bridges, canals and the like. The important thing for Bashō is that the great sage led an ambulatory life. He capitalizes on a legend about Gyōgi's use of chestnut wood for a walking-stick in order to establish a natural ''fit'': the Amidist sage walked about with the help of a stick made of a kind of wood that means ''tree of the Western [Paradise]'' when analyzed as a written character.[16] Implicit in this motif of Gyōgi as walker is, of course, the whole going/distancing structure of the entire passage. The link with Saigyō, considered one of the great peregrinating poets of the past, is also evident. And Bashō's presentation of himself as writing this while on a poetic journey completes the sequence of identifications.

A minor recapitulation and expansion of theme occurs in the reference to Gyōgi's use of chestnut wood for the support pillars in his house. There is a neat parallel between the walking-stick (''tsue'') and the pillars (''hashira''), both of which are used for support by Gyōgi; he stays close to Amida's wood whether indoors or out, whether at home or on the road. At the same time, the motif of support and reliance carries the imagery back to the opening sentence and its reference to the world-despising monk discovered seeking refuge under the chestnut tree. Between the opening line and the mention of Gyōgi there has also been the indirect glimpse—via the terse scrap from Saigyō's poem about horse chestnuts—of that poet standing in the mountains and relying there on the nuts of that tree for basic sustenance. These are all interwoven and reinforcing strands. Each in its own way, as well as the group collectively, emphasizes reliance, dependence, and being sustained.

The correspondence between Bashō's selection of images and what had come to be the central principle of Amidist piety is remarkable. It is true, as Kitagawa points out, that this piety had undergone a long development and had developed in various directions;[17] but in spite of various doctrinal and socio-religious forms, there was always in Amidism the basic and early symbolized motif of reliance and dependence upon Amida. This was translated into Amida's utter and total reliability. Bashō would not have had to explain the point to his readers: walking-sticks and pillars made of Amida's wood were eminently dependable.

There is one other, a third, thing Bashō seems to have known about Gyōgi, namely, that his reputation was that of a seer, in fact, an extraordinary one. In the *Nihon ryō-iki*, which, as we have seen, was a critically important text for the spread of Buddhism in early Japan, Gyōgi was presented as the most important religious personality. And his most distinguishing characteristic was possession of the "heavenly eye," or "penetrating eye" (*tengen*). In the *Nihon ryōi-ki* this capacity of Gyōgi for sight beyond that of ordinary people plays an important role. Because of it he can see behind immediate events to the whole karmic chain of causality that brought them into being. He is the "seer" who verifies and validates the way the system of karmic reaction takes effect; his sight transcends that of ordinary mortals and is, in fact, that of a heavenly being, the highest in the six-staged taxonomy of medieval Buddhism. His is a shamanic skill wed to the Buddhist scheme of reincarnation. With his heavenly eye Gyōgi can see the karmic chain of rebirths or incidents antecedent to any event or phenomenon witnessed in the present.

The stories about Gyōgi in the *Nihon ryōi-ki* are roughly hewn gems; they make their point directly and with minimal finesse. The following episode is one that was cited earlier to demonstrate the supernatural skill Gyōgi possessed:

> In the old capital in the village surrounding Gangō-ji, there was once a ritual gathering of Buddhists who had invited His Eminence Gyōgi to expound the dharma to them for seven days. Both clergy and laymen gathered to listen to his preaching. In the audience listening to his sermon there was one woman who had on her hair the body-oil of a wild boar. Gyōgi saw this and reproached the woman with the following words: "To me that smells awful. The woman has blood spread on her hair. Take her away from here." With that the woman was greatly ashamed and went away. Our ordinary eyes see nothing more than oil on such a woman's head. The farseeing eye of a sage, however, sees clearly the blood of the slain animal. Right here in Japan, such a one is an incarnation of the Buddha, a divine one in disguise.[18]

Gyōgi's attitude is equally imperious in another episode, one in which his penetrating eye enables him to see why a certain woman's child frets and cries incessantly during his sermons. He tells the woman to throw the child into a stream of water. The following ensues:

> Although terribly apprehensive about this, the mother could no longer stand the child's bawling and threw him into the deep stream. The child sank but then surfaced again, treading water and moving his arms about. Then he looked wide-eyed at his mother and reproached her: "How terrible! I was planning to get three more years of food out of you!" Now really dumbfounded, the woman returned to the congregation and listened again to what was being taught about the dharma. Venerable Gyōgi questioned her: "Did you throw the child away?" She said she had and went on to give the details, after which Gyōgi explained things as follows: "In a previous lifetime you borrowed from a certain man but failed to return what you received; so that man was born as your child and was finally getting repaid by getting his food from your body. In your earlier life that child was your creditor."[19]

From these episodes it is not immediately evident how Gyōgi gained his wide following among the common people. Perhaps there was an attractive charisma even in his forbidding characteristics; moreover, it cannot be doubted that his explanations made certain aspects of life and the world suddenly intelligible and even "just"—by the theodicy of karma.

Almost nine centuries—and a glaringly obvious difference in literary finesse—separate the *Nihon ryōi-ki* from Bashō's *Oku no hosomichi*. But, in spite of the profound differences, in both cases Gyōgi is presented as a seer extraordinary. I suspect that the seventeenth-century poet relied on his readers' knowledge of Gyōgi as seer to make his allusion to him more meaningful. Even in Bashō's text, Gyōgi is one who sees the true origins of the chestnut, its derivation in Amida's Western Paradise; he still sees around the corners of the ordinary, diurnal world to grasp things other men miss. By Bashō's time and through Bashō's craft, all the rusticity in the earlier account has been worn away; Gyōgi has become a gentle sage and seer.

The fact that he has remained a seer is emphasized in Bashō's text by the sudden, telling comparison between Gyōgi and the "men of the world" mentioned in the concluding haiku. The juxtaposition is swift and sharp; Gyōgi's extraordinary *sightedness* is contrasted with their abysmal *sightlessness*:

yo no hito no   Men of the world
mitsukenu hana ya   Fail to see its blossoms:
noki no kuri   Chestnut of the eaves.

The point is in the vivid contrast. Gyōgi, the holy man with an extraordinary capacity for sight, sees even the paradisal origin of the chestnut and acts accordingly, whereas men of the world (''yo no hito'') fail to see (''mitsu-kenu'') even something as obvious as the blossoms of the chestnut by the eaves. The paradox is patent: he who belongs to Amida's world also sees this one clearly, whereas those who belong only to this world see neither very well.

Although that is the general principle, its specific application is far from clear. What does it mean to Bashō to be a ''person of the world''? Would he include or exclude himself? Is it really a religious notion, or is it strictly an artistic one, in the modern sense? Moreover, is Bashō himself not surprisingly modern in spite of his citation of exemplary figures from the past and his reveries on religious symbols? These and related questions deserve some attention even if the answers must finally be left open, an invitation to further study.

In working toward tentative answers to some of these questions, we do well to recall that though Bashō is known for his travel diaries, it was not until 1684 that he made his first important journey, and only during the last decade of his life was there a close connection between his pilgrimages and his poetry. Perhaps a good deal of the motivation for his travels came, in fact, from his growing fame and from the sheer pressure of people wanting to learn the way of haiku from the age's acknowledged master. Undoubtedly, the journeys were undertaken partially in order to escape from these pressures and from the fact that society may have begun to asphyxiate Bashō's art.

There was something else involved too. Concerning the first journey, that of 1684, Makoto Ueda writes:

> He had made journeys before, but not for the sake of spiritual and poetic discipline. Through the journey he wanted, among other things, to face death and thereby to help temper his mind and his poetry. He called it ''the journey of a weatherbeaten skeleton,'' meaning that he was prepared to perish alone and leave his corpse to the mercies of the wilderness if that was his destiny. If this seems to us a bit extreme, we should remember that Bashō was of a delicate constitution and suffered from several chronic diseases, and that travel in seventeenth-century Japan was immensely more hazardous than it is today.[20]

We know from other sources—especially the journal of his companion, Sora—that Bashō was widely recognized wherever he went. Thus, there may have been some poetic hyperbole in his image of himself dying alone and unseen. But Bashō's dying—even surrounded by admirers—was clearly one of the possible consequences of the rigorous journeys.

It would be wrong, then, to picture Bashō as having merely adopted a romantic persona as a ploy to capture the sympathy and credulity of later generations. On the contrary, there is adequate evidence that during these years he suffered from anxiety about his creativity;[21] and this anxiety focused on what he took to be the necessity of escaping from social pressures and the suffocation of his art by its own success. In such circumstances, the exemplary role of the inja (literally, "hidden one"), or recluse, had great appeal. In classical times, figures such as Nōin (998–1050) and Saigyō constituted the model; they were poets and also Buddhist monks who led a comparatively ambulatory life.

For Bashō, as we have seen, Saigyō was of prime importance. What it meant to Saigyō to be an inja can be seen in some of the following materials.[22] Having served as a guard in the retinue of Retired Emperor Toba, Saigyō at age twenty-three decided to "throw the world away" ("yo o suteru"):

> During the time I was coming to a decision about leaving secular life, I was on Higashiyama with a number of people and we were composing verses expressing what we felt about the gathering mists there:

> sora ni naru   A man whose mind is
> kokoro wa haru no   At one with the sky-void steps
> kasumi nite   Inside a spring mist
> yo ni araji tomo   And begins to wonder if, perhaps,
> omoitatsu kana   He might step out of the world.[23]

It is quite clear from Saigyō's writing at the time that rejecting the world entailed both losses and gains. It was not strictly a matter of jettisoning all things of concrete value in the hope of gaining spiritual benefit. In Saigyō's case, the desire to make of world-rejection something that would be a fillip to the poetic vision clearly entered in. He traded off involvement in society in order to enrich his relationship with the natural world and to create the best conditions for his poetry.

This awareness was present when he made his initial decision; already there was a sense of the paradox:

> Written when I was petitioning Retired Emperor Toba to grant me his permission to leave secular life:

> oshimu tote   So loath to lose
> oshimarenubeki   What really should be loathed:
> kono yo kawa   One's vain place in life,
> mi o sutete koso   We maybe rescue best the self
> mi o mo tasukeme   Just by throwing it away.[24]

Running throughout Saigyō's poetry is the supposition that a world-rejecting posture is a sine qua non for the capacity for a special clairvoyance, one which is both religious and aesthetic. Saigyō repeatedly insists that he has through his reclusive life come to see the world and society in a new way:

haruka naru	Boulder-encircled
iwa no hazama ni	Empty space, so far away that
hitori ite	Here I'm all alone:
hitometsutsu made	A place where man can't view me
monoomowabaya	But I can review all things.[25]

The implication seems to be that according to Saigyō's set of values it is only by the conscious positioning of one's self within the depths of the forest—in spite of the loneliness and suffering this entails—that focus and perspective can be gained. Distance from society is necessary in order to understand even it; by contrast, proximity to the world leads to certain blindness.

That it is the "worldly" man who is blind is the notion that impressed Bashō. It made increasing sense to him as he grew older and as its paradoxes seemed verified by his own experience. As he (literally) moved in the ambit of the religious pilgrim, he discovered that his poetic vision was newly stimulated. The linkage between movement and vision is important. From the Buddhist perspective, the danger in worldliness lies in its false fixity, its refusal to live in accordance with the underlying movement and mutability (mujō) of all things. The advantage in world-rejection lies in the mobility it provides and the clairvoyance that comes from this. This seems congruent with the point made by Hans Jonas that, in the case of sight, the cognitive feat depends on movement: "We should not be able to 'see' if we had not previously moved."[26]

Given that so much of the most important imagery in classical Buddhism is of sight and vision, it is easy to see how in the Buddhist structure there was a nexus between enlightenment (however defined) and the practice of pilgrimage. The mundane is not so much evil as it is spiritually dangerous because easily routinized, a world of settled but seriously impaired sight. Because pilgrimage breaks the charm of the ordinary, it serves the purposes of the Buddhist vision.

Of course, in such a context aesthetic vision is virtually the same thing as religious vision. In the cultural context of Japan the weight of tradition invites the two into synthesis; it is not a matter of the religious and artistic being conceptually indivisible for the medieval Japanese mind but of the two being *consciously* and *deliberately* joined. And this is the tradition into which Bashō fits as well. In the passage we have considered, his selection of both Saigyō and

Gyōgi must be more than just fortuitous. Concerning Gyōgi I have argued that he stands in the tradition of the paradigmatic seer who looks with ease into the land of the dead, moves with his penetrating eye into the complex former lives of people who stand before him, and—at least in Bashō's prose—sees the paradisal origins of natural phenomena. Gyōgi's capacity as clairvoyant is shamanic in nature; but it is wed to the cosmology of Buddhism. Kitagawa rightly considers him a very important figure and astutely observes: "It was from this tradition, the Buddhist fusion with primitive shamanism and divination, that the creative impulse was elicited in the Heian period as well as in the subsequent history of Japanese religion."[27] Bashō, too, tapped into, and gave renewed life to that creative impulse.

The juxtaposition and mergence of Gyōgi with Saigyō in the same passage of the *Oko no hosomichi* reinforces the same points from within the tradition of the Buddhist inja, the monk who is not only seer but also poetic visionary. Thus, in Bashō's prose the two stand together to form one paradigm, that of the visionary who is simultaneously religious and aesthetic.

It remains to ask to what extent Bashō's very self-consciousness about all this is really an indication that he might be more modern than medieval. In Japanese scholarship there is considerable discussion about whether Bashō, in spite of his seventeenth-century dates, is the quintessential medieval figure or someone in whom something distinctively modern can be discerned.[28] My approach would be to ask whether the distinction between medieval and modern might not be less sharp in Japanese history than it is in the West. The materials we have considered suggest the following observations.

First, when Gyōgi (of the eighth century), Saigyō (of the twelfth century), and Bashō (of the seventeenth century) are compared, there are some areas in which there seems more affinity of world view between the latter two than between the former. Whereas Gyōgi's vision is literally supernatural and "miraculous" through his possession of a shamanic ability assimilated to the *siddhi* or "powers" of classical Buddhism, Saigyō and Bashō both live in a world of relatively reduced and "naturalized" epistemic possibilities. This is to say that some of the features we in the West ordinarily associate with the naturalistic perspective of modernity are already present, at least implicitly, in the world of the twelfth-century Saigyō. Karma, rebirth, and the rest are there, of course, in Saigyō's world as they are in that of Bashō; and dreams are full of revelatory possibilities. But no claims are made for a clairvoyance enabling one to see into the details of other lives and into the Paradise of Amida. Thus, modernity has come more as a gradual and gentle change of perspective than a crisis necessitating a radical critique of the religiously shaped episteme.[29]

This agrees with my second observation, namely, that the image of the artist/poet as religious seer carries the weight of the Japanese medieval tradition and is not, as is its counterpart in the West, a distinctively modern phenomenon.[30] In the West the emphasis on the poet as *vates*, or "seer," is largely an aspect of developing Romanticism. It is a synthesis that came into being after the Renaissance and the growth of science had already radically changed the episteme of the West. For, as M. H. Abrams has so clearly demonstrated in his *Natural Supernaturalism*, Romanticism "took shape during the age of revolutions,"[31] an idea expressed within a year of the fall of the Bastille by the philosopher C. L. Reinhold who then wrote: " . . . the most striking and distinctive characteristics of the spirit of our age is a convulsion of all hitherto known systems, theories, and modes of conception, of an inclusiveness and depth unexampled in the history of the human spirit."[32]

It was in such a context of revolution and change that, according to Abrams, the poet was seen by the Romantics as a seer: " . . . to the Romantic poet, all depends upon his mind as it engages with the world in the act of perceiving. Hence the extraordinary stress throughout this era on the eye and the object and the relation between them."[33] In an important sense the poet was to receive and revivify religious functions from an archaic past. So Carlyle, in discussing "The Hero as Poet," expands on the significance of the Latin term *vates*, which he takes to mean poet, prophet, and seer. And Ruskin expresses something very close to what we have observed in the medieval Japanese tradition when he writes: "The greatest thing a human soul ever does in this world is to *see* something, and tell what it *saw* in a plain way. . . . To see clearly is poetry, prophecy, and religion—all in one . . . ; [it is to be] a Seer."[34]

The parallel with the Japanese counterpart is interesting; but there is also a striking difference, inasmuch as the "seeing" function in the case of the Romantic poets of the West takes on the prophetic role as well, which on the one hand makes it the inheritor of a weighty Western tradition and, on the other, links it historically to the revolutionary events of the modern Western experience. For, as Abrams points out: " . . . at the formative period of their lives, major Romantic poets—including Wordsworth, Blake, Southey, Coleridge, and later, after his own fashion, Shelley—shared the hope in the French Revolution as the portent of universal felicity, as did Hölderlin and other young radicals in Germany."[35] Even when these millennarian expectations were disappointed, "Romantic thinking and imagination remained apocalyptic thinking and imagination, though with varied changes in explicit content."[36] So strong was this interest in historical events of the future that in Wordsworth even the figure of the hermit is made meaningful as the survivor of some future deluge and catastrophe—and as such becomes "the prophetic figure *par excellence.*"[37]

The role of the Buddhist seer, by comparison, is less related to the events of a specific epoch. In the case of Gyōgi, clairvoyance was thought to extend into the past so as to make visible the shape of karmic patterns. But even more typical is the insistence of poets such as Bashō that our greatest loss lies in failing to see the natural things near at hand and before our eyes. Being attached to the world leads to such an occlusion of the eye and mind.

Whatever modernization has meant in Japan, it seems not to have been accompanied by the same motif of a revolutionary sweeping away of the past. The language used to describe the changes of modernity has not been pervaded by notions of radicality and intensity. And this difference is perhaps not a minor one, a slight variation from the western pattern; it may indeed have made the whole process of becoming modern significantly and interestingly different from ours. Shaped by its own specific tradition, the Japanese experience deserves continuous attention and study.

NOTES

1. *"Floating Phrases and Fictive Utterances"*

* Arthur Waley, *The Life and Times of Po Chü-i, 772−846*, p. 207. My colleague Shirleen S. Wong helped me locate the original in Pai Chü-i, *Pai-shih Ch'ang-ch'ing chi*, vol. 2, p. 921.

1. Eugenio Montale, "Xenia," p. 329.

2. Saigyō, poem no. 2103 in *Sanka-shū*. Also in Ishida Yoshisada, *Shinkokin-waka-shū* as poem no. 1844. Translation in my *Mirror for the Moon: A Selection of Poems by Saigyō (1118−1190)*, p. 85. Kawada Jun estimated that this poem was written in or around the year 1180. If so, Tankai, who had been a longtime friend of Saigyō, had already been dead for six years. See Watanabe Tamotsu, *Saigyō Sanka-shū zenchūkai*, p. 1053.

3. Calculations at the time were as follows: It was widely, although erroneously, assumed that Śākyamuni had died 3,000 years prior to the year 1052—that is, 1,000 years for the period of pristine dharma and 2,000 years for that of the counterfeit dharma. In Japan it seemed to many that the third period, that of the finalized dharma (*mappō* or *masse*), must have begun in 1052 because during that year the Shingon temple Chōkoku-ji (popularly known as Hase-dera) burned to the ground. This was also a period during which the military was gaining increased power, and there was considerable violence on the part of mercenaries hired by temples (so-called warrior monks [*sōhei*]).

4. For instance, in his "Bendōwa" Dōgen wrote: "Those who are in the schools that stress doctrines like to make much of terminology and the various aspects of things, but in the true Mahayana there is no differentiating of 'true dharma,' 'counterfeit dharma,' and 'finalized dharma.' This is to say that those who practice the way also realize it." Dōgen, "Bendowa," p. 91. Translation mine.

5. See Jien, *The Future and the Past: A Translation and Study of the Gukanshō, an Interpretative History of Japan Written in 1219*. See also Charles H. Hambrick, "Gukanshō: A Religious View of History."

6. Poem no. 970 in *Sanka-shū*. Trans. in my *Mirror for the Moon*, p. 45.

7. See especially Fung Yu-lan, *A History of Chinese Philosophy*, 2:321−325 for materials from the *Wei-shi Erh-shih Lun*, which was important in the Hossō school in Japan and undoubtedly is the basis for much of this discussion of the relationship between dreams and reality.

8. Poem no. 1606 in *Sanka-shū*. Trans. in my *Mirror for the Moon*, p. 68.

9. Minamoto Takakuni, *Konjaku-monogatari-shū*, 22: 52−53. Translation in Marian Ury, *Tales of Times Now Past, Sixty-Two Stories from a Medieval Japanese Collection*, pp. 30−31.

10. See Kyōkai, *Miraculous Stories from the Japanese Buddhist Tradition: The Nihon Ryōiki of the Monk Kyōkai*, trans. Kyoko Motomochi Nakamura, pp. 280–283.

11. One of the most important discussions of this problem as experienced by Saigyō is that by Ienaga Saburō in his *Nihon shisōshi ni okeru shūkyōteki shizenkan no tenkai*, especially p. 14 ff. For a summary of Ienaga's position and an analysis from a different point of view, see part 2 of my "Saigyō and the Buddhist Value of Nature." For a comprehensive account of ways in which various people in this period handled the problem, see Herbert Plutschow, "Is Poetry a Sin? *Honjisuijaku* and Buddhism versus Poetry." The voluminous literature on this in Japanese is cited at appropriate places in the following pages. A work of particular value, however, is Manaka Fujiko, *Kokubungaku ni sesshu sareta Bukkyō*. I am grateful to Professor Konishi Jin'ichi for directing me to this work.

12. Plutschow, "Poetry a Sin," p. 207.

13. Po was so revered in Japan that stories about an imagined journey of his from China to Japan came into being and even became the subject of a nō play; see "Haku Rakuten" in Arthur Waley, *The Nō Plays of Japan*, 248–257.

14. See Nagai Giken, "Kyōgen kigo ni tsuite" and Shirato Waka, "Kyōgen kigo ni tsuite." An important related essay is Yamada Shōsen, "Chūseigoki ni okeru waka-soku-darani no jissen."

15. It is found, for instance, in the opening sentences of the *Shaseki-shū* and rendered as "mots fous" and "langage raffiné" by Hartmut O. Rotermund in his translation (Mujū Ichien, *Collection de sable et de pierres: Shasekishū*, p. 41). See also note 3 above.

16. For a discussion of the need for this, see Conrad Totman, "English-Language Studies of Medieval Japan: An Assessment."

17. Konishi Jin'ichi, for instance, defines the medieval period, or "chūsei," in Japan as extending from the tenth to the nineteenth century. "Chūsei to gendai," *Kokubungaku* 18, 11 (September 1973):34 ff. See also his *Michi: chūsei no rinen*.

18. See my discussion of this in the introduction to *Mirror for the Moon*, pp. xiii-xxvi.

19. Maruyama Shūichi, *Honji-suijaku*.

20. Kyōkai, *Nihon ryōi-ki*, pp. 52–53. Translation mine.

21. Kūkai, *Kōbō Daishi chosaku zenshū*, 3: 76–78. Translation by Yoshito S. Hakeda, in *Kūkai: Major Works*, pp. 138–139.

22. Tetsuo Najita, *Japan: The Intellectual Foundations of Modern Japanese Politics*, p. 27. Masao Maruyama points out that the study of Neo-Confucian thought had been the preserve of Zen monks earlier in Japan, but they had made it conform to Buddhist doctrines. Now, however, thinkers such as Fujiwara Seika (1561–1619) and Hayashi Razan (1583–1657) forsook the Buddhism of their families and came to criticize it. (Masao Maruyama, *Studies in the Intellectual History of Tokugawa Japan*, pp. 13–14). With respect to National Learning, or Kokugaku, H. D. Harootunian sees it—rightly, I think—as a nativism that "represents the invention or 'eruption' of a new mode of discourse." See his "The Consciousness of Archaic Form in the New Realism of Kokugaku." Quote p. 63. It was, at least according to the arguments of Toshio Kuroda, not until this late date that a Confucian theory of Shinto and the National Learning School made it possible for Shinto to be perceived by the Japanese as an

independent religion. Throughout the medieval period Shinto was drawn "into the Buddhist system as one segment of it, and its religious content was replaced with Buddhist doctrine, particularly *mikkyō* and Tendai philosophy." (Toshio Kuroda, "Shinto in the History of Japanese Religion," p. 11).

23. Many fine examples of this are displayed in John M. Rosenfield, Fumiko E. Cranston, and Edwin A. Cranston, *The Courtly Tradition in Japanese Art and Literature: Selections from the Hofer and Hyde Collections.*

24. Sei Shōnagon, *The Pillow Book of Sei Shōnagon*, trans. Ivan Morris, pp. 53 and 233.

25. *Taishō-shinshū-Daizō-kyō* (hereafter cited as *T*), 9.1 ff.

26. *T* 14.537 ff.

27. This is especially clear from Hayami Tasuku's fine study, *Heian kizoku shakai to Bukkyō.*

28. An example of this "veneer" theory is Shuichi Kato, *A History of Japanese Literature: The First Thousand Years.*

29. Within the vast literature on this topic, see especially Victor Turner, *The Ritual Process: Structure and Anti-Structure*; Mary Douglas, *Natural Symbols: Explorations in Cosmology*, pp. 19—39; and John Skorupski, *Symbol and Theory: A Philosophical Study of Theories of Religion in Social Anthropology*, pp. 161—173.

30. See Yuasa Yasuo, *Shintai: Tōyōteki shinjin-ron no kokoromi.*

31. *Kōbō Daishi chosaku zenshū* 1:41—58; translation in Kūkai, *Kūkai: Major Works*, trans. Hakeda, pp. 225—234.

32. See especially Alasdair MacIntyre, "Epistemological Crises, Dramatic Narrative, and the Philosophy of Science."

33. This is not to deny that there are times when the didactic element is a formal exercise to meet the demands of a censor or may even be ironically intended.

34. *T* 32.576, b and c. Translation by Yoshito S. Hakeda, *The Awakening of Faith Attributed to Aśvaghosha.*

35. This phrase appears in Japanese literature, for instance, in chapter 55 of the *Tsurezure-gusa*; see Nishio Minoru, *Hōjō-ki, Tsurezure-gusa*, p. 218.

36. Minoru Kiyota explores the implications of this in a number of areas of Kūkai's thought and Shingon practice in his *Shingon Buddhism: Theory and Practice.*

37. Kūkai, *Kūkai: Major Works*, trans. Hakeda, p. 74.

38. See part 2 of my "Saigyō and the Buddhist Value of Nature."

39. Explained in "Bendōwa," p. 83.

40. Poem no. 1080 in *Sanka-shū*; Poem no. 1674 in *Shinkokin-shū*; Trans. in my *Mirror for the Moon*, p. 49.

41. Poem no. 363 in *Shinkokin-shū*. Translation mine.

42. Yoshitaka Iriya, "Chinese Poetry and Zen," p. 59.

2. *In and Out the Rokudō*

1. I am here applying a point made by Alasdair MacIntyre, namely, that the move from medieval to modern in the West was one in which "the specific character of religion becomes clearer at the cost of diminishing its content." Alasdair MacIntyre, "Is Understanding Religion Compatible with Believing?"

2. Max Weber, *The Religion of India: The Sociology of Hinduism and Buddhism*. p. 121.

3. The most important study of this topic to date in a Western language is Paul Mus, *La lumière sur les six voies: tableau de la transmigration bouddhiques*. Mus's study deals primarily with Sanskrit sources. Note that a virtually synonymous term for *liu-tao/rokudō* in East Asia is *liu-ch'ü/rokushu*.

4. *T* 9.2c. Leon Hurvitz, trans., *Scripture of the Lotus Blossom of the Fine Dharma*, p. 5.

5. *T* 32.579.c. Yoshito S. Hakeda, trans., *The Awakening of Faith Attributed to Aśvaghosa*, p. 70.

6. *T* 46.15.b.

7. *T* 48.293.a.

8. *T* 84.42.a and 84.57.c. Genshin, "Genshin's Ojo Yoshu: Collected Essays on Birth into Paradise," trans. A. K. Reischauer, p. 26 ff.

9. *T* 82.16.a. Dōgen, "Dōgen's *Bendōwa*," trans., Norman Waddell and Masao Abe, p. 134.

10. *T* 83.729.a. and 83.733.a.

11. One particularly interesting but somewhat idiosyncratic use of the rokudō is at the end of the *Heike-monogatari* in the section entitled "Rokudō no sata" ("The Passage Through the Six Realms") wherein the court lady Kenreimon-In tells the story of her lifetime as a synopsis of the whole taxonomy since during it she had gone from the heights to the depths. Takagi Ichinosuke, *Heike-monogatari-shū*, 33:434—440; and Hiroshi Kitagawa and Bruce T. Tsuchida, trans., *The Tale of the Heike*, pp. 774—779.

12. Watsuji Tetsurō, "Zoku Nihon seishinshi kenkyū," p. 394.

13. Takagi Ichinosuke, *Man'yō-shū*, 4:178—179. Translation mine.

14. See chapter 6 for a consideration of the relevance of these variations for Zeami's thought and nō drama.

15. Erik Zürcher, *The Buddhist Conquest of China: The Spread and Adaptation of Buddhism in Early Medieval China*, 1:11—12. See also Inoue Mitsusada, *Nihon kodai no kokka to Bukkyō*, p. 201 and Hayami Tasuku, *Heian kizoku shakai to Bukkyō*, p. 187 ff.

16. Translations of this work into Western languages are by Hermann Bohner, in Kyōkai, *Legenden aus der Frühzeit des japanischen Buddhismus* and by Kyoko Motomochi Nakamura, in Kyōkai, *Miraculous Stories from the Japanese Buddhist Tradition: The Nihon Ryōiki of the Monk Kyōkai*. The translations of the sections that follow are my own, however.

17. Taketori Masao, in Ienaga Saburō, ed., *Nihon Bukkyō-shi*, 1:164.

18. This would certainly be the more generally accepted view within Japanese scholarship; it is also that of Kyoko Motomochi Nakamura in her introduction to her translation and in her *Ryōi no sekai*. My hypothesis that there may be more "system" in it than meets the eye was initially proposed in my review of Nakamura's translation entitled "Kyōkai and the 'Easternization' of Japan: A Review Essay."

19. The text translated here is from the volume entitled *Nihon ryōi-ki* in the series Nihon koten bungaku taikei, pp. 54 and 55. (Hereafter cited as *NRK*). On the relationship of Kyōkai's work to the two mentioned precursors in China, see Shirato Waka, "Nihon ryōi-ki ni okeru inga-ōhō-shisō: toku ni sono keifu ni tsuite."

20. *NRK*, pp. 306 and 307.

21. Kūkai, *Kūkai: Major Works,* trans. Yoshito S. Hakeda, introduction, p. 9.

22. Joseph M. Kitagawa, "Kūkai as Master and Savior."

23. Thomas S. Kuhn, *The Structure of Scientific Revolutions.* On the way in which Kuhn's theory answers certain questions earlier posed by R. G. Collingwood and its wider use in historical studies, see Stephen Toulmin, *Human Understanding: The Collective Use and Evolution of Concepts,* especially p. 98 ff.

24. In making this distinction I am in no way suggesting that the cosmology of Buddhism was "scientific" whereas that of medieval Christianity was "religious." On the contrary, it seems to me that, on the basis of work by Wittgenstein, Quine, Kuhn, MacIntyre—in spite of their diversity—we now have ample grounds for rejecting the simplistic evolutionism in the Comptean hypothesis that some epochs are "religious" or "metaphysical" whereas others might be "scientific" or "positive."

25. Richard Gombrich finds that even before the closure of the Pali canon " . . . the very rigor of the doctrine of self-reliance had called into being an alternate, parallel system, by which there were ways out." Richard Gombrich, " 'Merit Transference' in Sinhalese Buddhism: A Case Study of the Interaction Between Doctrine and Practice," pp. 203–219.

26. *NRK*, pp. 120–121.

27. On the element of poetic justice in karma theories, see Herbert Fingarette, *The Self in Transformation: Psychoanalysis, Philosophy, and the Life of the Spirit,* pp. 171 ff.

28. *NRK*, pp. 392–397.

29. Scholars have noted the emphasis on genpō in the *Nihon ryōi-ki* in contrast to its more limited role in Chinese precursors. See, for instance, Inoue, *Nihon kodai no kokka to Bukkyō,* and Shirato, "Nihon ryōi-ki ni okeru inga-ōhō-shisō," p. 337 ff., and Kyōkai, *Miraculous Stories,* p. 32 ff.

30. *NRK*, pp. 268–271.

31. See especially Maruyama Shūichi, *Honji-suijaku* and Toshio Kuroda, "Shinto in the History of Japanese Religion." My "Saigyō and the Buddhist Value of Nature" depicts the way in which arguments for the Buddha-nature of plants and trees (*sōmoku-jōbutsu*) forged accommodation through the formal debates of this era, whereas W. Michael Kelsey's "Salvation of the Snake, the Snake of Salvation: Buddhist-Shinto Conflict and Resolution," demonstrates other ways in which this theme pervades the legendary literature of this period.

32. There is, I suspect, a good deal of verbal play in the Japanese "reading" of Kyōkai's text and in its homiletic use. Here, for instance, the subtle difference between *saru* and *sari* embodies the whole episode's depiction of changed perceptions concerning this girl. "Saru," the original appellation, was intended as a term of disgrace and implied that she was pretending, monkey-fashion, to be something she was not, that is, a sage. Later, the sari, or "ashes of the Buddha," became part of her name, a metonymy for her bodhisattva-hood. In public esteem she moved from being thought pretentious to being thought of as one who humbly hid her divine status from others. Verbal subtlety such as this is not uncommon in the *Nihon ryōi-ki.*

33. *NRK*, pp. 368–371.

34. *NRK*, pp. 134–137. This fits naturally into accounts of En no Gyōja as the founder of the Shugendō.

35. *NRK*, pp. 264–265. The episode immediately following the one translated here reinforces the notion of Gyōgi's capacity to see the course of others' transmigrations. In it he tells the mother of a squalling child that this is retribution for the fact that in an earlier life this same child had been someone whose things she borrowed but did not return. *NRK*, pp. 264–266.

36. Kyōkai, *Miraculous Stories* p. 78 and Nakamura, *Ryōi no sekai*, p. 181 ff. See also Inoue, *Nihon kodai no kokka to Bukkyō*, p. 198.

37. On the antiquity of the divine eye as an organ that sees former lives, see David J. Kalupahana, *Causality: The Central Philosophy of Buddhism*, p. 106.

38. Kitagawa, *Religion in Japanese History*, p. 45.

39. Alasdair MacIntyre, "Epistemological Crises, Dramatic Narrative, and the Philosophy of Science," p. 467.

40. As a creative intellectual force Buddhism certainly seems to have been in retreat during the Tokugawa period. This accounts for the considerably different intellectual milieu that emerges in the essays edited by Tetsuo Najita and Irwin Scheiner, *Japanese Thought in the Tokugawa Period 1600–1868: Methods and Metaphors*.

41. *NRK*, pp. 414–415.

42. *NRK*, pp. 450–451.

43. Kuhn, *The Structure of Scientific Revolutions*, p. 68.

44. Ozawa Tomio, *Mappō to masse no shisō*, p. 61 ff.

45. Hayami Tasuku, *Heian kizoku shakai to Bukkyō*, p. 217.

46. See Kitagawa, *Religion in Japanese History*, pp. 82–85 for the relationships of these figures.

47. *T* 46.15.b

48. Hayami, *Heian Kizoku shakai to Bukkyō*, p. 217.

49. Hayami Tasuku, *Jizō shinkō*, p. 104.

50. See Mujū Ichien, *Shaseki-shū*, pp. 102–113, for example. Hayami, *Jizō Shinkō*, p. 121.

51. Marinus Willem de Visser, *Ancient Buddhism in Japan*, 1:103.

52. Watsuji Tetsurō, "Zoku Nihon seishinshi kenkyū," p. 393.

53. Genshin, *Ōjō-yō-shū*, p. 42. Translation mine.

54. Bando Shōjun , "Nihon bungaku ni arawareta inga-shisō:*Ōjō-yō-shū*," p. 341.

55. Ibid., p. 346 ff.

56. *T* 46.54.a.

57. Tamura Yoshirō in Tamura Yoshirō and Umehara Takeshi, *Bukkyō no shisō: zettai no shinri*, p. 105 ff. This is an especially valuable exposition.

58. Nichiren, "Kanjin-Honzon-shō," p. 706.

59. See Manaka Fujiko, *Koku-bungaku ni sesshu sareta Bukkyō*, especially p. 72 ff.

60. In addition to earlier, classic, studies of this by Huizinga and Callois, see also Victor Turner, "Liminal to Liminoid in Play, Flow, and Ritual: an Essay in Comparative Symbology." Important related and recent studies by Japanese scholars are sections in Yokoi Kiyoshi, *Chūsei minshū no seikatsu bunka*, and Yamazaki Masakazu, *Geijutsu, henshin, yuge*.

61. Actually it appears that closer, more contextual studies of mappō may force us to revise radically the common conception in Western writings that it is an index to the pessimism and "darkness" of medieval Japan. On the contrary, mappō may have

functioned conceptually and affectively as the extenuating circumstance that made optimism more accessible.

62. Kajiyama Yūichi in Ueyama Shunpei and Kajiyama Yūichi, *Bukkyō no shisō: sono genkei o saguru*, p. 27.

63. Ibid., p. 57. See also Yokoi Kiyoshi, *Chūsei Minshū no seikatsu bunka*, p. 85 ff.

64. Yanagida Seizan, *Zen shisō*, p. 140.

65. *T* 47.497.b. Translation by Ruth Fuller Sasaki in Lin-Chi, *The Recorded Sayings of Ch'an Master Lin-chi Hui-chao of Chen Prefecture*, p. 7.

66. *T* 47.497.c. Translation by Sasaki in Lin-Chi, *Recorded Sayings*, pp. 9–10. Yanagida's comment is in his "Zen to inga," p. 415.

67. *T* 48.293.a and b. Translation is from Zenkei Shibayama, *Zen Comments on the Mumonkan*, pp. 33–34. (I have made minor changes in the translation.)

68. *T* 47.496.c. Translation by Sasaki in Lin-Chi, *Recorded Sayings*, p. 3.

69. *T* 47.497.b. Translation by Sasaki in Lin-Chi, *Recorded Sayings*, p. 7.

70. Kitanishi Hiroshi in Ienaga Saburō et al., *Nihon Bukkyō-shi*, 2:129–132. See also Ichiro Hori, "On the Concept of *Hijiri* (Holy-Man)."

71. In this way they meet MacIntyre's criterion for a tradition, namely, that "what constitutes a tradition is a conflict of interpretations of that tradition, a conflict which itself has a history susceptible of rival interpretations." MacIntyre, "Epistemological Crises," p. 460.

72. H.D. Harootunian, "The Consciousness of Archaic Form in the New Realism of Kokugaku," p. 63.

73. Ibid., p. 93.

3. *Inns and Hermitages*

1. Ivan Morris, *The World of the Shining Prince: Court Life in Ancient Japan*, p. 110. See also Earl Miner, *An Introduction to Japanese Court Poetry*, p. 154 ff. The poem in question compares all of human life to blossoms that quickly flutter down and dreams that evaporate with dawn. Because of the veneration given Kūkai (774–835), popular piety often attributed it to him, but Roy Andrew Miller more accurately sees it as a later work, possibly composed by Kūya (903–972) or Senkan (918–983); see his *The Japanese Language*, p. 127. Important studies of mujō in Japanese include Kobayashi Hideo, "Mujō to iu koto;" Karaki Junzō, *Mujō*; Nishida Masayoshi, *Mujōkan no keifu* and *Mujū no bungaku*.

2. Within the extensive literature on structuralism I am indebted especially to Jacques Ehrmann, *Structuralism*; Robert Scholes, *Structuralism in Literature*; and Fredric Jameson, *The Prison-House of Language: A Critical Account of Structuralism and Russian Formalism*.

3. Helen Craig McCullough, *Tales of Ise: Lyrical Episodes from Tenth-Century Japan*, p. 25.

4. This is not to deny the earlier presence of this theme in literary works composed by Japanese in the Chinese language, especially in the *Chitei no ki (Ch'ih-t'ing chi)* written by Yoshishige no Yasutane in 982. It is merely to note that the effective entry of this theme into Japanese literature as such seems to be a late rather than middle Heian

development. It should also be noted that my insistence here on a thematic parity between temporal and spatial aspects of mujō is partially derived from the thought of Watsuji Tetsurō. See my "Buddhist Emptiness in the Ethics and Aesthetics of Watsuji Tetsurō."

5. See Origuchi Shinobu, "Nyōbō bungaku kara inja no bungaku e."

6. See Ishida Yoshisada, *Inja no bungaku* and *Chūsei sōan no bungaku*; Satō Masahide, *Inton no shisō: Saigyō o megutte;* Okumura Kōsaku, *Inton kajin no genryū*; and Fukuda Hideichi, *Chūsei bungaku ronkō*, pp.438–453. For Chinese precedents see Li Chi, "The Changing Concept of the Recluse in Chinese Literature." As a matter of fact, the hut of the recluse monk appears as a symbol of impermanence (*anicca*) already in the earliest Indian collection of Buddhist poetry, the *Theragāthā* of the Pali canon. There we find, for instance: "This is your old hut; you desire a new hut. Discard the hope of a hut; a new hut will be painful again, *bhikku.*" Verse 57 in K. R. Norman's new translation, *The Elders' Verses*. Here the exchange of one hut for another clearly suggests transmigration through a series of lives.

7. Ishida, *Chūsei sōan*, p. 15 ff.

8. Quotations here are from the translations by Donald Keene in his *Anthology of Japanese Literature* (New York: Grove Press, 1955), p. 197, pp. 198–199, p 206, and pp. 209–210, respectively. The original texts are from Kamo no Chōmei, "Hōjō-ki" in Nishio Minoru, *Hōjō-ki, Tsurezuregusa*, p. 23, p. 25, pp. 26–27, and p. 41, respectively.

9. Although Keene translates these as "hinges," it is likely that they were a type of metal joinery. The original has: "tsugime goto ni kakegane o kaketari."

10. Poem no. 388 in *Sanka-shū*. See translation also in my *Mirror for the Moon: Poems by Saigyō*, p. 16.

11. For another treatment of this in terms of philosophical discussions within medieval Japanese Buddhism, see part 2 of my "Saigyō and the Buddhist Value of Nature," pp. 239–246 especially.

12. Ishida, *Chūsei sōan*, p. 15.

13. Poem no. 2175 in *Sanka-shū*. Trans. in my *Mirror for the Moon*, p. 91.

14. Here as translated by Donald Keene, *Essays in Idleness: the Tsurezuregusa of Kenkō* (New York: Columbia University Press, 1967), p. 11. The original is in Nishio Minoru, *Hōjō-ki, Tsurezure-gusa*, pp. 98–99.

15. Matsuo Bashō, *Bashō bun-shū*, p. 193. Translation mine.

16. Gaston Bachelard, *The Poetics of Space*, p. 32.

17. Donald H. Shively, "Bashō—the Man and the Plant," p. 146.

18. Ibid., p. 148. For an example, see the end of the play *Izutsu* translated by Karen Brazell.

19. Ibid., pp. 153–4.

20. Shigeru Nakayama, *A History of Japanese Astronomy: Chinese Background and Western Impact*, p. 59. See also Hayami Tasuku, *Heian kizoku shakai to Bukkyō*, pp. 94–97.

21. The term *shukugō* (or *sukugō*), for example, appeared in the Chinese version of the *Abhidharma-kośa* and was known in Japan already in the Nara period. As a term it was employed in the *Nihon ryōi-ki* (Part I:8): see Kyōkai, *Miraculous Stories from the Japanese Buddhist Tradition: The Nihon Ryōiki of the Monk Kyōkai*, p. 118. On the

terms involved here, see Morohashi Tetsuji, ed., *Dai Kan-Wa jiten*, 3:1038D; Nakamura Hajime, *Bukkyōgo dai-jiten*, 1:670.

22. Mezaki Tokue, *Hyōhaku*, p. 241.

23. Poems no. 820 and 821 in *Sanka-shū;* Trans. in my *Mirror for the Moon*, p. 37.

24. See Takeoka Katsuya, *Ōchō bunka no zanshō*, pp. 131–149.

25. Poems no. 978 and 979 in Ishida Yoshisada, ed., *Shinkokin waka-shū: zenchūkai*.

26. Yokomichi Mario and Omote Akira, *Yōkyoku-shū*, pp. 55–56. Translation mine.

27. For examples in India see Mircea Eliade, *Yoga: Immortality and Freedom*, p. 257 and part 1 of Wendy Doniger O'Flaherty, "Asceticism and Sexuality in the Mythology of Śiva," especially p. 312 ff.

28. The possiblity of the historical influence of certain Tantric Buddhist materials—mediated in Japan through Shingon—upon this development cannot be discounted. Even without the catalyst of precedents derived ultimately from India, however, the transformations and values discussed here would likely have come into expression by virtue of the inner logic of the structure of the symbols for mūjo.

29. *Bashō bun-shū*, pp. 91–92. Translation mine.

30. For an account of Bashō bypassing a parentless child and the controversy concerning this, see Donald Keene, "Bashō's Journey of 1684," especially p. 135.

31. *Natural Symbols: Explorations in Cosmology*, p. 95.

32. Although there were numerous examples of common-law type marriages between Japanese monks and women, it was in the case of Shinran (1173–1263) that a priest took up, and affirmed, marriage and ordinary family life. This made for a radical change in Japanese Buddhism, although the shukke pattern remained the ideal as laid down in the codes.

33. Although Bashō does not permit the women to follow him, there is a clear sense in what he writes that some kind of parity and communitas was established between the clerics and the women. His haiku on the occasion suggests that these prostitutes may, like the moon, be enlightened, an inversion of ordinary values. See Victor W. Turner, *The Ritual Process: Structure and Anti-Structure*, especially chapter 5, "Humility and Hierarchy: The Liminality of Status Elevation and Reversal."

34. Wm. Theodore de Bary in his introduction to Saikaku Ihara, *Five Women who Loved Love*, p. 16.

35. For a review of the varieties of marriage within early court society of Japan, see William McCullough, "Japanese Marriage Institutions in the Heian Period," pp. 103–167.

36. Perhaps it would not be out of place to look for the continuation of these two topoi in the contemporary Japanese novel. Certainly the inn has continued to be the locus for action and perhaps even a symbol of transient life in modern novels. Kawabata Yasunari's *Snow Country* would be only one of many examples. The hermitage is, admittedly, less clearly identifiable in modern fiction. However, although Abe Kōbo would himself reject such a carryover from past literature into his own writing, it is not altogether impossible to see a residual iori structure in books such as *Woman of the Dunes* and *The Box Man*.

4. *Symbol and Yūgen*

1. William Carlos Williams, *Pictures from Brueghel and Other Poems*, p. 127.

2. Robert H. Brower and Earl Miner, *Japanese Court Poetry*, p. 231. See also Yasuda Ayao, *Uta no fukasa*, pp. 7–23 and Konishi Jin'ichi, *Michi: chūsei no rinen*, p. 47.

3. Brower and Miner, *Japanese Court Poetry*, p. 233.

4. *Ibid.*, p. 257.

5. Sen'ichi Hisamatsu, *The Vocabulary of Japanese Literary Aesthetics*, pp. 4–5. For more on the sociopolitical upheavals in this period see Oscar Benl, *Die Entwicklung der japanischen Poetik bis zum 16. Jahrhundert*, p. 63 especially, and the introduction to my *Mirror for the Moon: A Selection of Poems by Saigyō (1118–1190)*.

6. George Steiner, "Text and Context" in his *On Difficulty and Other Essays*, p. 9. Although in what follows I assume that we can and must discuss Japanese verse as a kind of written "text," Clifton W. Royston has rightly reminded us of the "oral nature of Japanese verse"; see his *"Utaawase* Judgments as Poetry Criticism."

7. In addition to Konishi's important studies in Japanese cited and employed in the following pages, I am also much indebted to his "Image and Ambiguity: The Impact of Zen Buddhism on Japanese Literature." This extremely important monograph has not yet begun to receive the attention it deserves.

8. Konishi Jin'ichi, "Shunzei no yūgen-fū to shikan."

9. See Watanabe Shōichi, " 'Yūgen' no shisō-kōzō," *Tetsugaku-rinrigaku Kenkyū*; Naka Seitetsu, "Korai fūteishō no karon to Bukkyō shumi"; and Manaka Fujiko, *Koku-bungaku ni sesshu sareta Bukkyō*. Professor Konishi brought Manaka's important work to my attention.

10. Stanley Weinstein, "The Beginnings of Esoteric Buddhism in Japan: The Neglected Tendai Tradition." See also Minoru Kiyota "The Structure and Meaning of Tendai Thought."

11. John M. Rosenfield, Fumiko E. Cranston, and Edwin A. Cranston, *The Courtly Tradition in Japanese Art and Literature,* p. 45 ff. See also Robert E. Morrell, "The Buddhist Poetry in the *Goshūishū.*"

12. Umehara Takeshi in Tamura Yoshirō and Umehara Takeshi, *Zettai no shinri: Tendai*, p. 244 ff.

13. The origin of a low opinion of the *Lotus* among Western scholars appears to be in Maurice Winternitz's *A History of Indian Literature*, 2:295–305; unquestioning acceptance of this opinion can be found in as recent a work as Arthur Danto, *Mysticism and Morality: Oriental Thought and Moral Philosophy*, pp. 78–83. In spite of recent and valuable new translations of this sutra, a real analysis of it either as a philosophical or literary treatise remains to be done. An important work that may eventually change this situation is Ōchō Enichi, ed., *Hokke no Shisō.*

14. The best study of this problem is Fujita Kōtatsu, "Ichijō to sanjō." Leon Hurvitz's translation of this valuable essay is entitled "One Vehicle or Three?"

15. See Stanley Weinstein, "Imperial Patronage in the Formation of T'ang Buddhism," p. 283 ff.

16. See Kumoi Shōzen, "Hōben to shinjitsu," for a discussion of the hazards involved in translating *upāya* as "means."

17. *T* 9.5.c. Translation mine.

18. *T* 9.19.b. Translation by Bunnō Katō et al., *The Threefold Lotus Sutra*, p. 127.

19. Erich Auerbach, *Mimesis: The Representation of Reality in Western Literature*, p. 49.

20. D. W. Robertson, Jr., *A Preface to Chaucer: Studies in Medieval Perspective*, p. 57.

21. Hans W. Frei, *The Eclipse of Biblical Narrative*, p. 14. In addition to Frei's important study, see also Karlfried Froehlich, " 'Always to Keep the Literal Sense in Holy Scripture Means to Kill One's Soul': The State of Biblical Hermeneutics at the Beginning of the Fifteenth Century," pp. 20—48.

22. Robertson, *A Preface to Chaucer*, p. 58.

23. Robertson, *A Preface to Chaucer*, p. 293.

24. Iris Murdoch, *The Fire and the Sun: Why Plato Banished the Artists*, p. 47.

25. Robertson, *A Preface to Chaucer*, p. 293. Emphasis mine.

26. Here I am pursuing further implications of Konishi's discussion of Richards in "Image and Ambiguity."

27. *T* 9.5.c. Translation mine. This insistence upon collapsing the distance between means and ends in the Mahayana is closely related to the development of the principle of *hongaku*, or original enlightenment. The best available study in a Western language is Bruno Petzhold, "Hon Gaku Mon und Shi Kaku Mon." The Zen master Dōgen (1200—1253), whose origins were in Tendai, pushed the logic of this to arrive at the principle of *shushō-ittō*, or "unification of practice and realization." See Dōgen, *Shōbōgenzō, Shōbōgenzō-zuimon-ki*, p. 83, and Dōgen, "Dōgen's Bendōwa," trans. Normal Waddell and Masao Abe,, p. 144.

28. *T* 9.15.a. Translation mine.

29. Winternitz, Danto, and others.

30. Leon Hurvitz, *Scripture of the Lotus Blossom of the Fine Dharma*, p. xxiii.

31. Fujita Kōtatsu, "Ichijō to sanjō," pp. 393—405; Leon Hurvitz takes issue with this, noting that statistically the number of references to emptiness in the *Lotus* is not impressive. See his "The *Lotus Sutra* in East Asia: A Review of *Hokke Shisō*," p. 723 and *Scripture of the Lotus Blossom*, p. xxiii. Certainly this is not a question that can be answered by statistics; "emptiness" is certainly *conceptually* very important in the *Lotus*. In addition to Fujita, see also Tamura Yoshirō and Umehara Takeshi, *Zettai no shinri: Tendai*, p. 70 ff.

32. The Major study of Chih-i in the West is Leon Hurvitz, *Chih-i*. Research by Sekiguchi Shindai, however, gives reason to suspect that Hurvitz's pioneering work ought to be used with some caution since it reflects the later ideas of Chan-jan (711—782) rather than those of Chih-i. See David W. Chappell, "Introduction to the 'T'ien t'ai-ssu-chiao-i'." A partial translation of the *Mo-ho chih-kuan* is N. A. Donner, "The Great Calming and Contemplation of Chih-i." In an important recent essay Robert Gimello has explicated the nature of *Shikan (śamatha vipaśyanā)* in order to demonstrate that facile assumptions that Buddhist meditation is a form of mysticism are unfounded. See his "Mysticism and Meditation." Although one may question whether *shi* or *śamatha* is "only the necessary prelude to an analytic discernment of the 'truths' of dependent origination and impermanence," (p. 181), Gimello's essay goes far to correct many wrong but widely held opinions.

33. Kusuyama Haruki, "Kango toshite no shikan."

34. Clifton W. Royston, "The Poetics and Poetry Criticism of Fujiwara Shunzei (1114–1204)," p. 386. See also Brower and Miner, *Japanese Court Poetry*, pp. 294–295 for a "platonized" interpretation of shikan.

35. Royston, *Poetics of Fujiwara Shunzei*, p. 384.

36. Ibid.

37. Manaka Fujiko, *Koku-bungaku ni sesshu sareta Bukkyō*, p. 223.

38. This phrase, although fairly common in the Mahayana, is conceptually important in the *Mo-ho chih-kuan*; see, e.g., *T* 46. 6a.

39. The text here translated is from Hayashiya Tatsusaburō, *Kodai chūsei geijutsu-ron*, pp. 262–263.

40. See the initial section of chapter 1, for a discussion of "kyōgen-kigo" and the problem faced by those wanting both literary and religious careers in this period of Japanese history.

41. Hara Ichirō, *Shi no shūkyō*, p. 153.

42. *T* 46.24.c.

43. Tamura and Umehara, *Zettai no shinri: Tendai*, p. 74. See also my discussion in "Buddhist Emptiness in the Ethics and Aesthetics of Watsuji Tetsurō."

44. *T* 46.24.b. and c.

45. This is precisely the stucture of shikan. Fung Yu-lan in his discussion of Chih-i noted that "to achieve Nirvana is the function of cessation; to return thence to the ordinary is that of contemplation." *History of Chinese Philosophy*, 2:377.

46. The question of "meaning" has been a much vexed one in contemporary philosophy; a good overview of issues involved and positions taken is Ian Hacking, *Why Does Language Matter to Philosophy?* I am not suggesting that the interest in language of a poet such as Shunzei was exactly in the same terms as that of modern philosophers, nor do I think he would have insisted on "indeterminacy" as completely as does Willard van Orman Quine in *Word and Object*. My point is merely that we can infer from their writings and from their practice as poets that Shunzei, Teika, and others—perhaps merely following a more general Japanese usage—rejected the idea that a given poem had a fixed or stable meaning. In fact, one of the most striking things about the *practice* of poetry in medieval Japan was the emphasis upon the creative possibilities in placing an existing poem in a collection (*shū*); without the change of a single syllable, a poem placed in a collection was given a new setting, a new sequence, and a new meaning as well. See Fujiwara Teika, *Fujiwara Teika's Superior Poems of Our Time*, trans. Robert H. Brower and Earl Miner. Likewise, it must be said that the development of *renga*, or "linked verse," was made possible by discovery of the creative possibilities when meaning is regarded as indeterminate. There may be a deep relationship between this and *muga*, or "no [determinate] self," in Buddhism.

47. Shin'ichi Hisamatsu, *Zen and the Fine Arts*, p. 49.

48. Shinkei, *Sasamegoto* in a version edited by Suzuki Hisashi in Haga Kōjirō, *Geidō shisō-shū*, pp. 193–194. Translation in Shinkei, "*Sasamegoto*, An Instruction Book in Linked Verse," trans. Dennis Hirota, p. 42.

49. Naka Seitetsu in his discussion of the *Korai fūteishō* makes a similar point by seeing this as an emphasis upon "michi," or "way," as a dynamic process. See Naka, *Korai Fūteishō*, p. 58.

50. Steiner, *On Difficulty*, p. 40.

51. Konishi, "Image and Ambiguity," p. 9.

52. Ibid., p. 15.

53. Tōkyō kokumin tōsho, ed., *Kokka taikei*, 10:495. Translation mine. Another reading for *wakezu* is *wakazu*.

54. *T* 9.19a—20b. Shunzei's poem is part of a sequence on the chapters of the *Lotus*.

55. This is the interpretation of Brower and Miner in *Japanese Court Poetry*, pp. 293—294. They write of Shunzei's use of "the vehicle of allegory." This, unless greatly qualified, is a misleading parallel with Western literary modes.

56. For a more extended discussion of how, by following the logic of hongaku, Chinese and Japanese thinkers in the T'ien-t'ai/Tendai tradition eventually affirmed the "Buddhahood of plants and trees," see part 1 of my "Saigyō and the Buddhist Value of Nature."

57. Poem no. 1968 in Ishida Yoshisada, *Shinkokin waka-shū: zenchūkai*, p. 842. Translation mine.

58. Kubota Jun, *Shinkokin kajin no kenkyū*, p. 304. For a more extended discussion of this poem, see Tsukudo Reikan, *Tsukudo Reikan chosaku-shū*, 1:9 ff.

59. Poem no. 363 in Ishida, *Shinkokin waka-shū*, pp. 168-169. Translation mine.

60. Brower and Miner, *Japanese Court Poetry*, p. 266. It is, of course, true that Shunzei used the word *yūgen*. Yet most Japanese scholars agree that this low statistical use does not invalidate its importance to him nor the fact that his use of it was initially the most important. In addition to the Konishi studies cited in the following pages, *yūgen* has received important consideration in Ōnishi Yoshinori, *Yūgen to Aware*; Nose Asaji, *Yūgen-ron*; and Haga Kōjirō, "Nihonteki na bi no seiritsu to tenkai: yūgen, wabi no keifu," in Haga Kōjirō, *Geidō shisō-shū*, pp. 3—42.

61. Tōkyō kokumin tōsho, ed., *Kokka taikei*. Translation mine.

62. Poem no. 515 in *Sanka-shū*; poem no. 362 in Ishida, *Shinkokin waka-shu*. Trans. in my *Mirror for the Moon*, p. 24.

63. Poem no. 2157 in *Sanka-shu;* Poem no. 625 in Ishida, *Shinkokin waka-shū*; trans. in my *Mirror for the Moon*, p. 88.

64. Kamo no Chōmei, *Mumyō-shō*. Translation here is by Hilda Katō, "The Mumyōshō of Kamo no Chōmei and Its Significance in Japanese Literature," p. 408.

65. Konishi Jin'ichi, "Shunzei no yūgen-fū to shikan," Translation mine.

66. Konishi Jin'ichi, "Yūgen no gen-igi." See also Konishi, *Michi: chūsei no rinen*, p. 44 ff.

67. Konishi, "Shunzei no yūgen-fū to shikan," pp. 111—112.

68. Brower and Miner, *Japanese Court Poetry*, p. 307.

69. See Tamura and Umehara, *Zettai no shinri: Tendai*, p. 227.

70. Ōnishi, *Yūgen to aware*, p. 100. Translation mine.

71. Konishi, "Image and Ambiguity," p. 1.

72. Yasuda, *Uta no fukasa*, p. 64.

73. Brower and Miner, *Japanese Court Poetry*, p. 295.

74. Kubota, *Shinkokin kajin no kenkyū*, p. 161.

75. This is developed more in my "Saigyō and the Buddhist Value of Nature."

76. Hisamatsu, *Zen and the Fine Arts*, p. 33.

77. The most penetrating discussion of this in a Western publication is Masao Abe, "Non-Being and *Mu*: the Metaphysical Nature of Negativity in the East and West."

5. *Chōmei as Hermit*

1. Richard B. Mather, "Vimalakīrti and Gentry Buddhism," and Paul Demiéville, "Vimalakīrti en Chine."
2. T. 11. 519–588.
3. My summary.
4. Charles Luk, *The Vimalakīrti Nirdeśa Sūtra*, p. 100.
5. Ibid.
6. Erik Zürcher, *The Buddhist Conquest of China*, 1:93 ff. Martin Collcutt tells how the T'ang practice of referring to the retreat of a Buddhist dignitary or lay scholar recluse as a *fang-chang* (hōjō) was based on a tradition according to which the pilgrim Wang Hsuan-t'se passed the ruins of a small cottage while in India. He was told that it was in this modest building that Vimalakīrti had debated Manjuśrī in the presence of thousands. Amazed, he measured the foundations and found them to be ten feet square. Martin Collcutt, *Five Mountains: The Rinzai Zen Monastic Institution in Medieval Japan*, p. 197. Kamo no Chōmei would appear to be tapping this tradition of the lay recluse when referring to his own hut as a hōjō; another tradition, both in China and Japan, used the term to designate the quarters of a Ch'an, or Zen, abbot of a monastery.
7. Arthur Waley, "The Fall of Loyang," p. 50.
8. Mather, "Vimalakīrti"; James D. Whitehead, "The Sinicization of the Vimalakīrtinirdeśa Sūtra."
9. Imanari Motoaki, "Ren-in Hōjō-ki no ron."
10. See, for example, the discussion in Itō Hiroyuki, *Chūsei no inja bungaku*, p. 107 ff.
11. Imanari, "Ren-in Hōjō-ki no ron," p. 121.
12. T 475.539.b. Trans. mine.
13. Ibid. Trans. mine.
14. Imanari, "Ren-in Hōjō-ki no ron," p. 122.
15. Kamo no Chōmei, "Hōjō-ki," p. 33. Trans. mine.
16. Ibid., p. 43. Trans. mine.
17. Ibid., p. 44. Trans. mine.
18. Ibid.

6. *Zeami's Buddhism*

1. Makoto Ueda, *Literary and Art Theories in Japan*, p. 70. For another approach to the problem considered in this chapter, see Gaston Renondeau, *Le Bouddhisme dans les Nō*. Renondeau gives more attention to specific things from specific schools which appear in nō.
2. Konishi Jin'ichi, *Nōgakuron kenkyū*, p. 11.
3. Hisamatsu Shin'ichi, "Yūgen-ron," p. 119.

4. Arthur Waley, *The Nō Plays of Japan*, p. 59.

5. Donald Keene, *Nō: The Classical Theater of Japan*, p. 27.

6. Paul Mus, La lumière sur les six voies: tableau de la transmigration bouddhiques, pp. 153–170.

7. Northrop Frye, *Anatomy of Criticism: Four Essays*, p. 207.

8. Ibid., p. 213.

9. Richard N. McKinnon, "Zeami on the Art of Training," p. 205.

10. Nose Asaji, ed., *Zeami Jūrokubushū hyōshaku*, p. 120.

11. Nishio Minoru, *Nihon bungeishi ni okeru chūseiteki na mono to sono tenkai*, p. 322.

12. See the introduction to my *Mirror for the Moon: A Selection of Poems by Saigyō*.

13. Dōgen, "Bendōwa," p. 83. See Dōgen, "Dōgen's Bendōwa," trans. Norman Waddell and Abe Masao, pp. 124–157.

14. I am indebted to Professor Kitayama Masamichi for this suggestion.

15. Nose, *Zeami Jūrokubushū hyōshaku*, p. 527. See also Konishi Jin'ichi, *Nōgakuron kenkyū*, p. 178–179 and a discussion of this in Richard B. Pilgrim, "Some Aspects of *Kokoro* in Zeami," especially p. 397.

16. Nose, *Zeami Jūrokubushū hyōshaku*, p. 192.

17. Zeami, "Zeami Jūroku Bushū, Kwadensho," trans. Michitarō Shidehara and Wilfrid Whitehouse, p. 199. See also Motokiyo Zeami, *The Secret of Nō Plays: Zeami's Kadensho*, p. 74 for another interpolation: "separate from the subject."

18. Nose, *Zeami Jūrokubushū hyōshaku*, p. 213. (I take "moteasobu" to have the sense of "taisetsu ni motenasu.")

19. See Frank Paul Hoff, "A Theatre of Metaphor: A Study of the Japanese Nō. Form."

20. Jacob Raz, "The Actor and His Audience: Zeami's Views on the Audience of the Noh," p. 265.

21. Konishi sees this as coming to a special fruition in the theories of Zenchiku: see his *Nōgakuron* kenkyū, p. 253 ff. Bruno Petzhold wrote concerning *hongaku* that "die Totalität der Dinge wird bejaht" in his "Hon Gaku Mon und Shi Kaku Mon" (p. 142).

22. Kamiyama Shumpei and Umehara Takeshi, *Nihon to Tōyō bunka*, pp. 171–172.

23. Nogami Toyoichirō, "Nōgaku gaisetsu," p. 13. See also Jin'ichi Konishi, *New Approaches to the Study of the Nō Drama*, p. 7. For exceptions to this see Anesaki Masaharu, "Yōkyoku ni okeru Bukkyō yōso," p. 152.

7. Society Upside-Down

1. Susanne K. Langer, *Feeling and Form*, p. 343.

2. The classic study in this field is Mikhail Bakhtin, *Rabelais and His World*. See also Robert M. Torrance, *The Comic Hero*.

3. Studies of kyōgen have long been overshadowed by those of nō; see Hayashiya Tatsusaburō, *Kabuki izen*, pp. 102–103.

4. Donald H. Shively, "*Bakufu* versus *Kabuki*," p. 231.

5. Text in Furukawa Hisashi, ed., *Kyōgen-shū*, Nihon koten zensho, vol. 83, pp. 110–112. Translations by Donald Keene, *Anthology of Japanese Literature* (New York: Grove Press, 1955), pp. 300–304.

6. Text in Furukawa Hisashi, ed., *Kyōgen-shū*, Nihon koten zensho, vol. 82, pp. 217–220.

7. Satake Akihiro, *Gekokujō no bungaku*, p. 137.

8. Ibid., p. 138.

9. Taguchi Kazuo, *Kyōgen ronkō*, p. 187 ff. Taguchi's work is a fine survey of modern scholarship on kyōgen.

10. Imamura Yoshio, "Shū Saku-nin [Chou Tso-jen] ni yoru kyōgen no chūgoku-yaku ni tsuite."

11. Also known as "Saru zatō."

12. John W. Hall, introduction to John W. Hall and Toyoda Takeshi, *Japan in the Muromachi Age*, p. 7.

13. In the case of Zeami there was not only patronage but also loss of the same, and exile; see Susan Matisoff, "Zeami's Kintōsho."

14. There are many studies employing the term *gekokujō*; among political historians it is usually applied to the so-called *sengoku* period (1477–1573), but cultural historians increasingly use it to describe social conditions in the whole of the Muromachi period. For an attempt to specify the meaning of the term see Fukuo Takeichirō, " 'Gekokujō' no ronri."

15. Fukuo, " 'Gekukujō' no ronri," p. 176.

16. See especially Yokoi Kiyoshi, *Chūsei minshū no seikatsu bunka*.

17. "Kammon gyoki," *Zoku gunshō ruijū* (hoi) 2:1, p. 427.

18. Northrop Frye, *Anatomy of Criticism: Four Essays*, p. 224.

19. Furukawa Hisashi, ed., *Kyōgen-shū*, Nihon koten zensho, vol. 83, pp. 207–332. See Omote Akira, " 'Tenshō kyōgen-bon' ni tsuite."

20. Y.M. Lotman and B.A. Uspensky as translated and quoted by Maria Corti in her "Models and Antimodels in Medieval Culture," p. 350.

21. See note 7 above.

22. Chieko Irie Mulhern, "Otogi-zōshi: Short Stories of the Muromachi Period," p. 196.

23. Ibid., p. 189.

24. Satake, *Gekokujō no bungaku*, pp. 109–110.

25. Jacqueline Golay, "Pathos and Farce: *Zatō* Plays of the *Kyōgen* Repertoire," p. 140.

26. Robert N. Bellah, "Religious Evolution," p. 82.

27. Donald Keene, *Nō: The Classical Theatre of Japan*, p. 46.

28. Zeami was propelled in this direction by his pursuit of the implications of Buddhist logic.

29. Makoto Ueda, *Literary and Art Theories in Japan*, pp. 101–13.

30. Victor W. Turner, "Metaphors of Anti-Structure in Religious Culture," p. 273.

31. Victor W. Turner, *The Ritual Process: Structure and Anti-structure*, p. 176.

32. James L. Peacock, *Rites of Modernization: Symbolic and Social Aspects of Indonesian Proletarian Drama*.

33. James L. Peacock, "Symbolic Reversal and Social History: Transvestites and Clowns of Java," p. 218.

34. Barbara A. Babcock, ed., *The Reversible World: Symbolic Inversion in Art and Society*, pp. 13–36.

35. A collection of these is in Conrad Hyers, *Zen and the Comic Spirit*.

8. Poet as Seer

1. Stephen Toulmin, *Human Understanding: The Collective Use and Evolution of Concepts*, p. 360. The influence here of the thought of Wittgenstein is clear.

2. Ibid., p. 299.

3. Ibid., p. 218.

4. Joseph M. Kitagawa, *Religion in Japanese History*, p. 19.

5. Joseph M. Kitagawa, "The Japanese *Kokutai* (National Community): History and Myth."

6. Joseph M. Kitagawa, "Kūkai as Master and Saviour."

7. "Stadiality" or "multi-leveledness" is a translation of *jūsōsei*, a concept set forth by Watsuji Tetsurō in his essay entitled "Nihon seishin," p. 314 ff.

8. The most important notion is that of *jita funi*, "self and other: not two," a position clearly different from that of monistic systems. The Buddhist position refuses to sacrifice either the harmony or the tension.

9. Matsuo Bashō, *Bashō bun-shū* pp. 76–77.

10. Makoto Ueda, *Matsuo Bashō*, p. 24 ff. The great change in Bashō scholarship came with the publication in 1943 of the journal of Bashō's companion Sora, which, in the words of Donald Keene, "came as a bombshell to Bashō Worshippers." See Keene's *World Within Walls: Japanese Literature of the Pre-Modern Era, 1600–1867*, p. 99 ff.

11. Poem no. 1290 in Saigyō, *Sanka-shū*.

12. Ueda, *Matsuo Bashō*, p. 137.

13. Modern scholarship holds, in contrast to Pound and Fenollosa, that although the written character presents itself visually, it is by no means a pictogram. For an interesting recent discussion of this in the context of poetic theory, see Andrew Walsh, *Roots of the Lyric: Primitive Poetry and Modern Poetics*, pp. 100–132. Bashō's own view is, of course, impossible to ascertain; his view here may be purely a literary construct.

14. See Inoue Kaoru, *Gyōki* and especially Hori Ichirō, *Hori Ichirō chosakushū*, pp. 423–463.

15. Kitagawa, *Religion in Japanese History*, p. 43.

16. The walking-stick (*tsue*) is symbolic as well as functional. For another instance of this, see Joseph M. Kitagawa, "Three Types of Pilgrimage in Japan," especially p. 162.

17. Kitagawa, *Religion in Japanese History*, p. 117.

18. Kyōkai, *Nihon ryōi-ki*, p. 264–265. Trans. mine.

19. Ibid., pp. 266–267. Trans. mine.

20. Ueda, *Matsuo Bashō*, pp. 25–26.

21. James H. Foard, "The Loneliness of Matsuo Bashō."

22. Bashō would have known of Saigyō through the latter's poetry and quite probably also through the hagiography called the *Saigyō monogatari*; on this, see my "The Death and the 'Lives' of Saigyō; The Genesis of a Buddhist Sacred Biography."

23. Poem no. 786 in *Sanka-shū*; trans. in my *Mirror for the Moon: Selected Poems by Saigyō*, p. 34.

24. Poem no. 2083 in *Sanka-shū*; trans. in my *Mirror for the Moon*, p. 84.

25. Poem no. 2079 in *Sanka-shū*; trans. in my *Mirror for the Moon*, p. 83.

26. Hans Jonas, "The Nobility of Sight: A Study in the Phenomenology of the Senses," p. 330.

27. Kitagawa, *Religion in Japanese History*, p. 45.

28. An important essay on this problem is Tomiyama Susumu, "Bashō ni okeru chūsei no keishō to danzetsu." Tomiyama argues for increasing distance between Bashō's posture and the medieval synthesis of poetry and Buddhism, although his argument is primarily from silence.

29. On a somewhat related point, Robert N. Bellah has written that in China and Japan "the reversal in primacy of contemplation and action was also taking place, even if pianissimo, so to speak, compared to the West." In his "To Kill and Survive or To Die and Become: The Active Life and the Contemplative Life as Ways of Being Adult," p. 71. The fact that it was "pianissimo" is, I think, important and accurate.

30. This point emerged in a discussion with Japanese scholars. See my "Seiyō ni okeru Nihon no Chūsei bungaku kenkyū no mondai to tenbō," and subsequent discussion in Meiji Daigaku, ed., *Gakujutsu Kokusai Kōryū Sankō Shiryoshū* (Tokyo, 1976), pp. 1–24.

31. M. A. Abrams, *Natural Supernaturalism: Tradition and Revolution in Romantic Literature*, p. 334.

32. *Ibid.*, p. 348. (Abrams's translation of Carl Leonhard Reinhold, *Briefe über die Kantische Philosophie*, 2 vols. [Leipzig, 1790], I, 12, 9.)

33. *Ibid.*, p. 375.

34. John Ruskin, *Modern Painters*, 3:268. Quoted in Abrams, *Natural Supernaturalism*, pp. 375–376. See also M. H. Abrams, *The Mirror and the Lamp: Romantic Theory and the Critical Tradition*.

35. M. A. Abrams, *Natural Supernaturalism*, p. 64.

36. *Ibid.*, p. 65.

37. Geoffrey H. Hartman, *The Unmediated Vision: An Interpretation of Wordsworth, Hopkins, Rilke, and Valéry*, p. 33. Saigyō is something of an exception to this within the ambit of Japanese culture; he commented directly on events in his day and often wrote verse on such things. See the introduction to my *Mirror for the Moon*.

JAPANESE NAMES AND TERMS

ashura 阿修羅

asobi 遊び

bakufu 幕府

Bashō 芭蕉

Bendōwa 弁道話

bonnō-soku-bodai 煩悩即菩提

bosatsu 菩薩

butsudō 仏道

chikushō 畜生

Daijō-kishin-ron 大乗起信論

daisōjō 大僧正

daruma-uta 達磨歌

Eguchi 江口

engaku 縁覚

Esashi Jūō 餌差十王

Fugen Bosatsu 普賢菩薩

Funa Benkei 舟弁慶

funi 不二

gaki 餓鬼

Gaki-zōshi 餓鬼草子

gekokujō 下剋上

genpō 現報

genshō-zoku-jisso 現象即実相

gesho 外書

genzai-mono 現在物

Gukan-shō 愚管抄

gyō 行

haibutsu-kishaku 排仏棄釈

haikai 俳階

haiku 俳句

Hakurakuten 白楽天

hana 花

hannya 般若

hashira 柱

hijiri 聖

hiyu 譬喩

hōben 方便

Hōjō-ki 方丈記

Hokke-kyō 法華経

hongaku 本覚

honji-suijaku 本地垂迹

ichinen-sanzen 一念三千

io, iori 庵

inja 隠者

irui-chūgyō 異類中行

jigoku 地獄

Jigoku-zōshi 地獄草子

jikkai 十界

183

jikkai-goku 十界互具

Jōdo 浄工

Jūji-kyō 十地経

juke-nyūkū 従仮入空

kabuki 歌舞伎

Kadensho 花伝書

kadō 歌道

Kagami otoko-emaki 鏡男絵巻

kaku 覚

kami 神

kami-nō 神能

Kammon gyoki 看聞御記

Kani Yamabushi 蟹山伏

Kanjin-Honzon-shō 観心本尊抄

kari 仮

kari 借り

katawara 傍

kazura-mono 鬘物

Kegon 華厳

Kegon-kyō 華厳経

keiko 稽古

keshin 化身

keshō 化生

Kinuta 砧

kire 切れ

kiri-no-mono 切りの物

kōan 公案

Kokin-shū 古今集

kokutai 国体

Konjaku-monogatari 今昔物語

Kōshoku gonin onna 好色五人女

Korai futeishō 古来風体抄

ku 苦

kū 空

kū-ke-chū 空仮中

kuge 公家

kuri 栗

Kusabira 茸

kyōgen 狂言

kyōgen-kigo 狂言綺語

kyoran-mono 狂乱物

Makashikan 摩訶止観

Makura-no-sōshi 枕草子

Man'yō-shū 万葉集

mappō 末法

Matsukaze 松風

matsuri 祭

matsurigoto 政

Michimori 通盛

muchū-mondō 夢中問答

muga 無我

muge 無礙

mujō 無常

mujū 無住

Mumyō-shō 無名抄

myō 妙

naikyō 内経

nembutsu 念仏

Nihonkoku genpō 日本国現報

　zen'aku ryōi-ki 善悪霊異記

Nihon ryōi-ki 日本霊異記

ningen 人間

Nōin 能因

nyorai 如来

odori nembutsu 踊念仏

Ōjō-yō-shū 往生要集

Oku no hosomichi 奥の細道

onna-mono 女物

onryō-mono 怨霊物

otogi-zōshi 御伽草子

Rakushisha-no-ki 落柿舎の記

rinne 輪廻

Rinzai-roku 臨済録

ritsu 律

rokudō 六道

rokudō-bakku 六道抜苦

roku-Jizō 六地蔵

roku-Kannon 六観音

rokudō-shishō 六道四生

ryōbu-shintō 両部神道

ryōi 霊異

Ryōjin-hi-shō 梁塵秘抄

sai 西

Saigyō 西行

Saihō-Jōdo 西方浄土

Sangō shiiki 三教旨帰

Sanka-shū 山家集

sanron 三論

santai 三諦

sarugaku 猿楽

Sarugae kōtō 猿替勾当

satori 悟

seidan 清談

setsuna 刹那

shaba 沙婆

shaba-soku-jakkō 娑婆即寂光

Shaseki-shū 沙石集

shiba 芝

shibashi 暫

shidai 四大

shishō 四生

shite 仕手

Shōbō-genzō 正法眼蔵

shōjūimetsu 生住異滅

shōmon 声聞

shujō 衆生

shukke 出家

shukugō 宿業

shukumei 宿命

shukuse 宿世

shura-mono 修羅物

shūshin-mono 執心物

shushō-ittō 修證一等

sōan 草庵

soku 即

sokushin-jōbutsu 即身成仏

sōmoku-jōbutsu 草木成仏

somuru 染むる

somuru 初むる

sue no yo 末の世

suku, shuku, yado 宿

sukuyō-dō 宿躍道

tairitsuteki 対立的

Takasago 高砂

Tanni-shō 歎異鈔

teishō 提唱

tengen 天眼

Tenshō kyōgen-bon 天正狂言本

tochi 橡   yamabushi 山伏

tsue 杖   yo 世

Tsurezure-gusa 徒然草   yojō 余情

ujō 有常   yo o suteru 世を捨てる

ukiyo 浮世   yūge-jinzū 遊戯神通

uta 歌   yūgen 幽玄

utsutsu 現   *Yuima-kitsu-gyō* 維摩詰経

waki 脇   yūjo 遊女

waki-no-mono 脇の物   yume 夢

wakezu 分けず   zaike 在家

Waranbe-gusa 童草   zatō 座頭

yakusō-yu 薬草喩   zazen 座禅

Yamabe 山部

BIBLIOGRAPHY

Abe, Masao. "Non-Being and *Mu*: The Metaphysical Nature of Negativity in the East and West." *Religious Studies* 11 (June 1975): 181–192.

Abrams, M. H. *The Mirror and the Lamp: Romantic Theory and the Critical Tradition*. New York: W. W. Norton, 1953.

————. *Natural Supernaturalism: Tradition and Revolution in Romantic Literature*. New York: W. W. Norton, 1971.

Anesaki Masaharu. "Yōkyoku ni okeru Bukkyō yōso." In Nogami Toyoichirō, ed., *Nōgaku zensho*. Tokyo: Sōgensha, 1942. 1:139–184.

Auerbach, Erich. *Mimesis: The Representation of Reality in Western Literature*. Princeton, Princeton University Press, 1953.

Bachelard, Gaston. *The Poetics of Space*. Trans. Maria Jolas. Boston: Beacon Press, 1969.

Bakhtin, Mikhail. *Rabelais and His World*. Trans. Hélène Iswolsky. Cambridge, Mass.: MIT Press, 1968.

Bando Shōjun. "Nihon bungaku ni arawareta inga-shisō: Ōjō-yō-shū." In Bukkyō Shisō Kenkyūkai, ed., *Inga*. Kyoto, 1978.

Bellah, Robert. "Religious Evolution." In William A. Lessa and Evon Z. Vogt, eds., *Reader in Comparative Religion: An Anthropological Approach*. New York: Harper and Row, 1965. Pp. 73–87.

————. "To Kill and Survive or to Die and Become: The Active Life and the Contemplative Life as Ways of Being Adult." *Daedalus* (Spring 1976), pp. 57–76.

Benl, Oscar. *Die Entwicklung der japanischen Poetik bis zum 16. Jahrhundert*. Hamburg: Otto Harrassowitz, 1951.

Brower, Robert H., and Earl Miner. *Japanese Court Poetry*. Stanford: Stanford University Press, 1961.

Chappell, David W. "Introduction to the 'T'ien't'ai ssu-chiao-i'." *The Eastern Buddhist* n.s. 9, 1 (May 1976):72–86.

Collcutt, Martin. *Five Mountains: The Rinzai Zen Monastic Institution in Medieval Japan*. Cambridge, Mass. and London: Harvard University Press, 1981.

Corti, Maria. "Models and Antimodels in Medieval Culture." *New Literary History* 10, 2 (Winter 1979):339–366.

Danto, Arthur. *Mysticism and Morality: Oriental Thought and Moral Philosophy*. New York: Harper Torchbook, 1972.

Demiéville, Paul. "Vimalakīrti en Chine." In *Choix d'études bouddhiques*. Leiden: E. J. Brill, 1973. Pp. 347–364.

Dōgen. "Bendōwa." In Nishio Minoru et al., eds., *Shōbōgenzō, Shōbōgenzō-zuimon-ki*. Nihon koten bungaku taikei, Vol. 81. Tokyo: Iwanami Shoten, 1966. Pp. 69–97.

————. "Dōgen's Bendōwa." Trans. Norman Waddell and Masao Abe, *The Eastern Buddhist* n.s. 4, 1 (May 1971): 124–157.

Donner, Neal A. "The Great Calming and Contemplation of Chih-i: Chapter 1, The Synopsis." Ph.D dissertation, University of British Columbia, 1976.

Douglas, Mary. *Natural Symbols: Explorations in Cosmology.* New York: Vintage Books, 1973.

Ehrmann, Jacques, ed. *Structuralism.* New York: Doubleday, 1970.

Eliade, Mircea. *Yoga: Immortality and Freedom.* Princeton: Princeton University Press, 1969.

Fingarette, Herbert. *The Self in Transformation: Psychoanalysis, Philosophy, and the Life of the Spirit.* New York: Harper and Row, 1963.

Foard, James H. "The Loneliness of Matsuo Bashō." In Frank E. Reynolds and Donald Capps, eds., *The Biographical Process: Studies in the History and Psychology of Religion.* The Hague and Paris: Mouton, 1976. Pp. 363–391.

Frei, Hans W. *The Eclipse of Biblical Narrative.* New Haven: Yale University Press, 1974.

Froehlich, Karlfried. " 'Always to Keep the Literal Sense in Holy Scripture Means to Kill One's Soul': The State of Biblical Hermeneutics at the Beginning of the Fifteenth Century." In Earl Miner, ed., *Literary Uses of Typology: From the Late Middle Ages to the Present.* Princeton: Princeton University Press, 1977.

Frye, Northrop. *Anatomy of Criticism: Four Essays.* Princeton: Princeton University Press, 1957.

Fujita Kōtatsu. "Ichijō to sanjō." In Ōchō Enichi, ed., *Hokke no shisō.* Kyoto: Heirakuji Shoten, 1969. Pp. 351–405.

————. "One Vehicle or Three?" Trans. Leon Hurvitz. *Journal of Indian Philosophy* 3, 1 and 2 (April 1975):79–166.

Fujiwara Teika. *Fujiwara Teika's Superior Poems of Our Time.* Trans. Robert H. Brower and Earl Miner. Tokyo: Tokyo University Press, 1967.

Fukuda Hideichi. *Chūsei bungaku ronkō.* Tokyo: Meiji Shoin, 1975.

Fukuo Takeichirō. " 'Gekokujō' no ronri." *Nihon Rekishi* 248 (January 1969): 174–176.

Fung Yu-lan. *A History of Chinese Philosophy.* 2 vols. Princeton: Princeton University Press, 1953.

Genshin. "Genshin's Ojo Yoshu: Collected Essays on Birth into Paradise." Trans. A. K. Reischauer. *Transactions of the Asiatic Society of Japan* 2d ser. 7 (1930): 16–97.

Genshin. "Ōjō-yō-shū." In Ishida Mizumaro, ed. *Genshin*, Nihon shisō taikei, vol. 6. Tokyo: Iwanami Shoten, 1970.

Gimello, Robert M., "Mysticism and Meditation." In Steven T. Katz, ed., *Mysticism and Philosophical Analysis.* New York: Oxford University Press, 1978.

Golay, Jacqueline. "Pathos and Farce: *Zatō* Plays of the *Kyōgen* Repertoire." *Monumenta Nipponica* 28, 2 (Summer 1973): 139–149.

Gombrich, Richard F. " 'Merit Transference' in Sinhalese Buddhism: A Case Study of the Interaction Between Doctrine and Practice." *History of Religions* 11, 2 (November 1970): 203–219.

Hacking, Ian. *Why Does Language Matter to Philosophy?* Cambridge: Cambridge University Press, 1975.

Haga Kōjirō, ed. *Geidō shisō-shū*. Nihon no shisō, vol. 7. Tokyo: Chikuma Shobō, 1971.

Hakeda, Yoshito S., trans. *The Awakening of Faith Attributed to Aśvaghosha*. New York: Columbia University Press, 1967.

Hall, John W. Introduction to John W. Hall and Toyoda Takeshi eds. *Japan in the Muromachi Age*. Berkeley: University of California Press, 1977. Pp. 1—8.

Hambrick, Charles H. "Gukanshō: A Religious View of History." Ph.D. dissertation, University of Chicago, 1971.

Hara Ichirō. *Shi no shūkyō*. Tokyo: Waseda Daigaku Shuppanbu, 1973.

Harootunian, H. D. "The Consciousness of Archaic Form in the New Realism of Kokugaku." In Tetsuo Najita and Irwin Scheiner, eds., *Japanese Thought in the Tokugawa Period: Methods and Metaphors*. Chicago: University of Chicago Press, 1978. Pp. 63—104.

Hartman, Geoffrey H. *The Unmediated Vision: An Interpretation of Wordsworth, Hopkins, Rilke, and Valéry*. New York: Harcourt, Brace and World, 1954.

Hayami Tasuku. *Jizō shinkō*. Tokyo: Hanawa Shinsho, 1975.

———. *Heian kizoku shakai to bukkyō*. Tokyo: Yoshikawa Kōbunkan, 1975.

Hayashiya Tatsusaburō. *Kabuki izen*. Tokyo: Iwanami Shoten, 1954.

———, ed. *Kodai chūsei geijutsu-ron*. Nihon shisō taikei, vol. 23. Tokyo: Iwanami Shoten, 1973.

Hisamatsu, Sen'ichi. *The Vocabulary of Japanese Literary Aesthetics*. Tokyo: Center for East Asian Cultural Studies, 1963.

Hisamatsu Shin'ichi. "Yūgen-ron." In *Hisamatsu Shin'ichi chosakushū: Zen to geijutsu*. Tokyo: Risōsha, 1970. 5:102—135.

Hisamatsu, Shin'ichi. *Zen and the Fine Arts*. New York and Tokyo: Kodansha International, 1974.

Hoff, Frank Paul. "A Theatre of Metaphor: A Study of the Japanese Nō Form." Ph.D. dissertation, Harvard University, 1965.

Hori Ichirō. *Hori Ichirō chosakushū*. Vol. 1. Tokyo: Miraisha, 1977.

Hori, Ichiro. "On the Concept of *Hijiri* (Holy-Man)." *Numen* 5 (1958): 128—160 and 199—232.

Hurvitz, Leon, *Chih-i*. *Mélanges chinois et bouddhiques*, vol. 12 (1962).

———. "The *Lotus Sutra* in East Asia: A Review of *Hokke Shisō*." *Monumenta Serica* 29 (1970—1971): 697—762.

———, trans. *Scripture of the Lotus Blossom of the Fine Dharma*. New York: Columbia University Press, 1976.

Hyers, Conrad. *Zen and the Comic Spirit*. Philadelphia: Westminster, 1973.

Ienaga Saburō, ed. *Nihon Bukkyō-shi*. 3 vols. Kyoto: Hōzōkan, 1967.

———. *Nihon shisōshi ni okeru shūkyōteki shizenkan no tenkai*. Tokyo: Sōkansha, 1944.

Ihara, Saikaku. *Five Women Who Loved Love*. Trans. Wm. Theodore de Bary. Rutland and Tokyo: Charles E. Tuttle, 1956.

Imanari Motoaki. "Ren-in Hōjō-ki no ron." *Bungaku* 42, 2 (1974):115—127.

Imamura Yoshio. "Shū Saku-nin [Chou Tso-jen] ni yoru kyōgen no chūgoku-yaku ni tsuite." *Bungaku* 24, 7 (1956):864—868.

Inoue Kaoru, *Gyōki*. Tokyo: Yoshikawa Kōbunkan, 1959.

Inoue Mitsusada. *Nihon kodai no kokka to Bukkyō*. Tokyo: Iwanami Shoten, 1971.

Iriya, Yoshitaka. "Chinese Poetry and Zen." *The Eastern Buddhist* n.s. 6, 1 (May 1973):54–67.

Ishida Yoshisada. *Chūsei sōan no bungaku*. Tokyo: Kitazawa Tosho Shuppan, 1970.

———. *Inja no bungaku*. Tokyo: Hanawa Shobō, 1968.

———, ed. *Shinkokin waka-shū: zenchūkai*. Tokyo: Yūseidō, 1967.

Itō Hiroyuki et al., eds. *Chūsei no inja bungaku*. Tokyo: Gakuseisha, 1976.

Jameson, Fredric. *The Prison-House of Language: A Critical Account of Structuralism and Russian Formalism*. Princeton: Princeton University Press, 1972.

Jien. *The Future and the Past: A Translation and Study of the Gukanshō, an Interpretative History of Japan Written in 1219*. Trans. and ed. Delmer M. Brown and Ichirō Ishida. Berkeley. University of California Press, 1979.

Jonas, Hans. "The Nobility of Sight: A Study in the Phenomenology of the Senses." In Stuart F. Spicker, ed., *The Philosophy of the Body: Rejections of Cartesian Dualism*. New York: Quadrangle, 1970. Pp. 312–333.

Kalupahana, David J. *Causality: The Central Philosophy of Buddhism*. Honolulu: University of Hawaii Press, 1975.

Kamiyama Shumpei and Umehara Takeshi, eds. *Nihon to Tōyō Bunka*. Tokyo: Shinchōsha, 1969.

Kamo no Chōmei. "An Account of My Hut." In Donald Keene, ed., *Anthology of Japanese Literature*. New York: Grove Press, 1955. Pp. 197–212.

———. "Hōjō-ki." In Nishio Minoru et al., eds., *Hōjō-ki, Tsurezure-gusa*. Nihon koten bungaku taikei, vol. 30. Tokyo: Iwanami Shoten, 1971.

Karaki Junzō. *Mujō*. Tokyo: Chikuma Shobō, 1965.

Katō, Bunnō et al., trans. *The Threefold Lotus Sutra*. New York and Tokyo: Weatherhill/ Kosei, 1975.

Katō, Hilda. "The Mumyōshō of Kamo no Chōmei and Its Significance in Japanese Literature." *Monumenta Nipponica* 23, 3–4 (1968):321–430.

Kato, Shuichi. *A History of Japanese Literature: The First Thousand Years*. Trans. David Chibbett. New York, Tokyo, and San Francisco: Kodansha International, 1979.

Keene, Donald. "Bashō's Journey of 1684." *Asia Major* n.s. 7, 1 and 2:133–144.

———. *Nō: The Classical Theater of Japan*. Tokyo and Palo Alto: Kodansha International, 1966.

———. *World Within Walls: Japanese Literature of the Pre-Modern Era 1600–1867*. New York: Holt, Rinehart, and Winston, 1976.

Kelsey, W. Michael. "Salvation of the Snake, the Snake of Salvation: Buddhist-Shinto Conflict and Resolution." *Japanese Journal of Religious Studies* 8, 1 and 2 (March–June 1981):83–113.

Kitagawa, Hiroshi, and Bruce T. Tsuchida, trans. *The Tale of the Heike*. Tokyo: Tokyo University Press, 1975.

Kitagawa, Joseph M. "The Japanese *Kokutai* (National Community): History and Myth." *History of Religions* 13, 3 (February 1974):209–226.

———. "Kūkai as Master and Savior." In Frank E. Reynolds and Donald Capps, eds., *The Biographical Process: Studies in the History and Psychology of Religion*. The Hague and Paris: Mouton, 1976. Pp. 319–341.

———. *Religion in Japanese History*. New York: Columbia University Press, 1966.

———. "Three Types of Pilgrimage in Japan." In E. E. Urbach, R. J. Zwi

Werblowsky, and Ch. Wirszubski, eds., *Studies in Mysticism and Religion*. Jerusalem, 1967. Pp. 155–164.

Kiyota, Minoru. *Shingon Buddhism: Theory and Practice*. Los Angeles and Tokyo: Buddhist Books International, 1978.

———. "The Structure and Meaning of Tendai Thought." *Transactions of the International Conference of Orientalists in Japan* 5 (1960):69–83.

Kobayashi Hideo. "Mujō to iu koto." In *Kobayashi Hideo zenshū*, vol. 8. Tokyo: Shinchō Shuppan, 1967.

Konishi, Jin'ichi. "Image and Ambiguity: The Impact of Zen Buddhism on Japanese Literature." Mimeographed. Tokyo, 1973.

———. *Michi: chūsei no rinen*. Tokyo: Kodansha, 1975.

———. *New Approaches to the Study of Nō Drama*. Tokyo: Tōkyō Kyōiki Daigaku Bungaku-bu Kiyō, 1960.

———. *Nōgakuron kenkyū*. Tokyo: Hanawa Shobō, 1961.

———. "Shunzei no yūgen-fū to shikan." *Bungaku* 20, 2 (February 1952):108–116.

———. "Yūgen no gen-igi." *Kokugo to kokubungaku* 20, 6 (June 1943):499–508.

Kubota Jun. *Shinkokin kajin no kenkyū*. Tokyo: Tōkyō Daigaku Shuppankai, 1973.

Kuhn, Thomas S. *The Structure of Scientific Revolutions*. Chicago: University of Chicago Press, 1962.

Kūkai. *Kōbō Daishi chosaku zenshū*. Ed. Katsumata Shunkyō. 3 vols. Tokyo: Sangibō Busshorin, 1968.

———. *Kūkai: Major Works, Translated with an Account of His Life and a Study of His Thought* by Yoshito S. Hakeda. New York: Columbia University Press, 1972.

Kumoi Shōzen. "Hōben to shinjitsu." In Ōchō Enichi, ed., *Hokke shisō*. Kyoto: Heirakuji Shoten, 1969. Pp. 321–351.

Kuroda, Toshio. "Shinto in the History of Japanese Religion." Trans. James C. Dobbins and Suzanne Gay. *Journal of Japanese Studies* 7, 1 (Winter 1981):1–21.

Kusuyama Haruki. "Kango toshite no shikan." In Sekiguchi Shindai, ed., *Shikan no kenkyū*. Tokyo: Iwanami Shoten, 1975. Pp. 181–200.

Kyōkai. *Nihon ryōi-ki*. Ed. Endō Yoshimoto et al. Nihon koten bungaku taikei, Vol. 70. Tokyo: Iwanami Shoten, 1967.

———. *Legenden aus der Frühzeit des japanischen Buddhismus*. Trans. Hermann Bohner. *Mitteilungen der Deutschen Gesellschaft für Natur- und Völkerkunde Ostasiens*, vol. 27 (1934–1935).

———. *Miraculous Stories from the Japanese Buddhist Tradition: The Nihon Ryōiki of the Monk Kyōkai*. Trans. Kyoko Motomochi Nakamura. Cambridge, Mass.: Harvard University Press, 1973.

LaFleur, William R. "Buddhist Emptiness in the Ethics and Aesthetics of Watsuji Tetsurō." *Religious Studies* 14 (June 1978):237–250.

———. "The Death and the 'Lives' of Saigyō: The Genesis of a Buddhist Sacred Biography." In Frank Reynolds and Donald Capps, eds., *The Biographical Process: Studies in the History and Psychology of Religion*. The Hague and Paris: Mouton, 1976. Pp. 343–361.

———. "Kyōkai and the 'Easternization' of Japan: A Review Essay." *Journal of the American Academy of Religion* 43, 2 (June 1975):266–274.

———. "Saigyō and the Buddhist Value of Nature." *History of Religions* 13, 2 (November 1973):93–128; 3 (February 1974):227–248.

————. "Seiyō ni okeru Nihon no chūsei bungaku kenkyū no mondai to tenbō." In Meiji Daigaku, ed., *Gakujutsu Kokusai Kōryū Sankō Shiryoshū*. Tokyo, 1976. Pp. 1—24.

Langer, Susanne K. *Feeling and Form*. New York: Charles Scribner's Sons, 1953.

Li Chi. "The Changing Concept of the Recluse in Chinese Literature." *Harvard Journal of Asiatic Studies* 24:234—247.

Lin-Chi. *The Recorded Sayings of Ch'an Master Lin-chi Hui-chao of Chen Prefecture*. Trans. Ruth Fuller Sasaki. Kyoto: The Institute for Zen Studies, 1975.

Luk, Charles, trans. and ed. *The Vimalakīrti Nirdeśa Sūtra*. Berkeley and London: Shambala, 1972.

MacIntyre, Alasdair. "Epistemological Crises, Dramatic Narrative, and the Philosophy of Science." *The Monist* 60, 4:453—472.

————. "Is Understanding Religion Compatible with Believing?" In Brian R. Wilson, ed., *Rationality*. Oxford: Basil Blackwell, 1977. Pp. 62—77.

Manaka Fujikō. *Koku-bungaku ni sesshu sareta Bukkyō*. Tokyo: Bun-ichi Shuppan, 1972.

Maruyama, Masao. *Studies in the Intellectual History of Tokugawa Japan*. Trans. Mikiso Hane. Princeton and Tokyo: Princeton University Press and University of Tokyo Press, 1974.

Maruyama Shūichi. *Honji-suijaku*. Tokyo: Yoshikawa Kōbunkan, 1974.

Mather, Richard B. "Vimalakīrti and Gentry Buddhism." *History of Religions* 8, 1 (August 1968):60—72.

Matisoff, Susan. "Zeami's Kintōsho." *Monumenta Nipponica* 32, 4:441—458.

Matsuo Bashō. *Bashō bun-shū*. Ed. Sugiura Shōichirō et al. Nihon koten bungaku taikei, vol. 46, Tokyo: Iwanami Shoten, 1959.

McCullough, Helen Craig, trans. *Tales of Ise: Lyrical Episodes from Tenth-Century Japan*. Tokyo: University of Tokyo Press, 1968.

McCullough, William. "Japanese Marriage Institutions in the Heian Period." *Harvard Journal of Asiatic Studies* 27 (1967):103—167.

McKinnon, Richard N. "Zeami on the Art of Training." *Harvard Journal of Asiatic Studies* 16, 1 and 2 (June 1953):200—225.

Mezaki Tokue. *Hyōhaku*. Tokyo: Kadokawa Shoten, 1975.

Miller, Roy Andrew. *The Japanese Language*. Chicago and London: The University of Chicago Press, 1967.

Minamoto Takakuni (supposed author). *Konjaku-monogatari-shū*. Ed. Yamada Yoshio et al. Nihon koten bungaku taikei, vols. 22—26. Tokyo: Iwanami Shoten, 1959.

Miner, Earl. *An Introduction to Japanese Court Poetry*. Stanford: Stanford University Press, 1968.

Montale, Eugenio. "Xenia." Reprinted in T. Weiss and Renée Weiss, eds., *Contemporary Poetry*. Princeton: Princeton University Press, 1974. Pp. 325—329.

Morohashi Tetsuji, ed. *Dai Kan-Wa jiten*. 13 vols. Tokyo: Taishūkan Shoten, 1955—1960.

Morrell, Robert E. "The Buddhist Poetry in the *Goshūishū*." *Monumenta Nipponica* 28, 1 (Spring 1973):87—100.

Morris, Ivan. *The World of the Shining Prince: Court Life in Ancient Japan*. New York: Alfred A. Knopf, 1969.

Mujū Ichien. *Collection de sable et de pierres: Shasekishū.* Trans. Hartmut O. Rotermund. Paris: Gallimard, 1979.

———. *Shaseki-shū.* Nihon koten bungaku taikei, vol. 85. Tokyo: Iwanami Shoten, 1966.

Mulhern, Chieko Irie. "Otogi-zōshi: Short Stories of the Muromachi Period." *Monumenta Nipponica* 29, 2 (Summer 1974):181–198.

Murdoch, Iris. *The Fire and the Sun: Why Plato Banished the Artists.* New York and Oxford: Oxford University Press, 1977.

Mus, Paul. *La lumière sur les six voies: tableau de la transmigration bouddhiques.* Paris: Institut d'Ethnologie, 1939.

Nagai Giken. "Kyōgen kigo ni tsuite." *Nihon Bukkyō-gakkai nenpō* 29 (October 1963):331–344.

Najita, Tetsuo. *Japan: The Intellectual Foundations of Modern Japanese Politics.* Chicago and London: The University of Chicago Press, 1974.

Najita, Tetsuo and Irwin Scheiner, eds. *Japanese Thought in the Tokugawa Period 1600–1868: Methods and Metaphors.* Chicago: University of Chicago Press, 1978.

Naka Seitetsu. "Korai fūteishō no karon to Bukkyō shumi." *Kenshin* 36, 12 (December 1941):44–60.

Nakamura Hajime, ed.. *Bukkyōgo dai-jiten.* 3 vols. Tokyo: Tōkyō Shoseki Kabushikigaisha, 1975.

Nakamura Kyōko. *Ryōi no sekai.* Tokyo: Chikuma Shobō, 1967.

Nakayama, Shigeru. *A History of Japanese Astronomy: Chinese Background and Western Impact.* Cambridge, Mass.: Harvard University Press, 1969.

Nichiren. "Kanjin-Honzon-shō." In Risshō Daigaku Nichiren Kyōgaku Kenkyūjo, eds., *Nichiren Shōnin ibun.* 1964–1965. 1:702–721.

Nishida Masayoshi. *Mujō no bungaku.* Tokyo: Hanawa Shobō, 1975.

———. *Mujōkan no keifu.* Tokyo: Ōfūsha, 1970.

Nishio Minoru. *Nihon bungeishi ni okeru chūseiteki na mono to sono tenkai.* Tokyo: Iwanami Shoten, 1976.

———, et al., eds. *Hōjō-ki, Tsurezuregusa.* Nihon koten bungaku taikei, vol. 30. Tokyo: Iwanami Shoten, 1971.

Nogami Toyoichirō. "Nōgaku gaisetsu." In *Nōgaku zensho.* Tokyo: Sōgensha, 1942–1944. Pp. 1–64.

Nonomura Kaizō, ed. *Kyōgen-shū.* Nihon koten zensho, vol. 81–83. Tokyo: Asahi Shimbunsha, 1956.

Norman, K. R., trans. *The Elders' Verses.* London: The Pali Text Society, 1969.

Nose Asaji. *Yūgen-ron.* Tokyo: Kawade Shobō, 1944.

———, ed. *Zeami Jūrokubushū hyōshaku.* Vol. 1, Tokyo: Iwanami Shoten, 1949.

Ōchō Enichi, ed. *Hokke no shisō.* Kyoto: Heirakuji Shoten, 1969.

O'Flaherty, Wendy Doniger. "Asceticism and Sexuality in the Mythology of Śiva." *History of Religions* 8, 4 (May 1969):300–337; 9, 1 (August 1969):1–49.

Okumura Kōsaku. *Inton kajin no genryū.* Tokyo: Kasama Shoin, 1975.

Omote Akira. " 'Tenshō kyōgen-bon' ni tsuite." *Bungaku* 24, 7 (1956):51–59.

Ōnishi Yoshinori. *Yūgen to aware.* Tokyo: Iwanami Shoten, 1940.

Origuchi Shinobu. "Nyōbō bungaku kara inja no bungaku e." In *Origuchi Shinobu zen-shū.* Tokyo: Chūō Kōronsha, 1959. 1:265–320.

Ozawa Tomio. *Mappō to masse no shisō*. Tokyo: Yūzankaku, 1974.

Peacock, James L. *Rites of Modernization: Symbolic and Social Aspects of Indonesian Proletarian Drama*. Chicago: University of Chicago Press, 1968.

————. "Symbolic Reversal and Social History: Transvestites and Clowns of Java." In Barbara A. Babcock, ed., *The Reversible World: Symbolic Inversion in Art and Society*. Ithaca: Cornell University Press, 1978. Pp. 209–224.

Petzhold, Bruno. "Hon Gaku Mon und Shi Kaku Mon." In *Studies in Buddhism in Japan*. Tokyo: The International Buddhist Society, 1939. Pp. 133–178.

Pilgrim, Richard B. "Some Aspects of *Kokoro* in Zeami." *Monumenta Nipponica* 24, 4 (1969):393–401.

Plutschow, Herbert, "Is Poetry a Sin? *Honjisuijaku* and Buddhism versus Poetry." *Oriens Extremus* 25, 2 (1978):206–218.

Po Chü-i (Pai Chü-i). *Pai-shih Ch'ang-ch'ing chi*. Peking, 1955.

Quine, Willard van Orman. *Word and Object*. Cambridge: Cambridge University Press, 1960.

Raz, Jacob. "The Actor and his Audience: Zeami's Views on the Audience of the Noh." *Monumenta Nipponica* 31, 3 (Autumn 1976):251–274.

Renondeau, Gaston. *Le Bouddhisme dans les Nō*. Tokyo: Hosokawa Print Co., 1950.

Robertson, D. W., Jr. *A Preface to Chaucer: Studies in Medieval Perspective*. Princeton: Princeton University Press, 1962.

Rosenfield, John M., Fumiko E. Cranston, and Edwin A. Cranston. *The Courtly Tradition in Japanese Art and Literature: Selections From the Hofer and Hyde Collections*. Cambridge, Mass.: Fogg Art Museum, 1973.

Royston, Clifton W. "The Poetics and Poetry Criticism of Fujiwara Shunzei (1114–1204)." Ph.D. dissertation, University of Michigan, 1974.

————. "*Utaawase* Judgments as Poetry Criticism." *Journal of Asian Studies* 34, 1 (November 1974): 99–108.

Ruskin, John. *Modern Painters*. 5 vols. New York: J. Wiley and Son, 1869 and 1872.

Saigyō. *Mirror for the Moon: A Selection of Poems by Saigyō (1118–1190)*. Trans. William R. LaFleur. New York: New Directions, 1978.

————. *Sanka-shū*. Ed. Itō Yoshio, Nihon koten zensho, vol. 78. Tokyo: Asahi Shimbun-sha, 1971.

Satake Akihiro. *Gekokujō no bungaku*. Tokyo: Chikuma Shobō, 1967.

Satō Masahide. *Inton no shisō: Saigyō o megutte*. Tokyo: Tōkyō Daigaku Shuppankai, 1977.

Scholes, Robert. *Structuralism in Literature*. New Haven: Yale University Press, 1974.

Sei Shōnagon. *The Pillow Book of Sei Shonagon*. Trans. Ivan Morris. 2 vols. New York: Columbia University Press, 1969.

Shibayama, Zenkei. *Zen Comments on the Mumonkan*. Trans. Sumiko Kudo. New York: Harper and Row, 1974.

Shinkei. "*Sasamegoto*, An Instruction Book in Linked Verse." Trans. Dennis Hirota. *Chanoyu Quarterly* 19 (1978):31–46.

Shirato Waka. "Kyōgen kigo ni tsuite." *Bukkyō-gaku seminā* 9 (May 1969):25–34.

————. "Nihon ryōiki ni okeru inga-ōhō-shisō: toku ni sono keifu ni tsuite." In Ōtani Daigaku Bukkyō Gakkai, ed., *Gō-shisō no kenkyū*. Kyoto: 1975. Pp. 320–345.

Shively, Donald H. "*Bakufu* versus *Kabuki*." In John W. Hall and Marius B. Jansen, eds., *Studies in the Institutional History of Early Modern Japan*. Princeton: Princeton University Press, 1968. Pp. 231–261.

————. "Bashō—The Man and the Plant." *Harvard Journal of Asiatic Studies* 16, 1 and 2 (1953):146–161.

Skorupski, John. *Symbol and Theory: A Philosophical Study of Theories of Religion in Social Anthropology*. Cambridge: Cambridge University Press, 1976.

Steiner, George. *On Difficulty and Other Essays*. New York and Oxford: Oxford University Press, 1978.

Taguchi Kazuo. *Kyōgen ronkō*. Tokyo, 1977.

Takagi Ichinosuke et al., eds. *Heike-monogatari-shū*. Nihon bungaku taikei, vols. 32 and 33.

Takagi Ichinosuke et al., eds. *Man'yō-shū*. Nihon koten bungaku taikei, vols. 4–7.

Takeoka Katsuya. *Ōchō bunka no zanshō*. Tokyo: Kadokawa Shoten, 1971.

Tamura Yoshirō and Umehara Takeshi. *Zettai no shinri: Tendai*. Tokyo: Kadokawa Shoten, 1970.

Tōkyō kokumin tōsho, ed. *Kokka taikei*. 28 vols. Tokyo: Kokumin kosho kabushiki-gaisha, 1927–31.

Tomiyama Susumu. "Bashō ni okeru chūsei no keishō to danzetsu." In Bukkyō Bungaku Kenkyūkai, ed., *Bukkyō bungaku kenkyū*. Kyoto: Hōzōkan, 1961. 10:157–180.

Torrance, Robert M. *The Comic Hero*. Cambridge, Mass.: Harvard University Press, 1978.

Totman, Conrad. "English-Language Studies of Medieval Japan: An Assessment." *Journal of Asian Studies* 38, 3:541–551.

Toulmin, Stephen. *Human Understanding: The Collective Use and Evolution of Concepts*. Princeton: Princeton University Press, 1972.

Tsukudo Reikan. *Tsukudo Reikan chosaku-shū*. 5 vols. Tokyo: Serika Shobō, 1976.

Turner, Victor. "Liminal to Liminoid in Play, Flow, and Ritual: An Essay in Comparative Symbology." *Rice University Studies* 60 (1974):53–92.

————. "Metaphors of Anti-Structure in Religous Culture." In *Dramas, Fields, and Metaphors: Symbolic Action in Human Society*. Ithaca: Cornell University Press, 1974.

————. *The Ritual Process: Structure and Anti-Structure*. Chicago: Aldine, 1969.

Ueda, Makoto. *Literary and Art Theories in Japan*. Cleveland: Press of Western Reserve University, 1967.

————. *Matsuo Bashō*. New York: Twayne, 1970.

Ueyama Shunpei and Kajiyama Yūichi, eds. *Bukkyō no shisō: sono genkei o saguru*. Tokyo: Chūō Kōronsha, 1974.

Ury, Marian, trans. *Tales of Times Now Past: Sixty-Two Stories from a Medieval Japanese Collection*. Berkeley: University of California Press, 1979.

Visser, Marinus Willem de. *Ancient Buddhism in Japan*. 2 vols. Leiden: E. J. Brill, 1928–1935.

Waley, Arthur. "The Fall of Loyang." In *The Secret History of the Mongols*. New York: Barnes and Noble, 1964.

————. *The Life and Times of Po Chü-i, 772–846*. London: Allen and Unwin, 1949.

————. *The Nō Plays of Japan*. New York: Grove Press, 1957.

Walsh, Andrew. *Roots of the Lyric: Primitive Poetry and Modern Poetics*. Princeton: Princeton University Press, 1978.

Watanabe Shōichi. " 'Yūgen' no shisō-kōzō." *Tetsugaku-rinri-gaku kenkyū*, March 1975. Pp. 112–134.

Watanabe Tamotsu. *Saigyō Sanka-shu zenchūkai*. Tokyo: Kazama Shobō, 1971.

Watsuji Tetsurō. "Nihon seishin." In *Watsuji Tetsurō zenshū*. Vol. 4. Tokyo: Iwanami Shoten, 1961–1963.

———. "Zoku Nihon seishinshi kenkyū." In *Watsuji Tetsurō zenshū*. Vol. 4. Tokyo: Iwanami Shoten, 1961–1963.

Weber, Max. *The Religion of India: The Sociology of Hinduism and Buddhism*. Trans. and ed. Hans H. Gerth and Don Martindale. New York: The Free Press, 1958.

Weinstein, Stanley. "The Beginnings of Esoteric Buddhism in Japan: The Neglected Tendai Tradition." *Journal of Asian Studies* 34, 1 (November 1974):177–191.

———. "Imperial Patronage in the Formation of T'ang Buddhism." In Arthur F. Wright and Denis Twitchett, eds., *Perspectives on the T'ang*. New Haven: Yale University Press, 1973. Pp. 265–306.

Whitehead, James D. "The Sinicization of the Vimalakīrtinirdeśa Sūtra." *Bulletin of the Society for the Study of Chinese Religions* 5 (Spring 1978):3–51.

Williams, William Carlos. *Pictures from Brueghel and Other Poems*. New York: New Directions, 1962.

Winternitz, Maurice. *A History of Indian Literature*. Trans. Subhadra Jhā. 2 vols. Calcutta: University of Calcutta, 1933.

Yamada Shōsen. "Chūseigoki ni okeru Waka-soku-darani no jissen." *Indo-gaku Bukkyō-gaku kenkyū*, March 1967, pp. 290–292.

Yamazaki Masakazu. *Geijutsu, henshin, yuge*. Tokyo: Chūō Kōronsha, 1975.

Yampolsky, Philip B., trans. *The Platform Sutra of the Sixth Patriarch*. New York: Columbia University Press, 1967.

Yanagida Seizan. *Zen shisō*. Tokyo: Chūō Kōronsha, 1975.

———. "Zen to inga." In Bukkyō Shisō Kenkyūkai, ed., *Inga*. Kyoto, 1978.

Yasuda Ayao. *Uta no fukasa*. Osaka: Sogensha, 1971.

Yokoi Kiyoshi. *Chūsei minshū no seikatsu bunka*. Tokyo: Tōkyō Daigaku Shuppan, 1975.

Yokomichi Mario and Omote Akira, eds. *Yōkyoku-shū*. Nihon koten bungaku taikei, vol. 40. Tokyo: Iwanami Shoten, 1960.

Yoshida, Kenkō. *Essays in Idleness: The Tsurezuregusa of Kenkō*. Trans. Donald Keene. New York: Columbia University Press, 1967.

Yuasa Yasuo. *Shintai: Tōyōteki shinjin-ron no kokoromi*. Tokyo: Sōbunsha, 1977.

Zeami, Motokiyo. *The Secret of Nō Plays: Zeami's Kadensho*. Trans. Chūichi Sakurai et al. Kyoto: Sumiya-Shinobe Publishing Institute, 1968.

———. "Zeami Jūroku Bushū, Kwadensho." Trans. Michitarō Shidehara and Wilfrid Whitehouse. *Monumenta Nipponica* 5, 2 (1942).

Zürcher, Erik. *The Buddhist Conquest of China: The Spread and Adaptation of Buddhism in Early Medieval China*. 2 vols. Leiden: E. J. Brill, 1972.

INDEX

Abrams, M. H., 163
Actors: in kyōgen, 139; in nō dramas, 126—129
Allegories, 86—87, 96; in *Lotus Sutra*, 85—87
Allusion, nature of, 95—96
Amida, 50, 51, 57; Western Paradise of, 51, 97, 154
Amidist Buddhism, 51, 57, 97; Matsuo Bashō and, 156—157; nō plays and, 117
Anatman, Indian Buddhist concept of, 29, 151
Animals, and transmigration, 29, 34—37, 121
Anitya (necessary change), law of, 60. *See also* Mujō
Anomalies. *See* Ryōi
Antistructure, 145. *See also* Symbolic inversion
Aseity, attribute of, 92
Asceticism, treatment of, in kyōgen, 134—135
Ashura (martial heroes), 28—29, 118; in nō plays, 120—121, 123, 124
Astrology, Indian, in Buddhist texts, 69—70
Auerbach, Erich, 86, 96
Avatamsaka-sūtra (Kegon-kyō), 54

Bachelard, Gaston, *Poetics of Space*, 68, 69
Bakufu, 133
Bankei (Eitaku), 147
Bashō. *See* Matsuo Bashō
Beauty, portrayal of, 97—98, 102
Bellah, Robert, 143
"Bendowa" (Dōgen), 127
Birth, modes of (rokudō shishō), 43, 44, 55

Blindness. *See* Sightedness versus sightlessness
Bodhisattva, 44, 45, 46, 50—51, 54—55, 125—126; of Compassion, 49—50; Earth-Store, 49—50; Śākyamuni Buddha as, 6; Samantabhadra, 93
Body-mind as a unity, 16—17, 21. *See also* Nondualism
Botanical metaphors, 69—69, 112, 126—127
Brower, Robert H., 80—81, 98, 101—102
Buddhism, Chinese, 14, 29, 61
Buddhism, Indian, 29
Buddhism, Japanese, 9—10, 11—14; comprehensiveness of, 26—27; versus Confucianism, 124—126; dance in, 57; dreams in tradition of, 6; "four characteristic states," 21; hegemony of, 9—14, 47, 59, 64—65; in Heian period, 16, 61; Hossō school, 5; ideals of, 124; in Kamakura era, 16; modern view of, 125; and poetry writing, 7—9; rivalries within, 58—59; role of, 27; versus Shinto, 124—126, 151; symbolization and, 20—25; as a theodicy, 27. *See also* Amidist Buddhism; Hinayanist Buddhism; Mahayana Buddhism; Shingon Buddhism; Tendai Buddhism; Zen

Change and impermanence. *See* Impermanence/instability; Mujō
Chien-chen, 15
Chih-i, *Mo-ho chih-kuan*, 50, 53—54, 83, 88, 90, 92
Children, and icons of Jizō, 50—51
Chinese Buddhism, 14, 29, 61
Chōmei. *See* Kamo no Chōmei
Chou Tso-jen, 135—136, 137
Chūjin, 22

Cold, yūgen and, 98
Comedy. See Kyōgen
Confucianism, 11, 13, 59, 111, 124−126
Consciousness, continuum of, 4−6
Conversation, 110−111
Copenetration, transcendence by, 49,
    52−53
Cosmology, Japanese Buddhist, 117−
    123; and nō drama, 120−123; order as
    a value of, 130, 143, 148; rokudō in,
    26−59
Courtesan(s), 69, 71−73; roles of, 74,
    77; as a symbol of impermanence/
    instability, 74, 75

Daijō-kishin-ron, 20−21, 128
Dance, in Amidist worship, 57
Darkness, yūgen and, 98
Death. See Dying
DeBary, William Theodore, 77−78
Depth of poetry. See Yūgen, aesthetic
    quality of
Dichotomies, interdependence of, 105.
    See also Nondualism
Didacticism in Japanese literature, 18−
    20, 79
Distance, and impermanence, 97, 100
Divination, 64
Dōgen, 22, 117, 128; "Bendōwa," 127;
    mappō theory opposed by, 3; and
    Nāgārjuna, 127; on poetry writing, 8;
    Zeami and, 128, 129
Douglas, Mary, 75
Dreams, Buddhist philosophy of, 4−7
Dualism. See Nondualism
Dutch Learning, 14
Dwelling places, mujō of, 61, 65. See
    also Hermit's hut; Traveler's inn
Dying: and Amidist belief, 51; and mobil-
    ity of dwelling place, 65

Eguchi (Kan'ami), 71−73, 93
Emotion, 105−106
Emptiness (únya), 87−88, 92
Enlightenment (satori), 20−21, 22
En no Gyōja, 46
Esashi Jūō, 134, 143
Essays in Idleness [Tsurezure-gusa]
    (Yoshida Kenkō), 67−68
Eye, penetrating. See Heavenly eye

Fenollosa, Ernest, 154
"Floating phrases and fictive utterances"
    (kyōgen kigo), 8, 90, 91, 95, 126
Freedom, of bodhisattva, 54−55
Frye, Northrop, 123, 140
Fujita Kōtatsu, 87
Fujiwara Shunzei, 4, 52, 81, 82, 89;
    Korai fūteishō, 83, 90−97, 126;
    Saigyō's dream of, 2; on status of Jap-
    anese poetry, 95
Fujiwara Teika, 81, 89, 97−98; emphasis
    on recognition of phenomena, 24; mujō
    in poetry of, 101
Fukuo Takeichirō, 138
Funa Benkei, 122

Gaki-zōshi, 52
Ganjin. See Chien-chen
Gekokujō, principle of, 138−139
Gekokujō no bungaku, 141
Genpō, 37−38, 40
Genshin, Ōjō-yō-shū, 51
Geomancy, Chinese, 64
Gesho ("outer books"), 11, 12
Ghosts, hungry, 28, 29, 120, 121; in nō
    plays, 121
Godlike figures (kami), 29; in nō plays,
    120, 122
Golay, Jacqueline, 142
Goshirakawa, Ryōjin-hi-shō, 52, 57
Gukan-shō (Jien), 3, 10, 30−31, 138
Gyōgi Bosatsu, 45−46, 155−159, 161;
    ambulatory life of, 45, 156, 159; as
    Amidist, 156; heavenly eye of, 45−46,
    157, 162, 164; linked to Saigyō by
    Bashō, 152−153, 156, 160−162; as
    seer, 157−159

Habitations. See Dwelling places; Her-
    mit's hut; Home; Traveler's inn
Haibutsu-kishaku movement, 14
Hakeda, Yoshito S., 21
Hakurakuten, 8−9, 122
Hall, John W., 137
Han-shan, 24
Han Yü, 18
Harootunian, H. D., 59
Heart Sutra, 128
Heavenly eye (tengen), 45−46, 157, 152,
    162, 164

Heian period, 13; literature of, 5, 10, 30, 32, 53; fusion of Shamanism and Buddhism in, 46

Hermit, life of, 113

Hermit's hut: in *Hōjō-ki* (Kamo no Chōmei), 111−113; impermanence of, 62−67; as literary topoi, 60−69, 76− 79; versus ordinary house, 63−65; Saigyō's descriptions of, 65−67; in relation to traveler's inn, 69, 76−79; Vimalakīrti and, 109−111

Hierarchical arrangement: of rokudō system, 119, 143, 147; of society, 143, 145−146, 147

Hierarchical mode of thought, 86, 88, 95, 108

Hinayanist Buddhism, 114

Hirata Atsutane, 59

Hisamatsu, Sen'ichi, 82

Hisamatsu, Shin'ichi, 93, 105, 117

Hisō-ten heaven, Genshin on, 51−52

Hōben, 84

Hoff, Frank, 130

"Hōjō-ki" (Kamo no Chōmei), 62−65; basics of, 109−110; hermitage in, 111−113; historical analysis of, 108− 115; Imanari Motoaki on, 111−113; metaphors in, 112; mujō in, 112; in relation to *Vilmalakīrti Sutra*, 108− 115

Hokke-kyō. See *Lotus Sutra*

Home, stability of householder in, 78−79

Hōnen, 52

Hongaku (original enlightenment), principle of, 20, 21−24, 128; and Buddhist theory of symbols, 22−24; and Zen, 23−24

Honji-suijaku, 11−12

Horse chestnuts, symbolism of, 152−154

Hossō school of Buddhist philosophy, 5

Hou-pao, 37

Householder(s), 78−79; Vimalakīrti as, 110

Hungry ghosts (gaki), 28, 29, 120, 121

Iconography, Japanese, bodhisattva in, 50−51

Ideographs, Bashō's use of, 153−154

Ikkyū, 147

Imanari Motoaki, "Ren-in Hōjō-ki no ron," 111−113

Impermanence/instability, 5, 88, 101; banana plants as symbol of, 68−69; Bashō and, 68−69; courtesan as symbol of, 74, 76, 78; and distance, 102; dwellings as symbols of, 60−79; hermit's hut and, 62−67; structure of, 60−79; in Teika's poetry, 101; Vimalakīrti and, 111. See also Mujō

Incarnations, 70. See also Rokudō system; Transmigration

Infiltration, salvation by, 49−50

Inn. See Traveler's inn

Intellectual framework of medieval Japan, 9−14. See also Literati

Interdependence: of dichotomies, 105; in nō drama, 131; of observer and observed, 100, 102−103, 104−105

Interpenetration of phenomena, 100, 106

Inversion: symbolic, 144−145; of values, 68

Iori. See Hermit's hut

Ippen, 57

Iriya Yoshitaka, 24

Irui-chūgyō, 55

Jakusen, reincarnation of, 47

Jien, 82; *Gukan-shō*, 3, 10, 138; use of mappō concept by, 3

Jigoku-zōshi, 52

Jizō, 49−50

Jomyo Koji. See Vimalakīrti

Jonas, Hans, 161

Juke-nyūkū, 92−93

Kabuki, 133

Kadensho (Zeami), 126−129

Kaijiyama Yūichi, 54

Kaku (enlightenment), 20−21

Kamakura era, Japanese Buddhism in, 16, 58−59

Kammon gyoki, 139−140

Kamo no Chōmei: on high medieval in Japanese history, 108−115; "Hōjō-ki," 62−65, 107−115; nondualism and, 114−115; and Vimalakīrti as recluse, 111; on yūgen, 99

Kan'ami, 138; *Eguchi*, 71−73, 93

Kani Yamabushi, 135

Kanjin-honzon-shō (Nichiren), 53

Kannon, 49—50
Karma/karmic causality, 27, 28; Amida's power to cancel, 51—52; anxiety about, 48—53; and gekukujō, 138; and individual responsibility, 29; inexorability of, 48—49, 125; in kyōgen, 134; in Kyōkai's stories, 30—49; in literature, 28; in nō dramas, 123; retributions and rewards of, 34—39. *See also* Rokudō system
Keene, Donald, 144
Kegon sutras, 53
Ki no Tsurayuki, 126
Kinuta, 122, 130
Kire (linguistic/conceptual break), 103— 104
Kitagawa, Joseph M., 32, 46, 150; on Gyōgi Bosatsu, 155—156, 162; *Religion in Japanese History*, 150
Koan, 56—57, 127. See also *Wu-men kuan*
Kokin-shū, 30—31, 126
Kokugaku movement, 47
Konishi Jin'ichi, 82, 83, 98, 100, 117, 131
Konjaku-monogatari, 6, 30, 50
Korai fūteishō (Fujiwara Shunzei), 83, 90—97, 126
Kōshoku gonin onna [Five Women Who Loved Love] (Saikaku), 77
Kōya, 57
Kuhn, Thomas S., *The Structure of Scientific Revolutions*, 33
Kūkai, 17, 18, 20, 21—22, 32, 150; *Sangō shiiki*, 12—13
Kusabira, 134, 135
Kyōgen, 54, 133—148; Chou Tso-jen on, 135—136; didacticism of, 19; as distinguished from nō drama, 125, 138— 139, 141, 144—146; evolution of, 137—138, 140; gekokujō principle and, 138—139; karma and transmigration in, 134; Marxist perspective of, 135—137; of Muromachi era, 140; versus otogi-zōshi, 141—142; ritualization of, 144—146; satiric nature of, 139—142; social role of, 139; symbolic inversion in, 144—145; in Tokugawa era, 136—137; view of change in, 138—139; world view of, 138—139; zatō plays, 136

Kyōkai: explanatory system of, 33—39; *Nihon ryōi-ki* (see *Nihon ryōi-ki*); writing of, 32—33

Language, two-tiered nature of, 17, 22—23
Lin-shi lu, 55
Literati, medieval Japanese: social and political influences on, 10—11; Vimalakīrti as model for, 109
Lotman, Y. M., 140
Lotus Sutra, 53, 82, 83, 84—88; hongaku principle in, 22; parables in, 85, 87, 95; idea of rokudō in, 27
Ludization of transmigration, 49, 54, 56—58. *See also* Kyōgen

McCullough, Helen Craig, 61
MacIntyre, Alsadair, 46
McKinnon, Richard N., 126
Mādhyamika (Sanron) literature, 100
Mahayana Buddhism, 84, 108, 114— 115, 125; bodhisattva in, 55; versus Christianity, 20; cosmology of, 118— 119; hell as temporary in, 119; on nirvana in relation to samsara, 115, 119, 125, 127, 129—130; nō drama and, 116—132; nondualism and, 53, 114— 115. See also *Vimalakīrti Sutra*
Makoto Ueda, 153; on Bashō, 152; on Gyōgi, 159
Makura no sōshi [Pillow Book] (Sei Shōnagon), 15
Manaka Fujiko, 89
Manjuśri, and Vimalakīrti, 110
Manuscripts, copying of, 15
Man'yō-shū (Ōtomo Tabito), 7, 28, 103
Mappō, theory of, 3, 54; Jien's use of, 3; Saigyō on, 3—4
Matsukaze, 122
Matsuo Bashō, 149, 151—162; on Gyōgi and Saigyō, 152—153, 156, 160—162; Makoto Ueda on, 152; *Oku no hosomichi* (Narrow Road to the Deep North), 74—76, 149, 151—164; "Rakushisha no ki," 68—69; and Saigyō, 152—153, 154—155
Ma-tsu Tao-i, 55
Meditation, 100, 103
Metaphors: botanical, 68—69, 112, 126— 127; in "Hōjō-ki," 112

Mezaki Tokue, 70
Michimori, 122
Military figures. *See* Ashura
Mimesis (Auerbach), 86
Mind and body as a unity, 16−17, 21. *See also* Nondualism
Miner, Earl, 80−81, 98, 101−102
Ming-pao chi, 31
Miracles, 33. *See also* Ryōi
Mobility: of hermit's hut, 65; social, and kyōgen, 138, 139
Mo-ho chih-kuan (Chih-i), 27, 50, 53−54, 82, 83, 88, 90, 92
Monogatari, rokudō in, 28
Moon, movement of, 70
Morris, Ivan, 60
Motoori Morinaga, 18−19, 59, 117
Mujō, 60−79, 101; in "Hōjō-ki" (Chōmei), 112; in human affairs, 61, 63; images of, in Teika's poetry, 101−102; in nature, 61, 63; symbol of, 61. *See also* Impermanence/instability
Mus, Paul, 120
Mulhern, Chieko Irie, 141
Murdoch, Iris, 86
Muromachi period, 13; kyōgen in, 133, 137−140

Nāgārjuna, 105, 128; and Dōgen, 127; Zeami and, 129
Naikyō ("inner scriptures"), 11, 12
Nakamura, Kyoko M., 33, 46
Naksatra (stopping places), 70
Nara period, 5
National Learning, 13
Negative, attribution of positivity to, 97, 99, 102
Nembutsu, 51, 57
Neo-Confucianism, 13, 14, 124
New Criticism, on didacticism in literature, 18
Nichiren, *Kanjin-honzon-shō*, 53
Nihon ryōi-ki (Kyōkai), 6, 12, 13, 30−49, 58, 108, 118; adopted as temple homilies, 32; didacticism of, 18, 19; on Gyōgi Bosatsu, 45−46, 155, 157−158; historical impact of, 32; rebirth in, 51; *Wu-men kuan* compared with, 57
Nirvana, 152; locus of, 51; and samsara, 115, 119, 125, 127, 129−130, 147−148

Nishio Minoru, 126
Nobility, portrayal of: in kyōgen, 139−141, 144−146; in nō drama, 146
Nō drama, 24, 30−31, 72, 116−132; audience, 132; and Buddhist values, 117, 124−126, 129, 130−132; and cosmology of medieval Japan, 120−123; as distinguished from kyōgen, 138−139, 141; evolution of, 137−138; protagonist in, 123, 124; ritualization of, 144−146; rokudō system and, 28, 120−123; structure of progression of plays in, 120; Tokugawa shogunate approval of, 143; training for, 127; view of change in, 138−139; world view of, 138−139; yūgen in, 128, 130−131; Zeami Motokiyo on, 117, 126−127; and Zen, 117, 127
Nōin, 160
Nondualism, 21, 53−54, 88, 97; hongaku and, 22−23; of mind and body, 16−17, 21−22; of states of consciousness, 4−6; in Tendai Buddhism, 88; in *Vimalakīrti Sutra*, 110, 113−114
Nose Asaji, 00

Observer, in relation to observed, 100, 102−103, 104−105
Ōjō-yō-shū (Genshin), 27, 51
Oko no hosomichi [Narrow Road to the Deep North] (Bashō), 74−75, 149, 151−164
Ōkura Toraaki, *Waranbe-gusa*, 145
Onishi Yoshinori, *Yūgen to aware*, 102−103
Order, as a value, 143, 148. *See also* Hierarchical arrangement
Otogi-zōshi (moralizing tales for children), 50, 141−142
Ōtomo Tabito, *Man'yō-shū*, 28

"Pai-chang and a Fox," 56−57, 147
Parables, in *Lotus Sutra*, 85, 87, 95
Peacock, James L., 145−146
Penalty, immediate (genpō), 37
Penetrating eye. *See* Heavenly eye
Perception, act of, 101, 102. *See also* Observer
Phenomena: emptiness of, 87−88, 92−93; interpenetration of, 100, 106
Piety, 39

Pillow Book. See *Makura no soshi*
Planets, movement of, 70
Plants. *See* Botanical metaphors
Plato, 86, 87, 89, 90
Platonism, 89, 90
Play: element of, 54; salvation as a form of, 54–58
Po Chü-i, 8–9, 122
Poetics of Space (Bachelard), 68
Poetry: Buddhist problems in relation to, 7–9; depth of (*see* Yūgen); lyric, Japanese (uta), 93
Poets: Buddhist clerics as, 7–9; Romantic, 163; as seers, 161–163
Po-jo yen-chi, 31
Pound, Ezra, 154
Practice, in relation to realization, 127
Prajñāpāramitā (Hannya) literature, 54, 100
Proletarian literature, kyōgen as example of, 135–136
Prophets. *See* Seers
Prostitutes. *See* Courtesans
Pure Land, 51–52

Rain, 95. *See also* Water images
"Rakushisha no ki" [Record of the House of Fallen Persimmons] (Sashō), 68–69
Raz, Jacob, 131
Reality, Buddhist philosophy of, 4–6
Recluse. *See* Hermit
Religion in Japanese History (Kitagawa), 150
Relinquishment of the world, 71
Ren-in. *See* Kamo no Chōmei
Republic (Plato), 86, 87
Retribution, karmic, 123
Reversal, ritualized, 144–146
Richards, I. A., 86
Ridicule, in kyōgen, 134–135
Ritual(s): body-expressive, 16–17, 21; Buddhist, 14, 15, 16–17, 57; ludic, 57; as mode of cognition, 16–17
Ritualization, of kyōgen and nō drama, 144–146
Rivalries, in Buddhism, 58–59
Robertson, D. W., Jr., 86
Rokudō system, 27, 28, 117–123; as arena of play, 54–58; as common sense, 59; dualism, 131; hierarchical

arrangement of, 28–29, 118–119, 130, 143, 147; nō drama and, 120–123; skepticism about, in kyōgen, 142–143; in twentieth-century Japan, 59; and Western Paradise of Amida, 51–52. *See also* Karma; Transmigration
Rokudō-bakku (escape from suffering in the six courses), 49–51
Rokudō shisho. *See* Birth, modes of
Royston, Clifton W., 89
Ryōgen, 22
Ryōi (anomalies), 33–45. See also *Nihon ryōi-ki* (Kyōkai)
Ryōjin-hi-shō (Goshirakawa), 52, 57

Saddharma-pundarika sūtra. *See* Lotus Sutra
Saga (Kamino), 47
Saigyō, 103–105; depth in poetry of, 81, 82; descriptions of hermitage, 65–67; dream poem of, 2–3, 4; on dreams and reality, 3–6; linked to Gyogi by Bashō, 152–153, 156, 160–162; on mappō concept, 3–4; on poetry writing, 2–3, 7, 9; rejection of world by, 160–161; *Sanka-shū*, 70, 71–72, 73; and symbolization, 24
Saikaku, *Kōshoku gonin onna* (Five Women Who Loved Love), 77–78
Saitō Mōkichi, 103
Śākyamuni Buddha, 6, 16
Salvation, 49, 54–58, 125, 129–130
Samsara (realm of transmigration): and nirvana, 51, 115, 119, 125, 127, 129–130, 147–148; bodhisattva in, 50
Sangha, 47
Sango shiiki (Kukai), 12–13
Sanka-shū (Saigyō), 70–72, 73
Santai. *See* Truth, stages of
Sarugae Kōtō, 136, 142
Sasamegoto (Shinkei), 93–94
Satake Akihiro, 141–142, 144
Satire. *See* Kyōgen
Satori (enlightenment), 20–21, 22
Secular society, versus religious reclusion, 113–115
Seer(s): artist as, 161–163; Gyōgi Bosatsu as, 45–46, 157–159. *See also* Heavenly eye

Sei Shōnagon, *Makura no sōshi* (Pillow Book), 15
Self-sacrifice, 41
Setsuwa, 30
Shamans/shamanism, 45, 46
Shaseki-shū, 28, 50, 135
Sheng-pao, 37
Shigeru Nakayama, 70
Shih-chiai hu-chü (jikkai goku), 53
Shikan (calm and contemplation), 90, 98; Chih-i on, 88; structure of, 99; and yūgen, 99, 100
Shingon Buddhism, 16, 21, 57
Shinkei, *Sasamegoto*, 93−94
Shinkokin-shū, 71
Shinran, 52
Shinto practices and values, 11−12, 43, 46, 124−126, 151
Shively, Donald, 68−69, 133
Shōbō-genzō, 27
Shukugō (karma from the past), 70
Shukumei (destiny), 70
Shunzei. *See* Fujiwara Shunzei
Sightedness versus sightlessness, 34−35, 45, 142, 158−159, 161, 163
Simplicity, 23
Six courses. *See* Rokudō system
Society: hierarchical arrangement of, 143, 145−146, 147; life in, 113; mobility in, 138, 139
Soku (identity) principle, 128
Soul, in transmigration, 29
Spring, 95; symbols of, 97−98, 101−102
Śrāvaka, 84
Steiner, George, 82, 94
Stopping places (naksatra), 70
Structure of Scientific Revolutions, The (Kuhn), 33
Subject, in relation to object, 100, 102−103, 104−105
Suddhipanthaka, Chōmei and, 114
Suffering, 109, 111, 125
Sung culture, 83
Sutras, 11; idea of rokudō in, 27; symbols and metaphors in, 15−16
Symbolic inversion, kyōgen as a form of, 144−146
Symbolization process: Buddhist critique of, 20−25; reversal of, 23−24

Symbols, Buddhist, 14−20; versus Buddhist critique of symbolization, 20−25; and hongaku principle, 23; in Japanese literature, 17−18
Symbol system, Buddhist, 14−25

Ta-ch'eng ch'i-hsin-lun (*Daijō-kishin-ron*), 27
Taguchi Kazuo, 135
Takasago, 122
Taketori Masao, 30
Tale of Genji, The, 30−31, 61
Tamura Yoshirō, 92
Tankai, 4
Tanni-shō, 27
Taoism, 11, 13
Tears, 34−35, 66
Teika. *See* Fujiwara Teika
Tendai Buddhism, 16, 22, 51−54, 128; yūgen in verse of, 80−106; and Zen, 82−83
Tengen. *See* Heavenly eye
Tenshō kyōgen-bon, 140
Ten worlds, copenetration of, 53
Tetsuo Najita, 13
Theater. *See* Kyōgen; Nō drama
Tokugawa era, 13, 47; Buddhist hegemony in, 59; changes during, 14; kyōgen in, 133, 136−137, 140−148
Toulmin, Stephen, 150
Transcendence, salvation by, 49, 51
Transmigration, 27−28; concept in twentieth century Japan, 59; in kyōgen, 134, 142−143; in Kyōkai's stories, 30−49; means of escaping suffering of, 49−, 58; mobility on earth and, 65; and rokudō taxonomy, 28−29, 118−119; social implications of, 47; soul in, 29; in Zen literature, 55. *See also* Rokudō system
Transpecification, 40, 55; Kyōkai's story and explanation of, 35−38
Traveler's inn, 69−79; conception of, 69; courtesans in, 69, 71, in relation to hermit's hut, 69, 76−79; as literary topoi, 60−79
Truth (santai): Buddhism and, 91−92: three stages of, 91−92, 93−94
Tsurezure-gusa [Essays in Idleness] (Yoshida Kenzo), 67−68

Turner, Victor, 145

Umehara Takeshi, 84
Upāya, 84
Uspensky, B. A., 140

Vimalakīrti: in "Hōjō-ki" (Chōmei),
107−111; silence of, 110
Vimalakīrti Sūtra, 16, 53, 54, 69; and
"Hōjō-ki," 108−111; nonduality in,
113−114
Vision: artistic, 161−162. See also Sightedness versus sightlessness; Heavenly
eye
Void. See Emptiness

Wakezu (absence of discrimination), 95
Waley, Arthur, 110, 117
Waranbe-gusa (Ōkura Toraaki), 145
Warriors. See Ashura
Water images, 66, 94−95, 153
Watsuji Tetsurō, 28, 51, 52, 59, 150
Wei-mo. See Vimalakīrti
Western Paradise of Amida, 51, 52, 97,
154
Women: courtesans (see Courtesans);
literature of, 62, 73
Wordplay, 110
Wu-men, "Pai-chang and a Fox," 56−
57, 147
Wu-men kuan, 27, 56−57, 147

Yado, meaning of, 70. See also Travel-
er's inn
Yama (king of land of dead), 51
Yamabushi, ridicule of, in kyōgen,
134−135
Yanagida, 55
Yin-yang, 134
Yoshida Kenkō, Tsurezure-gusa (Essays
in Idleness), 67−68
Yoshishige Yasutane (Jakusen), 7, 47
"Yūgaku shudō kempū" (Zeami), 128
Yūgen, aesthetic quality of, 52, 82−106:
Konishi Jin'ichi's interpretation of, 98;
and meditation, 103; and nō drama,
128, 130−131; Onishi on, 102−103;
origins of, 100; and shikan, 99, 100;
Shunzei's concept of, 93, 98−99, 101
Yūgen to aware (Ōnishi), 102−103
Yuima. See Vimalakīrti
Yuima-gyō. See Vimalakīrti Sutra

Zato plays, 136
Zazen, 22, 100
Zeami Motokiyo, 24, 108, 138; Kadensho, 126−129; on nō drama, 117,
126−129; use of Zen vocabulary by,
127, 128
Zen, 20, 23−24, 83−84; introduction to
China, 103; and nō drama, 127; Rinzai,
147; and Tendai Buddhism, 82; transmigration in literature of, 55
Zürcher, Erik, 29

Designer: UC Press Staff
Compositor: Trend Western
Printer: Braun-Brumfield
Binder: Braun-Brumfield
Text: Times Roman
Display: Times Roman